STUDIES IN HISTORY, ECONOMICS AND PUBLIC LAW

EDITED BY THE FACULTY OF POLITICAL SCIENCE
OF COLUMBIA UNIVERSITY

Number 324

THE NAPOLEONIC WARS AND GERMAN
NATIONALISM IN AUSTRIA

THE NAPOLEONIC WARS AND GERMAN NATIONALISM IN AUSTRIA

BY

WALTER CONSUELO LANGSAM

AMS PRESS
NEW YORK

COLUMBIA UNIVERSITY
STUDIES IN THE
SOCIAL SCIENCES

324

This Series was formerly known as
Studies in History, Economics and Public Law.

Reprinted with the permission of Columbia University Press
From the edition of 1930, New York
First AMS EDITION published 1969
Manufactured in the United States of America

Library of Congress Catalogue Card Number: 75-82236

AMS PRESS, INC.
NEW YORK, N. Y. 10003

To

MY PARENTS

WHO SACRIFICED EVERYTHING
THAT MY WAY MIGHT BE
MADE THE EASIER

ERRATA

Page 161, footnote 1
Page 168, footnote 3
Page 171, footnote 2
Page 186, footnote 1, line 4, third
     and seventh words, with apostrophes
Page 191, footnote 2
Page 192, footnote 1
Page 197, footnote 1
In each of these instances, for Bibl *read* Srbik.

PREFACE

MUCH has been written upon the rise of a nationalism in
"regenerated Prussia" during the early years of the nineteenth century, and upon similar developments in other European areas, notably Spain. The synchronous growth of a
national feeling among the people of German Austria, that is,
among the people living within the confines of the present
Republic of Austria, has been disregarded, however, if not
actually denied. Perhaps this is due to the relatively lesser
part which nationalism played in Austria as compared with
its rôle in Prussia and Spain. Perhaps it is due to the circumstance that the appearance of a German nationalism in
Austria was only one phase of a general feeling of hatred for
all things French, or at least all things Napoleonic. After
all, German Austria, as the nucleus of the heterogeneous
Habsburg possessions, was situated in a naturally non-
nationalistic environment. Moreover, the fortunes of the
Habsburg monarchy never sank so low, during those years,
as did the fortunes of the Prussians and the Spaniards. The
Treaty of Tilsit reduced Prussia to the rank of a third-rate
power, and the negotiations at Bayonne led to the seating
of a Bonaparte on the throne of the Spanish Bourbons—but
in 1809, at Aspern, a Habsburg army still was able to inflict
upon Napoleon one of the greatest military defeats of his
career. Admitting, then, that nationalism was less evident
in Austria than in other parts of Europe, it becomes important, nevertheless, to recognize its existence — for the
nationalism of 1806 to 1815 was the root from which grew
the powerful nationalist feeling of 1848, and of later years.

7

For the purposes of this study it has seemed best to begin with the year 1806 because of the great Austrian regeneration that took place after the humiliating events of 1805, namely, the defeats of Ulm and Austerlitz, and the signing of the Treaty of Pressburg. The year 1815, on the other hand, has seemed a convenient stopping-place because of the fate which overtook German nationalism at the Congress of Vienna. This Congress, of course, witnessed the triumph of Metternich, and there was little place for nationalism in that statesman's political " system."

In the untranslated quotations throughout the volume the original spellings generally have been retained as they were found in the documents quoted. Elsewhere, the names of persons have, in most cases, been given in the English form. Sometimes, however, as in the instance of Friedrich von Schlegel, this seemed hardly desirable. The word "Austria" has been used to mean German Austria, though, on occasion, where there is no possibility of misconception, it has been used to designate the entire Habsburg monarchy. Chief emphasis, moreover, has been placed upon developments in Vienna, for the imperial city unquestionably took the lead in all spiritual and intellectual movements of early nineteenth-century Austria.[1]

The author is deeply grateful to the several teachers, colleagues and friends whose interest in his work led them to give so generously of their time and counsel: To Professor Carlton J. H. Hayes of Columbia University under whose guidance the work was completed; to Professors Gottlieb Betz and J. Bartlet Brebner of Columbia University,

---

[1] *Cf.* Schlossar, Anton, "Die 'Wiener Zeitschrift' von J. Schikh und F. Witthauer" in *Zeitschrift für Bücherfreunde*, vol. v, no. 2, p. 465 : "The sum-total of literary life in the early decades of the nineteenth century was concentrated in Vienna; the provincial capitals were of almost no moment in this regard."

and Mr. Joseph E. Wisan of the College of the City of New York, all of whom read and carefully criticized the entire manuscript; and to Professors Nelson P. Mead and Holland Thompson of the College of the City of New York who encouraged and befriended him in ways too numerous to mention.

WALTER C. LANGSAM

COLUMBIA UNIVERSITY, MARCH, 1930.

CONTENTS

CHAPTER I

The Concept of Nationalism in Austria

THE dawn of the year 1806 saw the Holy Roman Empire tottering on its foundation. The crown of Charlemagne evidently was slipping from the emperor's brow. His power and prestige in the future would rest solely upon his family possessions—upon the Habsburg dominions. These dominions comprised a motley assortment of lands and peoples: Magyars and Slovaks in Hungary, Czechs in Bohemia, Italians in the southwest and Poles in the northeast, Ruthenes to the east and Croats and Slovenes to the south. The heart of the Habsburg possessions, however, was German Austria —Austria proper—consisting of the crown lands of Upper and Lower Austria, Styria, Carinthia and Salzburg, with a total of about five million German-speaking inhabitants. Until December 26, 1805, the Tyrol and Vorarlberg also had been part of this Austria, but the Treaty of Pressburg of that date had assigned them to Bavaria. The capital of German Austria, as also of the entire empire, was Vienna— *die Kaiserstadt*. Vienna reflected the heterogeneous character of the Austrian monarchy, and was proud of its cosmopolitanism. The Viennese prided themselves upon the circumstance that foreigners felt quite at ease in their midst.[1]

One of the bonds of union of the various elements of the Habsburg monarchy was an intense love and patriotism for the monarchy, and a deep love for the Habsburg dynasty. The various peoples felt that their state owed much of its

---

[1] Rohrer, J., *Versuch über die deutschen Bewohner der österreichischen Monarchie*, 2 vols. (Vienna, 1804), vol. ii, p. 160.

13

greatness to the Habsburgs personally. From the days of Count Rudolph in 1273 down to Francis the Good in 1806. the Habsburgs had extended the prestige of the land along with the power of their family. The Habsburgs, moreover, had been among the staunchest upholders of the religion of a majority of their subjects, of Roman Catholicism. And in spite of occasional quarrels and differences between them, the Church usually had supported their " Apostolic Majesties ". Tradition, too, glorified the imperial family, and, generally speaking, the Habsburgs had ever been paternalistic and benevolent and solicitous of the welfare of their subjects. In addition, the German Austrians in particular were proud of the German blood in the veins of the Habsburgs, and of the fact that these rulers had extended their German might over many other peoples. The other German branches, such as the Bavarians and Prussians, could not boast of similar achievements.

The Austrian Government, of course, had to cope with the difficult task of reconciling the conflicting interests of the numerous linguistic groups under its control without arousing the jealousy or ill-will of any one of them. Its policies had to be " imperial " rather than " national " because the monarchy was naturally non-nationalistic. No special preferences could be shown and no particular sensibilities must be hurt. For the Austrian authorities to have adopted a nationalist policy of one sort or another, if they had been aware of the existence of such a spiritual force as nationalism, would have been an undertaking equivalent to the one of dancing upon the proverbial basket of eggs. Truly, the German Austria of 1806 would appear to have offered but an unfavorable environment for the growth of nationalism!

In the early years of the nineteenth century, however, the German-speaking inhabitants of the Habsburg monarchy were so frightened at the thought of Napoleon's power and of French invasions, that they seem to have been driven into a desire for a closer friendship with other people who spoke the same language as they, and who had a similar culture and a similar set of historical traditions to uphold and defend. Thus there was provided a point of contact which eventually made possible the development of a feeling of " common peopleness " with the Germans in other parts of the Holy Roman Empire. In their hour of need the German Austrians began to realize that they had more in common, spiritually, with the people who lived north of them, than with those with whom they were politically united, to the east and south. Not that all these Austrians ever thought of a change in the political status of Central Europe—they were hardly ready for that. Besides, some of the Germans were too religious to think of upsetting or breaking away, without supreme provocation, from any form of government which Providence had seen fit to place over them.[1] But once a number of the German Austrians realized, or believed, that they were one with the Germans of the *Reich* in the matters of language, culture and historical traditions, that is, when they became conscious of their own German " nationality ", there soon developed a definite form of cultural nationalism among them. In other words, they began to feel a supreme love and reverence for the language, literature, customs, traditions, laws and heroes of their nationality. From this it was only a step, if a big step, to a condition of mind among certain of the Austrians in which they were supremely loyal

---

[1] This was true especially of the Tyrolese and other mountain folk. In 1809, when the Austrians were trying to stir up the Tyrolese to revolt against Bavaria, they made special efforts to prove to these people that they were absolved from their allegiance to King Maximilian because the Bavarian authorities had violated certain terms of the Treaty of Pressburg under which the Tyrol had been ceded to them. See *infra,* p. 123n.

to the ideal of a politically unified and sovereign state made up of members of the German nationality—to the ideal of a German national state. And that is the sense in which "nationalism" is to be understood in this study: First, a feeling of cultural unity and identity with a definite group of people, and then a desire for a political union with them in a distinct national state, loyalty to which would be above all other possible human loyalties.[1]

Such ideas naturally had to overcome an enormous inertia in Austria before they could gain any ground. A number of factors, however, combined in the years following 1805 to supply an impetus to the rise of nationalism among the Austrians. First, Napoleon's troops, as they marched across the continent, and therefore across Austria, carried with them and spread the contagious concept of nationalism along with the notions of "liberty, equality, fraternity". Secondly, Napoleon's arrogance was becoming unendurable to self-respecting Austrians, and it helped to make them so much the more conscious of the need for a united German stand against the "outsider". Again, the distress into which the "fatherland" was plunged gave rise to considerable theorizing on the nature and meaning of a fatherland, and the desire for revenge made many receptive to any doctrine which implied retribution for insults and injuries. Further, the struggles of the patriotic Spaniards, which people had so often been allied with the Austrians, against their foreign oppressors, served as an inspiring example that seemed well worth emulating. In addition, a group of Austrian intellectuals led the way in a movement for a closer spiritual understanding and relationship between the common "descendants of Hermann", whether they lived within or without Habsburg territories. Finally, there came to power

[1] This conception of nationalism is based upon the first of the essays in Prof. C. J. H. Hayes' *Essays on Nationalism* (New York, 1926).

in Austria, at this particular time, a group of younger leaders who had a broader outlook and newer ideas of politics than had the members of the old school, like Colloredo and Thugut, who had been in control until 1805.

Under these circumstances it is not surprising that writers and thinkers about 1806 should have begun to appreciate and emphasize certain recent ideas and concepts regarding peoples and their loyalties. The concept of " fatherland ", and the importance of personal friendships and language as ties to the fatherland soon came to be defined and discussed. Thus, in a so-called letter " From Adolph to William " which appeared in a Viennese magazine in 1808, " Adolph " was made to inveigh against the idea of a world citizenship and of internationalism, saying:

The age cries out to me to become a citizen of the world, and a thousand living voices re-echo the call. " Citizen of the world " —the phrase has no meaning for me! The heart of a human being is too narrow for a world! The individual is forever bound to one nation by the force of eternal bonds—by his love for the ground that sustains him, by his circle of friends, by the language whose hallowed sounds he has essayed to repro-duce from the first babblings of his childhood. Verily, a human being can have only one fatherland![1]

Or again, a government proclamation in 1809 spoke of the need for unity and complete cooperation among all good citizens in one last great contest against France for political freedom and for everything " sweet and sacred " that was embraced within the meaning of the word " home " and the " concept of one's own fatherland ".[2] Still another written

---

[1] *Lebens-Accorde, Zeitschrift von Freyherrn von Putlitz* (Vienna, 1808), pp. 82-83. The editor of this magazine was a Prussian, but the periodical, as indicated, appeared in Vienna.

[2] " *Um Alles dasjenige . . . was nur immer die Heimath, und der Begriff eines eigenthümlichen Vatterlandes (sic) Süsses und Heiliges*

discussion of the word " fatherland " appeared in 1811, in the form of an introduction to a history of the Landwehr, that emergency militia called into being by a special proclamation of Emperor Francis in June, 1808.[1] The author of the volume was Franz Kurz, pastor at St. Florian in Upper Austria, and withal a popular historian in his day.[2] Kurz maintained [3] that every human being, save for a few " unfortunates ", had and loved a fatherland. It was in the fatherland, he said, that one completed the cycle of birth, life and death. During the course of this cycle one learned to love the soil, the laws and the people, and one became intimately acquainted with and fond of the customs and traditions that prevailed among one's people from time immemorial.[4] Upon further reflection Kurtz reached the conclusion that men have not always had a fatherland. The savage or barbarian, he wrote, really had no fatherland, for the place of primitive man's birth and the scene of his activities did not deserve this " beautiful name ". Those barbarians who lived by the chase had their " fatherland " wherever they could find game most plentiful. Those who were shepherds wandered from plain to plain, worshipping

in sich fasst." From an unsigned proclamation dated 1809, in Wiener Staats-Archiv, Staatskanzlei Vorträge, Faszikel 270. This proclamation was written during the armistice in 1809 and was intended to spur the people on to greater sacrifices and efforts in the event of a renewal of armed hostilities. The fact that it was never published, since the Peace of Vienna was signed before the armistice expired, does not diminish its importance as an illustrative document. In future references the Staats-Archiv will be cited W. S. A.

[1] Landwehr Patent, June 9, 1808.

[2] Wurzbach, C., Biographisches Lexikon des Kaiserthums Österreich, 60 vols. (Vienna, 1856-1890), vol. xiii, pp. 421-422. This work will be cited in the future as Wurzbach.

[3] Kurz, Franz, Geschichte der Landwehre in Österreich ob der Enns, 2 vols. (Linz, 1811).

[4] Ibid., vol. i, p. 1.

whatever piece of ground bore the necessary grasses for their flocks. The savages who lived on plunder, he continued, were little better than beasts of prey. They were not human beings and did not deserve to have a fatherland. To these uncouth and primitive groups who could not possibly be the citizens of any state, Kurz added those unfortunate individuals who were designated as slaves or serfs. Neither of these classes possessed a fatherland, since the slave lived for his master, and the serf for his lord. Neither the one nor the other was capable of a noble love of the fatherland.[1]

Other writers took cognizance of the fact that customs, traditions, laws and even religion differentiated one group of people from another, and that every individual preferred these attributes as they existed among his own people, to those of any and every other people. In 1809 a " native Austrian " endeavored to prove, rightly or wrongly, that Emperor Francis had gone to war with Napoleon in that year in order to preserve for posterity " our name, our language, our customs, our traditions, in a word, our fatherland." [2] The same pamphleteer, in another connection, also remarked upon the close relationship between the particular political system of one's native land, and such elements as " the language that one speaks, the religious beliefs in which one is raised, the customs and habits that one acquires through one's association with one's fellows, the native occupations and amusements—in short, everything that is valuable and dear to men." [3] This relationship, he continued, was happiest when a nation was governed by a native ruler—a man who had the same national upbringing (*National-erziehung*) as his subjects, who " knew what distinguished

---

[1] Kurz, *op. cit.*, p. 2.

[2] *Warum wird der jetzige Krieg geführt? Von einem österreichischen Landmanne* (Vienna, 1809), pp. 28-29.

[3] *Ibid.*, pp. 19-20.

them from all other peoples ", and who respected their peculiarities of religion, usages and habits.[1]

Closely bound up with this attitude of praise for things native was, of course, an attitude of slight for things foreign. Thus, one author discoursed bitterly upon the danger of the " spoiling " of a certain excellent language by " contamination " with foreign, and therefore inferior, ones.[2]   Another admitted that the knowledge of foreign languages was profitable as a key to unlock some literary treasure chests, and that the study of foreign tongues offered a good opportunity for mental training (!), but averred that an ability to speak the native language well transcended all other linguistic desiderata.[3]   " Should an individual," continued this scribe, " by any chance, be able to master foreign tongues—and we Germans seem to have been quite adept in this respect—well, then let him do so.   Charles V was reported to have said that whoever speaks four languages should count as four persons. . . . But let one beware lest, in a wasteful attempt to master other languages, one end by speaking them all, including one's own, wretchedly." [4]   Since he was writing about 1813, this patriot naturally also found occasion to make a reference to contemporary conditions : If any German will insist upon learning some foreign tongue, he advised, then let him scrupulously avoid the ill-equipped jargon of the enemy,

---

[1] *Warum wird der jetzige Krieg geführt? Von einem österreichischen Landmanne*, pp. 20-21.

[2] *Ibid.*, p. 14.

[3] *Unser Volk. Ein Blick in Vergangenheit und Zukunft* (Vienna, 1813?), pp. 51 *et seq.* Though this sixty-page, anonymous pamphlet is undated, it is listed in the catalog of the *Wiener Stadtbibliothek* as being of 1813. Various references in the text leave no doubt as to its having appeared at least in the period with which we are concerned, if not in that exact year. Similarly, the text indicates clearly that the author was an Austrian subject.

[4] *Ibid.*

of the French. Their language possessed neither euphony nor rhythm, freedom nor breadth. Others were bad enough. Why pick the worst? [1]

The habit of adopting foreign fashions and modes of dress was attacked in the same manner. Shafts were directed against that " glaring stupidity ", that " curious mixture of modesty and pride ", the " national weakness " for underestimating the worth of native things and preferring borrowed plumage. The complaint was made that too many people were wearing foreign clothes and adopting outlandish habits in the ridiculous belief that this would make them appear cultured and refined.[2] " Frenchified ladies " were berated, while the nation's daughters were criticized for seeking to find favor in the eyes of the native men by the adoption of foreign modes of dress and alien habits.[3] In fact, the men and women of the land were urged to readopt the truly dignified " native costumes " of the " days of old ".[4] Above all, it was clearly pointed out that the life work of every man should consist in striving for perfection in the characteristics of his own nation.[5]

Soon, too, there were recorded complaints concerning a

[1] *Unser Volk, op. cit.*

[2] *Ibid.*, pp. 20 *et seq.* Also various poems by Matthias L. Schleifer (1771-1842), the son of a Lower Austrian innkeeper. Schleifer lived in Vienna for a number of years, studying law with the aid of a stipend from the emperor. He later occupied a number of official positions in various Austrian cities. He was well-known and popular. *Cf.* Chapter IV for some of his verses, and Goedecke, Karl, *Grundriss zur Geschichte der deutschen Dichtung*, 2 ed. (Leipzig, Dresden, Berlin, 1898), vol. vi, pp. 552-554 for his life. In the future this work will be cited Goedecke.

[3] *Unser Volk*, pp. 56-57.

[4] A movement in this direction was approved by Empress Maria Ludovica, and furthered by the popular authoress Caroline Pichler. See *infra*, p. 103, and Hottenroth, F., *Handbuch der deutschen Tracht* (Stuttgart, 1892), p. 873.

[5] *Unser Volk*, pp. 20 *et seq.*

lack of uniformity in various phases of German development
and life. The question was asked: How could one expect
to find a "common spirit" among a people which was
brought up amidst the most diversified casts of thought and
feeling?[1] Further, the lack of "national vitality" worried
some patriots, while the disappearance of a supposed
"national solidarity" of bygone days was cause for concern
to others.[2] The absence of a truly national system of education, the best means for developing a "common spirit" was
bewailed. It was reasoned that before a people could adopt
a united stand on any matter, this people must recognize
itself as being one nation, and cherish itself as such. It was
argued that the "common spirit"[3] which was so essential
to a really national development could only be engendered
by appeal to a number of vital elements: to everything that
might bring the individual members of a people into closer
touch with one another, and remind them that they were all
organs of *one* great body; to everything that might make
them more familiar with the excellencies inherent in their
uniqueness, as well as with the outstanding achievements
that they had to their credit as a national group; and ulti-
mately by an appeal to certain generally known and recognized "national interests".[4] While other countries were
actively engaged in bringing to the realization of every child,
youth and man the eternal greatness of the particular nationality to which he belonged, chided a German Austrian nationalist in 1809, the members of the German nationality were
subject to influences which were calculated much more to

[1] *Unser Volk*, p. 7.

[2] *Ibid.*, p. 4. The author of the pamphlet here indicates that these
complaints, coming from his contemporaries, were "loud, general and
just".

[3] The pamphleteer employs this *English* phrase himself. *Ibid.*, p. 7.

[4] *Ibid.*

estrange them from their fatherland than to instil in them a special reverence and love for it.[1]

Much of the blame for the absence of a feeling of pride in and loyalty to the ideal of the fatherland, among the natives, was attached to the educational system of the Germans. Whereas the simplest solution was to teach the children of the nation to love the things that were characteristic of their people, the prevalent educational system among the Germans provided an intellectual training, said the critics, that was anything but national. The arts and sciences, and learning in general, according to contemporary writers, failed to furnish a genuine understanding and appreciation of the true national greatness. Learning remained confined within the walls of school buildings or within restricted circles of scholars, instead of being diffused throughout the land by educated men, wise parents, capable teachers and improved institutions. The function of these agencies should be to make known to all classes those peculiarly German national institutions which had stood the test of time. Everything that was great and good in the national character ought to have been presented in a manner to make the youth of the country burn with a desire to emulate their forebears. All the marvelous labors that had been accomplished through individual efforts in that vast area in which German was the predominant language, ought to have been taken up by a united nation and carried on to perfection. There was no reason, in spite of an admitted limitation of material means, why the forty universities and equally numerous art academies of the land should not have yielded first-rate products.[2]

[1] *Unser Volk*, p. 8.

[2] *Ibid.*, pp. 8, 51-55. That there was something wrong with the school system of Austria would seem to have been realized even by the Austrian Government, judging by such things as Count Saurau's report on intellectual training, rendered to Francis from Graz on March 16, 1808. *W. S. A., Kaiser Franz Akten, Fasz. 70.*

Here again, the patriots of 1809 insisted, the actual conditions were disappointing. The schools of the country had
customarily treated even the *history* of the fatherland, the
national history, with an incomprehensible coldness and indifference. Whereas the national history should have been
studied with especial thoroughness, treated most lovingly, and
" painted in glowing colors ", it was treated with a degree of
interest no more intense than that with which the history of
any other area was surveyed. Sorry to say, several of the
leading universities were badly injuring their reputations by
a mistaken universalism and an unreasonable impartiality.
Great German accomplishments were recorded and recited
without any warmth, or imagination or national pride! Intellectual worth " was being treated as coldly by the men of
the nation, as were the deeds and virtues of the ancestors."
Modesty ever was one of our characteristics, continued the
dissatisfied ones, and the ability to give due credit to foreign
achievements was a desirable " national virtue ". But was
it just to clip the very wings upon which the soul was borne
aloft to the heights of greatness? True greatness should
not fear to appear immodest.[1]

Along with this insistence upon a more intensive study of
national history, came the demand for a systematic national
hero worship and for the building up of an appropriate
national literature. That poetic talent was not wanting was
amply proved, it was claimed, by the existence of men like
Goethe. The real difficulty, it seemed, was a shortage of
national subject matter. Constant separations and splittings
had brought things to such a pass that what appealed to one
part of the nation was distasteful to another. Charles the
Great, for example, though one of the greatest of German
national heroes, was never mentioned in old Saxon songs
except as a ruthless conqueror and hated enemy. Again, the

[1] *Unser Volk*, pp. 13-15.

songs that inspired the Protestants in their divine services or encouraged them in battle, were naturally obnoxious to those whose religion was at variance with theirs. Even such recent and powerful war-songs as those of Alois Gleim,[1] it was contended, could not become really " national hymns " for the Germans, because they celebrated a hero [2] who, perhaps, more than any other hero preceding him, led German against German, brother against brother, in battle. Other poems and epics, such as the battle songs of the Swiss, were limited in their appeal to restricted areas, while such instances as the bravery and prowess of the Hansa towns remained totally unsung. True, the Song of the Nibelungs did possess some interest of a national scope, but, like so many of the good things produced by the fatherland, it had fallen into the limbo of oblivion and unfamiliarity. But perhaps this was just as well, since the Song's interest lay chiefly in the tragedy of the disruption of German might and unity through the unholy wedge of internal strife. It might prove stimulating, but it had no unifying influence.[3]

Among the writers and thinkers of the period who made such reflections upon the spiritual development of their nation, there were some who were quite aware of the circumstance that the Habsburg domains embraced members of different nationalities. They frequently made a special point of differentiating between the various peoples who happened to be living under the common sceptre of the Habsburgs, but they naturally did so in as inoffensive a manner as possible. For example: In its issue of August 12, 1808, a Viennese newspaper, the *Vaterländische Blätter für den österreich-*

---

[1] Johann Wilhelm Ludwig Gleim (1719-1803). His "Songs of a Prussian Grenadier" were among the best of his works.

[2] The reference is to Frederick the Great of Prussia, who was glorified by Gleim in such poems as "The Victor of Rossbach".

[3] *Unser Volk*, pp. 16 *et seq.*

ischen Kaiserstaat,[1] carried an article under the heading of
" A Survey of Literary Activity in Austria during the Years
1806 and 1807." [2]   The survey was introduced by this noteworthy paragraph:

The present essay is concerned with the literary efforts of the
years 1806 and 1807. Actually the attention is centered on
Austria, leaving it to others to catalogue the works of the remaining peoples in the widespread empire of Austria. Distinct
peoples, though they may all obey one mild sceptre, though they
may all enjoy the blessings of the same wise government, are
nevertheless segregated by differences in speech, in customs, in
habits, even, to a certain extent, in laws. Only the native (*der
Eingeborene*), only the one versed in the national language and
national customs, is capable of accurately portraying the intellectual movement of his nation (*seiner Nation*).

Finally, many of the German Austrians felt themselves
drawn more closely to their fellow-Germans outside the
limits of the Austrian Empire than they did to their fellow-
subjects—the Magyars and the rest. Of course, that was no
reason why Magyars and Czechs and Slavs should not help
the Austrians in their attempt to preserve and defend the
traditions of the " German nation " against Napoleon or anyone else.[3]   All help was welcome, and the number of Ger-

[1] The *Vaterländische Blätter* appeared from May 10, 1808 until the
close of 1820. Its editor in 1808 was John Michael Armbruster, an
active Francophobe propagandist, who, though born in Württemberg,
was now in the employ of Austria. *Cf.* Wagner, K., " Die Wiener
Zeitungen und Zeitschriften der Jahre 1808 und 1809 ", in *Archiv für
österreichische Geschichte* (Vienna, 1915), vol. civ, pp. 240 n. 3 and 235
n. In the future this article will be cited *A. f. o. G.*, vol. civ.

[2] *Vaterländische Blätter für den österreichischen Kaiserstaat*, August
12, 1808: " Übersicht der literarischen Thätigkeit in Österreich während
der Jahre 1806 und 1807." In the future the *Blätter* will be cited *Vat. Bl.*

[3] E. g. in *Denkwürdigkeiten Wiens während des Krieges zwischen
Österreich und Frankreich im Jahre 1805 von Freiherrn von P. Gaheis*
(Vienna, 1808), p. 14.

man pamphlets and proclamations praising the "brave Bohemians", the "loyal Hungarians" and the "good Italians" might well have been as great as the number praising the "courageous German brothers". In fact, though this was true more especially where the government was concerned directly, many of the verses and proclamations were written with a view to being acceptable for use, in translation, in all of the Habsburg lands. Nevertheless, there were those among the Austrians of these years who imagined and wrote of a "powerful German nation united under one supreme head", embracing even the Germanic-speaking Dutch and Swiss, but excluding Hungarians, Slavs and Italians.[1]

The concept of nationalism, then, was present in the German Austria of 1806 to 1815. With no attempt to depreciate the importance of such factors in Austrian life as dynastic loyalty, we shall see, in the following pages, that the dominant nationalism was German nationalism, and that it was present even among a fairly large section of the Austrian "masses". Since the government in Austria was so absolute and powerful at the time, it is necessary to begin with a summary of the attitude of the authorities toward the phenomenon.

[1]Cf. the vivid peroration concluding *Unser Volk*, pp. 58-60.

CHAPTER II

1809: Governmental Stimuli

On the eleventh of August, 1804, Francis II, Emperor of the Holy Roman Empire, announced by patent that henceforward he was also to be known as Francis I, Hereditary Emperor of Austria. Two years later, on August 6, 1806, the Holy Roman Empire ceased to be, though Francis continued to reign as Emperor of Austria for three more decades—until 1835. And while he reigned, others ruled.

"Franzl", as the Viennese were wont to call him, was kind-hearted and sincere. He loved peace and was willing to sacrifice much in order to avert the calamity of war. He was also a pious man, and devoted to his subjects. Private misfortune pursued him relentlessly. All these factors combined to make him popular with his subjects, especially with the sentimental Viennese. They never missed an occasion to display their loyalty and affection. Indeed, the mere sight of Francis frequently was sufficient to dispel from among them, at least temporarily, any feelings of dissatisfaction which they might entertain. Thus the popular welcome accorded him upon his return to Vienna after the catastrophe of 1809 was a remarkable demonstration of loyalty and faithfulness. Gloom and pessimism made way for joy and hope, while much of their lost courage and confidence was restored to the staid burghers of the " German capital ".[1]

An interesting contrast between Francis and Napoleon is presented by their respective attitudes toward pomp and

[1] Varnhagen von Ense, K. A., *Ausgewählte Schriften*, vol. ii, div. i: *Denkwürdigkeiten des eigenen Lebens*, 3 ed. (Leipzig, 1871), pt. ii, p. 307. Also entry for November 27, 1809 in Rosenbaum's *Tagebuch*, a manuscript diary in the *Nationalbibliothek* in Vienna.

display. Napoleon actually was vexed because Francis
appeared in public with so little ostentation. Upon his entry
into Vienna in 1805 the French ruler is said to have ex-
claimed to one of the city delegates who came to meet him:
"*Voyez comme je suis entouré.*" [1] But "Franzl's" simplicity
only endeared him all the more to his Austrians. As one of
them wrote: Napoleon's pomp " may be quite necessary in
Paris with its vain and flippant population which can only
discern the majesty of its rulers in red velvet robes; but a
German looks for much more than mere external embellish-
ments in his chief." [2]

Despite all this, however, and even though he preferred
the German tongue to any other of the numerous languages
in which he could converse,[3] Francis was not a German
nationalist. He could not afford to be, if he hoped to hold
his diversified domains together. As a Habsburg he might
be a symbol of unity to any number of nationalities. As a
German he would mean but little to the Magyars, the
Bohemians or the Italians. Accordingly, Francis remained
simply the scion of the Habsburgs, benevolent, cosmopolitan,
conservative. And his conservatism, which remained with
him even in the hectic days of 1809, must have exasperated
many a patriot. In reply, for example, to an offer of John
Michael Armbruster to edit an unsubsidized popular news
sheet for the purpose of " electrifying the people " and teach-
ing them a true love of the fatherland, Francis wrote that the
business of newspapers was to " narrate " not to discuss.[4]

---

[1] *Die Franzosen zu Wien—Eine historische Skizze nach den Berichten
eines Augenzeugen entworfen durch M. I. C. H.* (Photopel, 1806), pp.
130-131.

[2] *Ibid.*

[3] Wurzbach, vol. vi, p. 217.

[4] *W. S. A., Vortrag des Vizepräsidenten der Polizey Hofstelle vom
15. Hornung, 1809,* and answer of Francis dated February 22, 1809.
Kabinets Akten 1809, Nummer 763. (*Hornung* = February).

Occasionally, however, he seemed to see things in a different light, going so far, in March, 1809, as to order the distribution in Salzburg of large numbers of any such pamphlets as were likely to "elevate the public spirit ".[1] Again, Francis' letter appointing Frederick Stadion imperial commissioner with the army that soon was to invade the lands of Napoleon's German allies, indicates that that diplomat was chosen because of his " knowledge of the spirit and resources of the Germans ". Moreover, the commissioner was ordered to lighten the burden of military occupation in these German lands by a " due regard and respect for the national honor, national inclinations and even national prejudices " of the Bavarians, the Saxons and so on.[2]

Having been forced to accept the humiliating Treaty of Pressburg on December 26, 1805,[3] Francis became aware of the fact that Austrian officialdom and administration were suffering from an unprecedented rottenness and inefficiency. This inefficiency had made possible, for example, the appointment as commander of the main body of troops of General vor. Mack, whom Napoleon called one of the most incapable officers in existence. Even the rank and file of the French army laughed at him for the way he surrendered at Ulm. *"Nous avons pris le général Mack comme une prise de tabac"*, they boasted.[4] Obviously, the emperor must reconstitute the

[1] *W. S. A., Resolut. Auguss., 12. März 1809, Kabinets Akten 1809, Nummer 2594.*

[2] Letter of Francis dated March 7, 1809 in *W. S. A., Dépôt Stadion, Acta Fr. Stadion.*

[3] By the terms of the treaty Emperor Francis ceded the Tyrol and Vorarlberg to Bavaria, Venetia to the Kingdom of Italy, and a number of counties and cities to Württemberg and to Baden.

[4] Mack was also popularly known, after his defeat, as the " old wardrum "—for one never heard anything of him except that he had been beaten. Many of Mack's officers demanded that he be hanged after the Ulm fiasco. See Thürheim, Lulu, *Mein Leben*, edited by René van Rhyn (Munich, 1913), vol. i, p. 159 and Wertheimer, Ed., " Zur Geschichte

whole official family without delay, and make the necessary preparations to renew the conflict with France in the near future. For that Pressburg was final no one believed—the sting was far too severe.[1] That the seeds of the next war already were sown was quickly realized.[2] And that the next war would be different from the previous ones was, as we shall see, rapidly becoming evident.

In 1805 a renewal of hostilities with Napoleon had been favored only by the government of Austria. Both people and army were reluctant to make further sacrifices. But in 1809 government, people and army were united in a fierce and fervent desire to engage in a final and decisive conflict with the hated Conqueror.[3] New policies had ushered in a new era in the four-year interim, and the first sign of the new departure was the resignation of Count Ludwig Cobenzl as Foreign Minister. It was only natural that he should quit after the fiasco of 1805. With him went other members of the Imperial Council — Kollenbach, Francis Colloredo,

Wiens im Jahre 1809", in *Archiv für österreichische Geschichte*, vol. lxxiv, p. 165. This article will be cited in the future as *A. f. o. G.*, vol. lxxiv.

[1] Wrote the Freiherr Kübeck von Kübau in a letter of February 15, 1806: "*Der Pressburger Friede vom 26. Dezember 1805 hat uns, ich meine Alle, die wir der Monarchie und dem Kaiserhause mit Liebe anhängen, mit Schmerz und Gram erfüllt.*" See *Tagebücher des Carl Friedrich Freiherrn Kübeck von Kübau*, edited by his son (Vienna, 1909), vol. i, p. 164.

[2] Thus, on February 15, 1806, Minister Finkenstein wrote to his sovereign, the King of Prussia, from Vienna: "*Le traité de Presbourg contient déjà le germe d'une nouvelle guerre.*" Quoted in Wertheimer, Ed., *Geschichte Österreichs und Ungarns* (Leipzig, 1890), vol. ii, p. 105 n. 4.

[3] On March 18, 1809 the French chargé d'affaires in Vienna, M. Dodun, wrote to the French Foreign Minister, M. Champagny: "*En 1805, la guerre était dans le Gouvernement, mais non dans l'armée ni dans le peuple; en 1809, elle est voulue par le Gouvernement, par l'armée et par le peuple.*" *Archives du Ministère des Affaires Etrangères à Paris, Autriche. Corresp. Pol., Vienne, 1809,* vol. 382, folio 138. In the future this reference will be cited *A. E. A. C. P.*

Lamberti, von Stahl and several more.   No less than twenty-five generals were retired.[1]   The emperor next appointed an entirely new government headed by the German-minded Count Philip Stadion, who specifically undertook the task of rendering the war of revenge a "national" one.[2]   Francis generously supported Stadion's ideas and policies, and it was this attitude of the emperor which allowed many patriots to read into his superficially " neutral " actions and words the ideals with which they themselves were imbued.   They felt that the German Emperor was the natural leader in the movement for German reunification.   And he, at least, did nothing that could be interpreted as un-German.

On January 6, 1808, Francis, having previously been widowed twice, sought consolation in a third marriage.   His cousin, Maria Ludovica Beatrice of Austria, became his empress.   She was the daughter of Archduke Ferdinand, captain-general of Lombardy, and the Archduchess Maria Beatrice d'Este.   Maria Ludovica had been destined for a convent, but her parents were forced to flee Italy with her in 1796—driven out by Bonaparte.[3]   Now, twelve years later, this descendant of the imperial Habsburgs and proud d'Estes, was Empress of Austria.   And she remembered.

The wedding presented a splendid opportunity for popularizing German raiments at the expense of foreign, especially French fashions.   Madame de Staël, who was in Vienna at the time because her friend August Wilhelm Schlegel happened to be there,[4] described the ceremony in her German

---

[1] Weiss, K., *Geschichte der Stadt Wien*, 3 ed., 2 vols. (Vienna, 1882-1883), vol. ii, p. 252.

[2] " *Il me paraît tout aussi nécessaire de rendre cette guerre nationale.*" *W. S. A., Vortrag des Grafen Stadion, Pressburg, 27. September 1808.*

[3] Wurzbach, vol. vii, p. 53.

[4] Mme. de Staël and her " Schli–Schla–Schlegel " were the objects of many jokes in Vienna at the time. *Cf.* Werner, R. M., "Aus dem Wiener Lager der Romantik", in *Österreichisch-Ungarische Revue*, n. s. vol. viii, p. 283.

memoirs. The church was filled with the highest state officials; with the mothers, wives and daughters of the "oldest Teutonic nobility". No one had purchased anything new for the festival. Everyone displayed what he possessed according to his means. Even the ladies were attired in inherited family garments. The spirit of ancient times presided over a magnificence that had been prepared by the centuries—but that did not entail a single new sacrifice on the part of the people.[1] Incidentally, the empress soon became an active advocate of the adoption by German women of an ancient, distinctive, Teutonic form of dress (*Tracht*).[2] In this endeavor she was ably supported by Caroline Pichler.[3]

Interestingly enough, the very day of the wedding was chosen by an old Viennese burgher for the drawing up of his last will and testament. Like so many others he felt that the marriage presaged a renewal of hostilities with France. But he was so pessimistic as to see in the approaching war the complete downfall and destruction of the monarchy.[4]

Within two months of the ceremony the French Ambassador in Vienna, Andréossy, wrote to Napoleon's Foreign Minister, Champagny, that the influence of the empress was rapidly becoming evident on all sides. There was much talk about reforms, he noted, and better men were being selected to serve in the various administrative departments of the government.[5] Four weeks later he reported: " The empress continues to arouse general admiration; she is seeking to

[1] Mme. de Staël, *De l'Allemagne* (Paris, 1845), p. 44.

[2] Nagl, J. W., *Deutschösterreichische Literaturgeschichte* (Vienna, 1914), vol. ii, p. 841.

[3] See *infra*, p. 103.

[4] Wertheimer, Ed., *Die drei ersten Frauen des Kaisers Franz* (Leipzig, 1893), p. 82.

[5] *A. E. A. C. P., Vienne, 1808*, vol. 381, folio 105, Andréossy to Champagny from Vienna, March 19, 1808.

revive the glory of the throne, and she is succeeding with much dignity. If circumstances favor her I do not doubt but that she will become a second Maria Theresa."[1] And a second Queen Louise, he might have added. Similar observations were made by the Prussian minister at Vienna, who marvelled at her talent for ruling, and considered her the directing genius at court.[2]

Maria Ludovica was immensely popular with her new subjects. They, too, hailed her as a second Maria Theresa, and frequently referred to her as *unsere liebe Landesmutter*. The whole populace was moved to tears when she, with the aid of the Archduke Charles and her brother Maximilian, fastened the flags of the six Viennese *Landwehr* battalions to their flag-poles, after men and banners had been blessed by the venerable Archbishop Count von Hohenwart.[3] Wild shouts of enthusiasm replaced the tears when she walked across the square from beautiful St. Stephen's to hand the standards over to the respective battalions.[4] The empress need but lead on—the masses were eager to follow!

And Maria Ludovica was also a brave woman. In the spring of 1809 nothing could frighten her except — the thought of peace![5]

[1] *A. E. A. C. P., Vienne, 1808*, vol. 381, folio 117, Andréossy to Champagny from Vienna, April 9, 1808.

[2] *Finkenstein an den König, Wien, 30. Juli 1808, Publicationen aus den k. Preussischen Staatsarchiven*, vol. vi, p. 523.

[3] *Briefe des jungen Eipeldauers an seinen Herrn Vettern in Kakran*, Vienna, 1809, 4. Heft, p. 46. Also Bergenstamm, A. von, *Materialien zur Geschichte der österreichischen Landesvertheidigung etc.* (Vienna, 1809), pp. 52-53. The newspaper called *Briefe des jungen Eipeldauers* will be cited in the future as *Eipeldauer*.

[4] Reichardt, J. F., *Vertraute Briefe ... zu Ende des Jahres 1808 und zu Anfang 1809*, edited by G. Gugitz (Munich, 1915), vol. ii, p. 55.

[5] " *Ich bin gar nicht kleinmüthig und fürchte nichts, als wenn man auf Frieden denkt.*" Letter of April 27, 1809 from Maria Ludovica to Archduke John, in Zwiedeneck-Südenhorst, H. von, *Erzherzog Johann von Österreich im Feldzuge von 1809* (Graz, 1892), p. 16.

More important than either Francis or Ludovica in directly arousing German nationalist sentiment among the Austrians was the Minister of Foreign Affairs, Count Philip Stadion.[1] Scion of an old Rhenish family, Stadion, like Stein, had been one of the few remaining free imperial knights whose ancestral lands had been sequestered by the advancing French. This fact probably explains his intense hatred of the French Government and Napoleon, though the antipathy seems not to have extended to the French people.[2] From a personal viewpoint the Count was better fitted than had been his predecessors to instil into the people an unprecedented enthusiasm, an almost fanatical confidence[3] and a powerful national spirit and loyalty. He was intensely patriotic, an aristocrat in thought and action, and withal straightforward, frank and courageous. He despised the censorship and the police spy system as being beneath the

[1] Stadion's appointment was probably due in large measure to the influence of the emperor's brother, Archduke Charles, who considered the Count without a peer in the business of handling foreign affairs. *W. S. A., Kaiser Franz Akten, Fass. 78a*, note of Archduke Charles to Francis, January 3, 1806, on the condition of the monarchy.

[2] *A. E. A. C. P., Vienne, Supplément pour 1809*, vol. 384, folio 169: " Suite des renseignements sur la Cour de Vienne, vers juillet 1809." Also *A. E. A. C. P., Vienne, 1807*, vol. 380, folio 413, Andréossy to Champagny, December 24, 1807: " *Il* [Stadion] *ne peut dans les circonstances les plus ordinaires déguiser sa haine pour tout ce qui tient au gouvernement Français.*" And also *W. S. A., Kaiser Franz Akten, Fass. 78e, Vortrag Stadions, Wien, 22. Jänner 1809, Beilage:* " *Mein erster Satz wird also dieser seyn: dass wir Krieg gegen Napoleon, nicht aber gegen Frankreich führen.*" Napoleon said that the appointment of Stadion filled him with " deep distrust " as to what the future held in store, *cf.* Perthes, C. T., *Politische Zustände und Personen in Deutschland zur Zeit der französischen Herrschaft*, 2 vols. (Gotha, 1869), vol. ii, p. 301.

[3] It was rumored among the people at the time that the Holy Virgin had appeared before a worshipper in St. Stephen's and prophesied a victory over the French forces in the campaigns of 1809. *Cf.* Lilienstern, Rühle von, *Reise mit der Armee im Jahre 1809*, 3 vols. (Rudolfstadt, 1810-1811), vol. ii, p. 184.

dignity of a great state, and he placed the opening of letters on a level with eavesdropping.[1]

Prone to be rather gay and light-hearted, enjoying more than was good for his reputation the company of women, and glorying in the name of *bon-vivant,* Count Stadion yet was filled with a determination to checkmate Bonaparte and to liberate Austria, to liberate " Germany ", from the bonds which were weighing so heavily upon them. To that end he concentrated all the powers of his remarkable and practical intellect, his great learning, his affability, his untiring energy, his talents and his will-power. From the point of view of statesmanship his greatest fault was probably his tendency to regard even the most serious matters too lightly and too optimistically. On the other hand he was quick to lose heart and courage when his plans went awry, or misfortune dogged his footsteps.[2]

The presence of a new spirit in the government soon became apparent in the form of a proclamation drawn up by Stadion and another member of the administration, named Baldacci, and issued on February 6, 1806. This document solemnly promised a freer intellectual life and hearty governmental support for all worthy and useful literary endeavors.[3] Moreover, the minister believed in " full freedom for books " because of their enormous influence in the welding of a national culture. This attitude was reflected in a fairly liberal, though detailed, ordinance issued in March, 1806, regarding the traffic in books. There were even circulated

[1] *W. S. A., Vortrag Stadions an Seine Majestät,* June 8, 1808.

[2] " *Man thut ihm nicht zu viel wenn man sagt: Er hat Alles, auch sich selbst zu leicht genommen.*" Memoir of Knesebeck, 1809. After the first five days of battle in 1809, with Regensburg in Napoleon's hands, he cried: " *Mon Dieu, mon Dieu, tout est perdu!* " Cf. Droysen, J. G., *Vorlesungen über das Zeitalter der Freiheitskriege,* 2 ed., 2 vols. (Gotha, 1886), vol. ii, p. 330.

[3] Wurzbach, vol. xxxvii, p. 39.

some rumors concerning the possible suspension of the censorship laws relating to newspapers and periodicals; but this much-needed relief failed to reach the stage of realization.[1] December 30, 1806, saw the appearance of a further reform decree, this time in connection with the printing of a set of rules and regulations governing the duties and obligations attaching to all governmental positions. Every official was requested either to read for himself, or to listen to a reading of, these rules once a year.[2] It was hoped thus to end the sloth and corruption which had been the bane of Austrian politics for so long. No more would the state hire officials " whose shortsightedness rendered them incapable of grasping the spirit of the age."[3]

Stadion also realized the value of propaganda, and kept emphasizing to the emperor the necessity for working on the " spirit of the nation "[4] and for creating an " electrified army ". To this end he demanded a general cooperation for the production of pamphlets and broadsides in great quantities. These might then, with the aid of the police, be " cast among the public ".[5] He further let it be known that he was heart and soul for the publication and spreading of any composition that would arouse national sentiment, and he indignantly protested against the withholding from publication of an article on the newly-created *Landwehr* which he himself

[1] Just, G., *Als die Völker Erwachten* (Vienna, 1907), p. 55.

[2] *W. S. A., Kaiser Franz Akten, Fass. 70*, paragraph 13 of *Vorschriften über die allgemeinen Pflichten und besonderen Obliegenheiten der Stellen und Beamten etc., Wien, 1807.*

[3] A criticism of the old group of officials made by Archduke Charles in the note to Francis of January 3, 1806, *op. cit.*

[4] *W. S. A., Vortrag Stadions*, October 22, 1808.

[5] *W. S. A., Staatskanzlei Korrespondenz, Fass. 73*, marginal annotation by Stadion on a note sent from Vienna by Aulic Councillor Hudelist, April 11, 1809. An Aulic Councillor was a member of the Aulic or State Council.

had revised.[1]   The skilled propagandist Gentz was notified
in August, 1808, that his services might be in demand shortly,
and on February 18, 1809, he was called to Vienna.[2]
Similarly, when the exiled nationalist Stein asked for permission to live in Prague, in 1809, Stadion supported his
request with the recommendation that the Baron be allowed
to live in Brünn instead, because he " soon might prove to
be exceedingly useful, and would then be close at hand." [3]
All writers, good and mediocre, were to be drafted for service
in a huge press campaign.

Moreover, encouraged by the many demonstrations of
patriotism taking place throughout the land every day,
Stadion ordered the careful collection of these "noble
strains " so as to make them known to the public at large.
It was a " double duty " to preserve these splendid proofs of
Austria's ability to outdo all other lands and peoples in true
patriotic exertions.   This gathered information was then to
be published in special booklets as well as in the Viennese and
provincial newspapers.   Eventually there might be gotten up
a sort of anthology of patriotic broadsides, pamphlets, proclamations, speeches, poems, etc.[4]

Despite his dislike of the censorship, Stadion was careful
to forestall any event which might dampen the public spirit.
Thus he forbade the performance or publication of a
tragedy entitled *Hannibal* because " after a series of constantly recurring appeals for revenge against Rome as the
oppressor of the freedom of the masses, the conclusion runs

[1] *W. S. A., Polizey Corresp. 1807-1810.   Noten an die Polizey Hofstelle,
Fasz. 2*, Stadion to Baron von Hager, vice-pres. of police, September 9,
1809.

[2] *Tagebücher von Friedrich von Gentz—Aus dem Nachlass Varnhagen's
von Ense* (Leipzig, 1861), pp. 63 and 66.

[3] *W. S. A., Vortrag Stadions*, January 17, 1809.

[4] *W. S. A., Polizey Corresp., op. cit.*, Stadion to Hager, March 10,
1809.

so far counter to all legitimate expectations as to leave Rome triumphant; her opponents, on the other hand, having to content themselves with impotent curses and the doubtful consolation of poison." And he rightly concluded that " as an example, this is anything but encouraging." [1]

As Foreign Minister, Stadion took it upon himself to maintain unbroken contact with the rest of Germany.[2] In this capacity he was ably assisted by his older brother, Frederick Lothar,[3] who, as Austrian minister to Bavaria, was able to keep Philip constantly in touch with conditions and sentiments in South Germany. The essence of their correspondence and conversations seems to have been noted down in two drafts in the elder Stadion's handwriting, entitled respectively, " General Observations Regarding the Impending War " and " Observations Regarding the March of the Imperial Austrian Troops through Germany." In the first of these documents it is pointed out that although *Germany* is an " aggregate of states " rather than one state, the *German nation* must always be considered as *one*. Accordingly, in the great task of freeing Germany from the foreign yoke which oppresses it, the èmperor occupies the position of overlord; the commanding officer of the emperor's troops becomes the generalissimo of Germany; and the General Headquarters is located in Vienna, the capital of Germany and of the German nation.[4] The second manuscript discusses the

[1] *Ibid.*, Stadion to Pres. of Police Summerau, June 29, 1808.

[2] *Allgemeine Deutsche Biographie*, 56 vols. (Leipzig, 1875-1912), vol. xxxv, p. 372. Cited in the future as *A. D. B.*

[3] Though Frederick Lothar Stadion was two years older than his brother, Philip, he gave up his rights of the first-born in order to devote himself to the Church. When Philip became foreign minister in Austria, he called on his equally German-minded brother to help him in the struggle against Napoleon. *Cf.* Perthes, *op. cit.*, vol. ii, pp. 311 and 320.

[4] *Allgemeine Gesichtspunkte über den bevorstehenden Krieg in Beziehung auf Deutschland*, 5⁰, quoted in Fournier, A., "Österreichs Kriegsziele

importance of winning over the people in the German lands that had to be crossed by Austrian troops to such an extent that the influence of the intriguing French Government may be banished forever.   To this end the Austrians should make it clear that their purpose is not to conquer Germany, but rather to combine with their " fellow-Germans " to drive the French tyrants from Germany, and to restore once again the ancient freedom and independence that was "Germania's ".[1]

Without doubt the Stadions hoped to find in Vienna " the German Emperor, the protector of the laws, the living representative of ancient glories, the symbol of German honor and its champion against foreign aggression! "[2]   On the other hand the whole attempt to arouse the German nation out of its lethargy provided one Dr. Karl Venturini, an ardent admirer of Napoleon, with welcome material for sarcastic comments in his *Chronicle of the Nineteenth Century*.   The volume for 1809 ridicules the Austrian Government for essaying the unheard-of in order to ensure victory.   The war against France, the Doctor wrote, was to become literally a German national war.   The people rather than the princes of Germany were to be " lured " into shaking off the bonds of customary obedience, and of blind reverence for such superiors as were not " legitimate ".   Independence, liberty, national honor, hitherto without meaning to the masses, were to be made powerful levers in rousing German might, and in uniting for a common purpose that German public opinion

im Jahre 1809 " in *Beiträge zur neueren Geschichte Österreichs*, booklet iv.   Fournier received the document from Count Rudolph Stadion, a descendant of Count Philip.

[1] *W. S. A., Dépôt Stadion, Acta des Herrn Grafen Friedrich von Stadion in Staats-Kriegs-und anderswärtigen Angelegenheiten aus den Jahren 1800-1810: Bemerkungen über den Marsch der kaiserl. königl. Österreichischen Armee nach Deutschland.*

[2] Wurzbach, vol. xxxvii, pp. 42-43.

which ever had been divided. "Writers a-plenty could be found who now announced that the Messiah of German freedom, of national independence, would come from Austria, from Vienna, that notorious paradise of *gourmands!*" [1] Incidentally, Venturini published his book at Altona, near Hamburg, and hence at a safe distance from Vienna!

Closely associated with Stadion in the task of awakening a German nationalism among the masses, were the Archdukes Charles and John, brothers of Emperor Francis. Charles was a " small, lively man, Austrian in mode of speech, a thoroughly kindly, genuinely German, splendid being." [2] The hero of several earlier campaigns (in 1796 and 1799), [3] Charles was hailed throughout the German lands as a great general and a savior of the fatherland. After his victories in 1799 a special medal—a Maltese cross bearing the inscription *Heil dem Retter Germaniens*—was struck in his honor. At that time, too, following the suggestion of the Princess Fürstenberg, German women and girls of every rank and class wore miniature crosses with a similar inscription. Their shawls, moreover, were embroidered in gold with a little verse declaring that Germany's daughters were proud to wear the symbol of Charles' victories—" no other ornament could adorn the wearer more becomingly." [3]

Appointed generalissimo of the imperial armies in 1805, Charles set about introducing urgent military reforms almost immediately. Close order drill was simplified. Incapable officers were dismissed. Pigtails were abolished. The hair was no longer to be powdered. Leggings were shortened so

[1] Venturini, K., *Chronik des neunzehnten Jahrhunderts, VI. Band, 1809* (Altona, 1811), pp. 89-90.

[2] He was so characterized in 1812 by a friend named Eichendorff. *Cf. Erzherzog Karl, Der Feldherr und seine Armee* (Vienna, 1913), p. 69.

[3] At Würzburg in 1796, at Ostrach, Stockach and Zürich in 1799.

[4] Criste, O., *Das Buch von Erzherzog Carl* (Vienna and Leipzig, 1914), p. 135.

as to allow freedom of movement in marching.   The pace
was quickened and a livelier manual of arms introduced.
The men were to be accorded better treatment with a view
to increasing their self-respect and sense of honor.   And for
the sake of greater mobility the forces were divided into nine
active corps and two reserve corps, while the artillery was
created a distinct branch of the army.[1]   Although, by virtue
of his reputation and reforms, he possessed the complete
confidence of the army, Charles was considered highly over-
rated by some people.   Thus, Herr von Baldacci, a close
adviser of the emperor, was firmly convinced of two things
in this connection.   First, that Napoleon was an utterly incapable and stupid general.   Secondly, that Napoleon would
have been routed on more than one previous occasion if only
the Archduke Charles had not been even more incapable.[2]
The German masses, however, felt as did the army.   And
their pride in their illustrious archduke reached a new high-
water mark when, upon the arrival of a Spanish government
vessel in Trieste on November 27, 1808, a rumor was circulated to the effect that the Spanish people had offered the
crown of Spain to Charles.[3]

Realizing the value of propaganda in converting the masses
to a new viewpoint, Charles was especially interested in the
dissemination of knowledge regarding military heroes and
military traditions.   He was particularly anxious to have the
history of the celebrated Hohenzollern Cuirrassier Regiment
become a familiar story to every citizen.[4]   Then, literally

---

[1] *Kübeck's Tagebücher*, a letter of May 30, 1807, vol. i, p. 210, and
Mayer, F. M., *Geschichte Österreichs*, 3 ed., 2 vols. (Vienna and Leipzig,
1909), vol. ii, p. 538.

[2] *Kübeck's Tagebücher*, vol. i, p. 270.

[3] Erzherzog Johann, "Feldzugserzählung" in *Mitt. des k. k. Kriegsarchivs*, Supplement 4 (Vienna, 1909), p. 9.

[4] *Min. des Innern, Polizeiarchiv, 1808, Fasz. 155*, quoted in Wagner,
K., "Die Flugschriftenliteratur des Krieges von 1809", in *Anno Neun,*
which is vol. v of *Bücherei des österreichischen Volksschriftenvereins*
(Brixen, 1912), p. 100.   See also *infra*, p. 103.

burning with zeal to smite the foe when the war finally came,[1] Charles issued a fiery army order under date of April 6, 1809. Though the order was written by Friedrich Schlegel, it really expressed the sentiments of Charles, exhorting the soldiers to rally around him and advance to the attack.

Companions-in-arms [it read] the eyes of the world, the eyes of all such as still possess a sense of national honor, are focused upon you. You shall not share the disgrace of becoming tools of oppression. You shall not fight, under distant skies, the endless wars stirred up by a consuming ambition. You shall not be doomed to annihilate innocent peoples. You shall not be forced to blaze the trail, over the dead bodies of slain defenders of their fatherland, to a ravished throne for a foreigner!— A happier lot awaits you: Europe seeks freedom beneath your standards. Your victories will loose its bonds. Those of your German brethren who are still in the ranks of the enemy await redemption at your hands. You are engaging in righteous combat, else I would not stand at your head.[2]

When Charles appeared in the camp of his troops on the day following the publication of this order he received a tremendous ovation. His humaneness and kindliness had endeared him to the hearts of all those veterans who in previous wars had seen him weep on the battlefields where German blood flowed so freely. The attitude of the enthusiastic soldiery is interestingly portrayed in a poem of the time written "by a grenadier". In prose metamorphosis its substance is as follows: The reappearance of Charles in the midst of his German hosts brings tears of joy to every veteran's eyes. Now German might will carry the flag of victory through fire and smoke—for Charles is leading the advance. The grenadiers, those hardy sons of battle, will

[1] *Gentz' Tagebücher*, p. 67.

[2] *Armee Befehl*, Vienna, April 6, 1809.

wade in blood, will push on and on for Charles, for Francis, for Germany! On to victory over the ground hallowed by Charles' former triumphs! On to the spot where once we conquered, and where Charles was moved to tears at the sight of his bleeding and mangled soldiers. God will protect those who are left behind while the grenadiers advance through peril and blood and death. God's blessing will be upon you, Charles, and upon us, and upon the fatherland. And then when the danger is past and the enemy banished forever, Charles will return in our midst, hailed by the liberated fatherland. Cries of gratitude and exaltation will pour forth from every hut. All sorrows will vanish and all eyes become moist with tears of joy. Then Germany's princes will once again draw closer to Francis. Then aged parents will revel in the possession of a sturdy German son, of Charles and of Francis.[1]

As to Charles' younger brother John, he was " the most German of all the archdukes." [2] " I am German, German with heart and soul " he had said of himself.[3] And since the " welfare and unity of Germany " meant more to John than anything else,[4] it is small wonder that the dissensions between the greatest German monarchies, Austria and Prussia, should have filled him with sadness. He worked diligently for an alliance with Prussia and never grew tired of emphasizing the need for fostering a true German national spirit.[5] He

[1] *An Erzherzog Carl zu seiner Ankunft bei der Armee. Von einem Grenadier* (Vienna, 1809).

[2] Lamprecht, K., *1809, 1813, 1815, Anfang, Höhezeit und Ausgang der Freiheitskriege* (Berlin, 1913), p. 10.

[3] Richter, H. M., *Geistesströmungen [in Österreich]* (Berlin, 1875), p. 337.

[4] Wurzbach, vol. vi, p. 285.

[5] Erzherzog Johann, *Denkschrift vom 15. Februar 1807*, quoted in Krones, F., *Zur Geschichte Österreichs, 1792-1816* (Gotha, 1886), pp. 69 *et seq.*

could pay no greater compliment than to call a person " German ". Indeed, when he first met that fiery advocate of a Greater Germany, Hans von Gagern, he recorded in his diary: " Gagern is with me; there is a German for you! " [1] And the Styrians and Carinthians, in whose midst he had spent many a happy month, were characterized by him as " faithful mountain folk of German origin ". [2]

The fire of nationalism which warmed the young prince's heart received constant replenishment through his contact with three powerful personalities—the historian Johannes von Müller, the publicist Friedrich von Gentz, and the patriot Josef von Hormayr. Müller was a native Swiss historian whose monumental and pioneer *History of the Swiss People* was one of John's two favorite works, the other being Herder's *Cid*. [3] In the History, as well as in many of his other writings, lectures and speeches, Müller strove constantly to awaken a community of spirit among the Swiss cantons—a " Swiss spirit " (*Schweizersinn*), he called it. He pointed out the inevitability of federation, and showed how united action had been resorted to again and again in times past when danger had threatened. He declared that only in unity could his compatriots hope to find salvation and happiness. The importance of a " national upbringing " was stressed, and the upper classes were urged to take the lead in the matter of patriotic activities. The masses would then follow suit quickly enough. [4]

[1] *Aus dem Tagebuch Erzherzog Johanns von Österreich 1810-1815*, edited by F. Krones (Innsbruck, 1891), entry of January 10, 1813.

[2] In a proposed proclamation to Inner Austria in case of a renewal of war in 1809, drawn up by John. *W. S. A., Kabinets Akten 1809*, September 15, 1809, *Beilage*.

[3] *A. D. B.*, vol. xiv, p. 287.

[4] Müller, J. von, *Sämmtliche Werke*, 40 vols. in 14 (Stuttgart, 1831-1835), vols. vii-xxiii *passim.*, especially vol. vii, pp. xvi and xxiii, and vol. xxiii, pp. 344-345.

Since John was hoping to achieve in Germany what
Müller was striving for in Switzerland, it was not unnatural
that the two men should be drawn toward one another. For
a number of years they corresponded frequently and intimately. The political opinions and ideas which they ex-
changed invariably dealt with the fascinating thought of
German unification. The archduke delighted in submitting
his various schemes for the attainment of this goal to the
historian for criticism and approval.[1] Both men became
more nationalistic because of their intercourse.

In a different, yet equally effective way, did Friedrich von
Gentz influence Archduke John. Born in Breslau, in 1764,
Gentz rose to fame as a publicist, and entered Prussian state
services in 1793. Four years later he greeted the new King
of Prussia, Frederick William III, with a brilliantly written
demand for the adoption of liberal national policies, for freedom of the press, and above all for a united Germany under
the dual control of Prussia and Austria. However, in view
of the terms of the Peace of Basel of 1795, Gentz' ceaseless
advocacy of war against Napoleon made his position in
Prussia untenable. In 1802 he entered the service of
Austria.[2] Within three years he became an " Austrian to
the fingertips ",[3] and more anti-French than ever.

Not that Gentz was an outspoken German nationalist.
The important thing to him was the establishment of a
European balance of power and the maintenance of law and
order. For, he wrote, " the state is neither the property of
an individual nor an arrangement left to the discretion of

---

[1] *A. D. B.*, vol. xiv, p. 287.

[2] *Brockhaus' Konversations-Lexikon*, 14 ed. (Leipzig, 1902), vol. vii,
p. 701. Cited in the future as Brockhaus.

[3] At least so he wrote in a letter of October 24, 1805 to Count Louis
Starhemberg, *cf. Mitt. des Instituts für österreichische Geschichtsforschung* (Innsbruck, 1886), vol. vii, p. 124.

peoples. It is an eternal society (*eine ewige Gesellschaft*), destined to tie together the past, the present and the future by an indissoluble bond; and in this sense it is of God." [1] From this it followed that Napoleon, who was interfering with the established order, must be overthrown, or at least checked. Accordingly, Gentz devoted twenty years of his life to the accomplishment of this task. But he felt that the restoration of the natural order of things was dependent upon the permanent dominance of a united and independent Germany. Neither Austria nor Prussia was powerful enough to maintain peace and quiet on the Continent. Only Germany could save Germany! Once in Vienna, therefore, he redoubled his efforts to bring about a speedy renewal of hostilities with France. Between 1804 and 1809 he published numerous memorials indicating the need for Austro-Prussian unity as a preliminary to German unity and European peace. Indirectly, therefore, his journalistic activities did much to arouse a national sentiment in others. In pleading for German unity he helped foster a spirit of German nationalism.[2]

It remained, however, to convert the peace-loving Emperor Francis to similar views. Gentz himself was unable to make great headway in this direction, but he soon discovered a valuable ally in Archduke John. Impelled to act for the same end by different yet compatible motives, the two men found little difficulty in working together. Gentz had an unbounded admiration for John. He marvelled at the prince's " great and truly regal thoughts " which were at the same time " so solid, so clear and so discreet." [3] John, on the other hand, appreciated Gentz' statesmanlike qualities

[1] *Aus dem Nachlass Friedrichs von Gentz*, edited by Prokesch-Osten (1867), vol. i, p. 287.

[2] Guglia, E., *Friedrich von Gentz* (Vienna, 1901), p. 240.

[3] *A. D. B.*, vol. xiv, p. 285.

and political acumen. The friends encouraged one another, and while Gentz prepared diplomatic memoranda, John corresponded with nationally-minded persons throughout the Germanies. Gentz also was responsible for the correspondence which developed between the archduke and Prince Louis Ferdinand, the " soul " of the national party at the court of Berlin.[1] And John, of course, had considerable influence in the counsels of the emperor, all the more since the empress had greater faith in him than in any other of the official advisers.

Of the last member of this triumvirate, Josef Freiherr von Hormayr, we shall say more later, in connection with the Tyrol. Suffice it to say here that he first met the archduke in the fall of 1800, though it remained for Johannes von Müller really to bring them together a year later.[2] The community of interest of the two like-aged German youths (they were born on the same day) presaged a firm friendship. Indeed, for almost a score of years, Hormayr remained John's chief lieutenant.[3] The one was as enthusiastic an advocate of German unity as the other. Moreover, since he was in no way directly connected with the reigning family, the Tyrolese patriot could afford to be bolder and more outspoken in his views than the archduke, without necessarily compromising or hampering the government in its diplomatic negotiations. A good summary of the Freiherr's aims and methods is given in an official French report of 1811 describing his activities:

[1] Guglia, *op. cit.*, p. 178.

[2] Krones, F., *Aus Österreichs stillen und bewegten Jahren, 1810-1812 und 1813-1815* (Innsbruck, 1892), pp. 182 *passim*.

[3] Wihan, J., " Matthäus von Collin und die patriotisch-nationalen Kunstbestrebungen in Österreich zu Beginn des neunzehnten Jahrhunderts ", in *Euphorion* (Vienna, 1901), suppl. vol. v, p. 106. This 100-page contribution is crowded with information on the literary and artistic developments in early nineteenth-century Vienna.

Baron Hormayr . . . has undertaken the editorship of a periodical called *Archives of Geography, History, Politics and Military Science*. Under this rather innocent-sounding title he continues to ape Thomas Paine in the preaching of revolutionary doctrines. These doctrines, he claims, should bring about the regeneration of Germany and the reunion of that vast country under one new constitution. Rarely does M. de Hormayr himself speak. Instead, he very cleverly quotes from many justly esteemed German writers who thought of anything but revolution. Even Luther is laid under contribution. Moreover, that the kind reader may be the better able to grasp the intentions of the compiler, the latter has printed in large type all such passages as seem to him to be at all applicable to the contemporary state of affairs. The favorite themes of these extracts are the *unity* and *indivisibility* of Germany, and the conservation of its *mores*, its usages and its language. As historian and imperial archivist M. de Hormayr has access to many details regarding the ancient unity of Germany of which we are entirely ignorant.[1]

Encouraged and supported by these personages, then, John felt, by 1807, that "the moment was approaching when Providence would give to Austria the means of rescuing distressed humanity." Austria, he thought, soon would liberate the German nation, put an end to the selfish plans of a foreign conqueror, and restore to the German people their ancient freedom and renown. Thereupon the internal regeneration of the German nation might proceed apace.[2] In anticipation of these happy events the archduke set about to spread a nationalist sentiment among the masses. He had

[1] *A. E. A. C. P., Vienne, 1811*, vol. 389, folio 64, *Bulletin de Vienne*, February 10, 1811. The *Bulletin* was a careful analysis and sketch of conditions and happenings in Vienna and Austria, which was sent to Paris from Vienna at frequent intervals. It was usually attached to a report of the French ambassador or chargé in Vienna.

[2] *Denkschrift des Erzherzogs Johann, 1807, op. cit.*

no fear of the masses—he loved them. And he had great faith in the efficacy of a truly " national uprising " to overthrow the power of foreign invaders. He centered his main hopes and plans, and lavished his especial love, on the sturdy German mountain folk in the Tyrol and in Styria. No other section, he felt, was better qualified to become the nucleus of a Greater Germany than this paradise of mountain majesty, this rocky embodiment of the rugged simplicity, self-reliance and power of Germania. He had travelled from one end of these provinces to the other, and was intimately acquainted with many of the simple, pious, devoted, straight-shooting inhabitants. When in Vienna, he lived in his own charming *Tirolerhaus* enclosed within the beautiful gardens of Schönbrunn.[1] He loved the Tyrolese and knew that he could count on them in any emergency. The affection was mutual, for " Prince Hans " was truly the " idol of the land ". " 'Twere a marvelous thing ", he dreamt, " could someone unite the whole Tyrol " and give it a constitution—a constitution flexible enough so that it could be adapted and made applicable to a larger area. Then, with the dice once cast, the people of the Alps would encourage the people of the German plain to assert their independence, and to become members of " a new federative body ". Verily, the tearing asunder of such a union would prove to be a most difficult task.[2]

John also cooperated effectively with the government in its campaign of propaganda by becoming the center and guiding spirit of a group from which poured forth one patriotic literary endeavor after another. He sought to make con-

[1] Hirn, J., " Literarische Vorläufer des Tiroleraufstandes 1809 ", in *Beiträge zur neueren Geschichte Österreichs* (Vienna, 1908), booklet iv, pp. 197 *passim.*

[2] Horstenau, E. Glaise von, *Die Heimkehr Tirols* (Vienna, 1914), pp. 58-59.

tacts with numerous persons who could popularize, through prose or verse, any steps which the government might find advisable to take in preparation for the inevitable war.[1] And he was himself a prolific contributor to various scientific and historical periodicals whose purpose it was to make the people more intimately familiar with the glory and grandeur of their national heritage and existence.[2] To this end he was also prominent in the movement for establishing provincial museums wherein could be preserved and displayed the relics and tokens of ancient greatness and prowess. And he encouraged prominent artists, like Russ, Krafft and Petter to choose national themes for their paintings. Moreover, not content with his own and his immediate circles' creations, he collected assiduously in 1808 and 1809 whatever England and Spain produced in the way of belabored indictments or satirical jokes against Napoleon and his methods. Most of this material was received, *via* Trieste, from Admiral Collingwood, commander of the British fleet in the Adriatic Sea. The archduke turned the English and Spanish papers over to his friend Hormayr, to Julius Schneller in Graz, to Friedrich Schlegel in Vienna, and to numerous other skillful propagandists, for translating and editing. The dauntless Viennese burgher Anton Strauss took charge of the publishing end of the enterprise.[3]

The inspiring example set by the Spanish nation in 1808 made John quite optimistic. In his reminiscences of the campaign of 1809,[4] this grandson of Maria Theresa recorded the observation that regardless of Napoleon's success in defeating the armies of the Spanish nation, France had found

[1] The creation of the *Landwehr* was conspicuous in this category.

[2] Arnold, R. F. and Wagner, K., *Achtzehnhundertneun* (Vienna, 1909), pp. vii-viii. In the future this will be cited *Achtzehnhundertneun.*

[3] *Ibid.*

[4] *Feldzugserzählung, passim.*

it impossible to " conquer the nation itself ". The spirit of the people was splendid in its unity. All were eager to die on the altar of the fatherland—but there was a lack of capable leadership. The nationalist generals allowed themselves to be drawn into a series of open-field battles, and on such a chess-board Napoleon was supreme. But Austria, John knew, had better generals. And Austria's people were Germans. Woe to Napoleon!

By 1809 then, the government of Austria was controlled by men of a decidedly nationalist bent. The emperor, it is true, at best was neutral. But the empress, Foreign Minister Stadion, Commander-in-Chief Charles, and the emperor's brother, Archduke John, were all positively German in their outlook, at least for the time being. Austria's cause after Pressburg, however, required more than a nationalist-minded governing group. It required a populace inflamed as only the fire of nationalism can inflame. This the government proceeded to secure, as has been said, by a well-organized campaign of propaganda. The war of liberation was to be a people's war, and the people were to be armed! In 1796 when a plan for the arming of the masses was presented to Count Colloredo, that trusted imperial councillor was horrified. " I can at any time stuff the mouth of a victorious enemy with a province," he said, " but to arm the people means literally to overturn the throne." And he took every precaution that the scheme might remain absolutely secret.[1] Thirteen years later, on the other hand, the Countess Thürheim could write: " Every man has been carrying arms ever since 1808." [2] For on June 9, 1808, the emperor had issued a patent virtually creating a nation-in-arms through the establishment of what was called the *Landwehr*.[3]

[1] Droysen, *Vorlesungen*, vol. ii, p. 319.

[2] Thürheim, *Mein Leben*, vol. i, p. 279.

[3] The organization of a new reserve system soon followed.

All men between the ages of 18 and 45 who were able to bear arms were made liable to service in the *Landwehr* unless they already were affiliated with the regular army or the reserve. The administration of the decree worked so as to allow of numerous exemptions, but many additional recruits were secured through voluntary enlistments. Vienna alone, for example, fitted out six volunteer battalions. Originally the *Landwehr* was intended solely for service on domestic soil, but before the war was over many of the *Landwehr-männer* gave up their lives on the battlefields in Bavaria and in Italy.

Who first conceived the idea of the *Landwehr* at the time is not known. There were a number of historical precedents, not the least important of which was Carnot's *levée en masse* in France. A French official observer in Vienna reported that a Swabian named Lehmann had conceived a plan for an " insurrection " in Hungary in 1807, but that it had failed of any important results because it was not suited to the peculiar laws and customs of the Hungarians. However, the same scheme, reproduced in the German provinces in 1808, as a sort of temporary conscription, under the name of *Landwehr,* had much better success.[1] But other sources name different originators.[2]

The effect of this new departure from its traditional policy was most gratifying to the government. The people reacted favorably and were delighted " to be permitted personally " to help in the future defense of the land.[3] " Hitherto the people believed that an insurmountable barrier separated the

---

[1] *A. E. A. C. P., Vienne, Suppl. pour 1809,* vol. 384, folio 170: " Suites des renseignements sur la Cour de Vienne."

[2] *Cf. Achtzehnhundertneun,* p. 279 and *W. S. A.,* copy of a letter of General de Grünne to Marshal Prince de Ligne, dated Pest, September 27, 1809, and attached to *Vortrag Metternich's* of January 13, 1810.

[3] *Vat. Bl.,* September 16, 1808, p. 301.

soldier class from all other classes in the state. . . . The institution of the *Landwehr* showed all subjects that the defense of the fatherland was no longer to remain a matter of concern solely for the professional soldier. It indicated that in certain cases this lot, with all its dangers, burdens and hardships, would fall to the civilian groups as well. The wall between defenders and defended was torn down." [1]   A closer consideration of the relation between the *Landwehr* system and the nationalism of the people must be left for another chapter. [2]

In order to create the desired spirit among the masses the government also utilized such events as the unveiling of a statue to the Emperor Joseph II in Vienna. This ceremony provided the opportunity for the appearance of a biography of Joseph, which contained some remarks regarding the construction of the statue. The book pointed out that hitherto the world's largest hard-metal statue made of one piece had been that of Louis XIV on horseback, located in Paris. Its creator had been a German genius. But now another German, the famous Tyrolese artist, Francis Zauner, had done even better. "The statue of Joseph II", wrote the enthusiast, "exceeds that of Louis XIV both in size and weight, and since it has attained the pinnacle of artistic perfection, it can be regarded as the grandest work of its kind anywhere on the face of the earth at the present time." [3]   One can almost visualize the flourishes with which the proud scribe recorded the fact that it was a German who had designed the statue, and that the completed masterpiece decorated a square in the heart of the leading German city! [4]

[1] *Ibid.*, p. 302.

[2] See *infra*, p. 114 *et seq.*

[3] *Lebensbeschreibung des Kaisers Joseph des Zweiten. Nebst einigen Nachrichten von der Errichtung seiner Bildsäule auf dem Josephsplatze* (Vienna, 1807), pp. 76-77.

[4] Vienna was frequently referred to, at the time, as "the leading German

The most powerful of all the means to which the government resorted in its attempt to stimulate a national feeling among its German subjects, however, was the printing press. This once more implied a departure from traditional lines and a further intellectual conversion of Francis. But Stadion was willing to assume the responsibility. He really appreciated the power of the press.

city ", *cf.* e. g. a letter of one Count Fechtig, dated at Vienna, November 6, 1809, referring to this city as *" die erste deutsche Residenzstadt "* The Order of Leopold was founded at this time to reward faithful servants of the fatherland. It was patterned after the Legion of Honor.

CHAPTER III

1809: THE PRINTING PRESS AND THE TREND OF LITERARY ACTIVITY

IN a court decree of October 12, 1792, Emperor Francis had complained bitterly that newspapers were being read almost universally by the general public, " and even by the very lowest ranks of the public, the peasants." [1] The spirit of this decree sounded the death knell of the liberal press laws of Joseph II, and inaugurated an inquisition of literary police that threatened to strangle Austrian intellectual life. Books suffered from the same incubus as newspapers. Censorship weighed down heavily upon both. An English traveler in Austria in 1805 was astounded at the conditions he witnessed:

No circulating libraries are allowed, they are suppressed by order of the government. No reading-rooms or clubs are permitted, and every book and every newspaper must pass through a censor's hands (probably not through his head) before it is permitted to be given to the purchaser or proprietor. The English newspapers are stopped many days at the post-office to pass through this formality. The consequence of this arbitrary prohibition is, that the public mind is dull and torpid, or rather no public mind exists! [2]

[1] Winckler, J., *Die periodische Presse Österreichs* (Vienna, 1875), p. 48.

[2] Reeve, H., *Journal of a Residence at Vienna and Berlin in the Eventful Winter 1805-1806*, publ. by his son (London, 1877), p. 26, entry of October 13, 1805.

It need hardly occasion wonder, then, to learn that after 1803 there existed only one political newspaper in Vienna, the *Wiener Zeitung*.[1]

Count Stadion, however, ushered in a change of policy. It was in his plans to make the Austrians conscious of their German nationality. He felt that the best way to accomplish this was to familiarize the German-speaking subjects of the Habsburgs with the art, science, literature and customs of all the Germans. *Die Pflege der Vaterlandskunde* became his chief concern—and it implied a loosening of the censorship regulations as well as greater democratization of the school system. Thus, on the one hand, the authorities pointed with a certain amount of pride to the fact that in 1806 only 179 out of 1629, and in 1807 only 169 out of 1407 imported books were prohibited.[2] On the other hand, Count Saurau and others were ordered to render reports on the general condition of the monarchy, especially in relation to education and educational facilities.[3] The new attitude was also reflected in a memorandum on the question of press censorship drawn up in Paris by Count Metternich, at that time Austrian Ambassador to France. Metternich had ample time and opportunity to study the effect of Napoleon's newspapers upon French public opinion, and he decided to call the attention of his government to the value of journalistic propaganda.

[1] *A. f. o. G.*, vol. civ, p. 231.

[2] Weiss, *Geschichte der Stadt Wien*, vol. ii, pp. 253-254.

[3] *W. S. A., Kaiser Franz Akten, Fasz. 70, Kabinetbefehl*, March 6, 1808, and *Bericht des Grafen Saurau* from Graz, March 16, 1808. In his report Saurau complained of the lack of *Volksschulen*, especially in the rural areas. Many districts, he said, had none of these at all, while in others the salaries were so low that the securing of good teachers was out of the question. And this in spite of the fact that the local school authorities recently had been ordered to increase the number of schools and make instruction available, especially for the lower classes. *Cf.* Weiss, *op. cit.*, vol. ii, p. 254.

Public opinion [he wrote to Stadion] is the most powerful of all agents; like religion, it penetrates the most hidden recesses, where administrative measures have no influence. To despise public opinion is as dangerous as to despise moral principles, and if the latter will rise up even when they have been almost stifled, it is not so with public opinion; the latter requires peculiar cultivation and a continued and sustained perseverance. Posterity will hardly believe that we have regarded silence as an efficacious weapon to oppose to the clamors of our opponents, and that in a century of words! . . .

The newspapers are worth to Napoleon an army of three hundred thousand men, for such a force would not overlook the interior better, or frighten foreign powers more, than half-a-dozen of his paid pamphleteers.[1]

Francis, too, finally realized the truth of these contentions. In his opening address to the Hungarian Diet at Pressburg on September 9, 1808, he promised to further the development and enriching of the splendid intellectual potentialities of the " various nations " under his rule.   This was to be done through " better educational facilities, greater freedom of the press, and the unhampered use of the cultural treasures of other countries." [2]

Upon the express command of the emperor, moreover, the newspaper called *Vaterländische Blätter für den österreichischen Kaiserstaat* was founded, on May 10, 1808.   In accordance with the advice of Baron Hager the sheet was

[1] Metternich to Stadion, Paris, June 23, 1808, quoted in *Memoirs of Prince Metternich 1773-1815*, edited by Richard Metternich, transl. by Mrs. Alex. Napier (New York, 1880), vol. ii, pp. 226-227.   In a letter of 1809 to Fr. Schlegel, Baron Kübeck, then a commissary in the army, wrote: " *Die Presse ist eine Riesenmacht, die nicht mehr zu überwinden und in einer nicht entfernten Zukunft gar nicht zu beschränken ist, und in welcher die ganze künftige Folge der sozialen Zustände der Menschheit wurzelt.   Wir selbst appellieren schon heute mitten unter den Waffen an diese höhere Macht.*" Quoted in Richter, *op. cit.*, p. 340.

[2] Quoted in Droysen, *op. cit.*, vol. ii, p. 320.

allowed considerable freedom in the use of statistical and other data which would serve to make known, and therefore to endear, the fatherland to the public.[1] Following the example set by Justus Möser in his *Osnabrückische Intelligenz Blätter* and in his contributions to Herder's *Fliegende Blätter*,[2] the *Vaterländische Blätter* described and discussed the customs and traditions, the laws and culture, the politics and industry, the art and literature, the history and heroes of the various parts of the monarchy, in particular of Austria. Edited until 1814 by J. M. Armbruster, the *Blätter* soon took rank as one of Austria's leading papers.[3] The fact that it discussed (though it did not criticize) governmental policies gave the paper an appearance of independence which fitted in well with its motto, " true, candid, modest," but which was quite deceptive. The *Blätter* also boldly announced that " the first condition of all culture is intellectual freedom," but carefully added that " whoever knows the Austrian censorship laws will recognize therein the wise liberality of the government which promulgated them." [4]

Francis was so well satisfied with the results of the *Blätter* that he ordered the founding of another paper, which, however, was to be devoted chiefly to replying to the attacks of foreign papers, and to furnishing papers from other countries with items of interest and importance regarding domestic affairs in Austria.[5] Furthermore, the government not only

---

[1] *A. f. o. G.*, vol. civ, p. 237. Pages 3 and 5 of the first volume of the *Blätter* are devoted to a discussion of its purpose and scope: " *Der Zweck dieser Blätter ist: die Bewohner der kais.-königl. Erbstaaten mit sich selbst näher bekannt zu machen und Vaterlandsliebe durch Vaterlandskunde zu befördern.*"

[2] *A. f. o. G.*, vol. civ, p. 238.

[3] *Ibid.*, p. 241.

[4] *Vat. Bl.*, August 12, 1808.

[5] *W. S. A., Abschrift eines höchsten Kabinetsschreibens an Freiherrn von Hager*, February 6, 1809.

sanctioned the founding of other newspapers and the printing of numerous pamphlets and tracts, but actually assisted in the wide-spread distribution of them.[1]   Truly, Austria's appeal to the " greater might " of the press was an earnest one.[2]

In addition to waging a veritable press war against all pro-French journals, during the course of which each side did its best to malign the other,[3] the Austrian papers were active along two other lines.   First, they devoted a good deal of time and space to material relating to the Spaniards and their heroic opposition to Napoleon.   The *Wiener Zeitung,* especially, drew news from the papers of Seville and from the *London Gazette,* the *Advertiser,* the *Morning Chronicle* and the *Times,* as well as from private sources.   The accounts of events which it then printed read quite differently from those presented in that part of the European press which was controlled by Napoleon.[4]   Spanish victories were always announced with great glee,[5] while the heroism of the Spaniards was pointed to as an example well worthy of emulation.[6]

[1] *A. f. o. G.,* vol. civ, p. 199.

[2] In spite of everything, however, the censorship system remained a bar to the printing of numerous "classical" works, and most of the Viennese publishers were only too glad to avail themselves of the opportunity to sell as many of the latter as they could when the occupying French lifted the ban temporarily. *Cf. ibid.,* pp. 303 *et seq.*

[3] *Ibid.,* pp. 260 *et seq.* The *Wiener Zeitung* was especially active in this field. By order of the Archduke John many of its articles were copied for insertion in the provincial newspapers, chiefly in Carinthia and Styria. *Cf.* Hamberger, J., "Die französischen Invasionen in Kärnten im Jahre 1809", in *XXXII. Jahresbericht der Staats-Oberrealschule zu Klagenfurt* (Klagenfurt, 1889), p. 13.

[4] Guglia, E., "Geschichte der Wiener Zeitung im Zeitalter der Revolution und Napoleon", in *Jubiläums-Festnummer der kaiserlichen Wiener Zeitung, 8. August 1703-1903,* pp. 23 to 33.

[5] Venturini, *Chronik,* vol. vi, p. 93.

[6] *Eipeldauer,* 1809, 5. Heft, pp. 42-43.

Secondly, the Austrian papers, directly or indirectly, stressed the German nationality of the Austrians. Thus, while the *Vaterländische Blätter* maintained that nature had endowed " the Austrians along with the rest of the Germans " with a thorough mind and a penchant for research,[1] the *Eipeldauer* used the phrases " we Viennese " and " we Germans " interchangeably,[2] and made it known to such people as were ignorant of the fact, that " our beloved Vienna " is also " an integral part of Germany ".[3] Or again, the *Eipeldauer* boasted : " And now we have a further proof that we Germans are just as good at inventing as the foreigners are. Recently the famous craftsman, Melzel, made a mechanical trumpeter who can stand independently in uniform on his two feet, and blow more beautifully than any real trumpeter." [4]

The *Sammler* occasionally was even more German in tone. Edited by Ignaz Franz Castelli,[5] the *Sammler,* as its name indicates, presented excerpts and anecdotes collected from every conceivable source—though the source was hardly ever noted. The issue of March 16, 1809, contained the following article entitled : " A Voice from the Past."

The memory of Martin Opitz,[6] greatest German poet of the seventeenth century, will linger on in his inspiring songs until the end of days. He was thoroughly convinced of the manifold superiorities of our language over any other, and earned everlasting credit for his work in cultivating it. When such a man

---

[1] *Vat. Bl.*, 1808, p. 228.

[2] *Eipeldauer*, 1809, I. Heft, p. 16.

[3] *Ibid.*, 2. Heft, p. 5.

[4] *Ibid.*, 1808, 7. Heft, p. 40.

[5] Castelli was born in Vienna in 1781. He became a poet and dramatic critic, who wrote war-songs in 1809 anl especially in 1812 and 1813. He also founded the Vienna *Tierschutzverein*. He died in 1862.

[6] Martin Opitz, born 1597 in Bunzlau in Silesia, perfected German verse, was made " von Boberfeld " by the emperor in 1628, died of pestilence in Danzig in 1639. *Cf.* Brockhaus, vol. xii, p. 607.

has something to say to the people, he deserves an attentive audience. Woe betide the Germans, if ever they bcome indifferent toward the voices of their forefathers. Should that time come, German thought, might and excellence would vanish from the earth.

In one of his works, the *Aristarchus*,[1] written in Latin [!], Opitz makes a remarkable appeal to his fellow-Germans. Every word of this entreaty, which deals with a cause of which mention cannot be made too often in our present circumstances, warrants the closest attention: " If pleas and asseverations have any power over you, I conjure you by your beloved motherland, Germania, by the halo of glory surrounding the deeds of your ancestors, to keep your mode of thought on a plane with the high station of your calling. Be as interested in your language, and as tenacious in preserving it, as the forefathers were interested and tenacious in the defense of their boundaries. Your ancestors, the brave Semnones, never hesitated to sacrifice their lives for altar and hearth. Though there is no need at present for your doing likewise, you at least ought to endeavor to reflect in pure language the unstained thoughts that fill your noble minds. Endeavor to hand down to your descendants that facility of expression in the native language which you inherited from your parents. Endeavor, finally, to outshine all other peoples as much in beauty of speech as you do in bravery and fidelity." [2]

Seven weeks after it published this excerpt, the *Sammler* brought to the notice of the public another work of Opitz'. With the expressed intention of entertaining its readers, the paper reprinted a " powerful and particularly timely selection from the poetry of the Germany of old," by " the father of German poetry ".[3] The first few lines of this poem, labelled " A German of the Days of Yore to his Countrymen ", were a call to

[1] *Aristarchus, De contemptu linguae Teutonicae.*

[2] *Der Sammler* no. 32, March 16, 1809, under *Notizen*.

[3] *Ibid.*, no. 53, May 4, 1809.

> Arise! Arise! Whoe'er loves German freedom
> Who will his sword for God unsheath.
> Empty boasts of brilliant wisdom
> Never accomplished knightly deed!

The *Sammler* also gave evidence that Father Jahn's [1] movement for the development of strong and healthy bodies among the youth of Germany, in preparation for the great day upon which the French would finally be ousted from German soil, also took root in Austria. Through the medium of an article on " National Education among the Ancient Germans ", it was pointed out that there was room for greater emphasis upon physical training in Austria.

Preparation for war [said the article] was the goal of both the mental and physical educational schemes of the ancient Germans. Whatever tended to develop strength, agility and courage in an individual was included in the schedule of training. Jumping and running were the chief exercises, while, according to Tacitus, the one and only sport in which these ancient Germans indulged, consisted in dancing around upon upturned spearheads.[2] Body and mind, then, were inured to the sight of danger and death. . . . The degree of perfection which these ancient Germans attained in jumping is indicated in the writings of Florus. According to this source, Teutobach, the King of the Cimbri, thought nothing of leaping over from four to six horses. Anyway, vaulting seems to have been one of the chief items in the educational system of our ancestors. This accounts for their ability to mount and dismount from their horses so rapidly, and for the superiority of the German over the Roman cavalry in all encounters between the two.

Whoever is strong and agile of body is also determined and sturdy of mind. Hence the mind must never be developed at

---

[1] Jahn's invention of modern gymnastics was one phase of the regeneration movement in post-Jena Germany.

[2] A reference to the "sword dance among upturned blades and sharpened spearheads."

the expense of the body. . . . Moreover, since the body should be the servant of the mind, it is essential that more attention be devoted to the development of the former, than has hitherto been the case among us.[1]

Important as they were, newspapers alone could not " electrify " the people sufficiently for the government's purpose. Stadion felt that it was " necessary, in cooperation with M. Gentz, with the police, and with our good and mediocre writers, to put out a large quantity of pamphlets, fly-sheets and so on, which we can then cast among the public." [2]   Some novel methods were employed to get the proper cooperation between police and writers: Several authors of scientific works were ordered to visit police headquarters, where they were asked to place their pens at the disposal of the government.   Regardless of what pleas they advanced to be excused, they were all obliged to compose timely tracts.[3]   On another occasion the editor of a purely literary paper was ordered to accept certain patriotic poems which had been submitted to him, but which he had rejected on the ground that printing them would convert his sheet into a political journal.   The censor told him that if he did not serve the public cause with all the means at his command, his publisher's license soon would be withdrawn.[4]

It was not long, then, before " all the scribes, good and bad, dedicated their genius to exalting the spirits of the people and to diminishing the glory of Napoleon " after the example set by " an important personage [Charles] in his proclamations ' To the Germans ' and ' To the German Nation '." [5]

[1] Der Sammler, no. 51, April 29, 1809.

[2] W. S. A., Staatskanzlei Korresp., Fasz. 73, marginal annotation by Stadion on a note to Hudelist, April 11, 1809.

[3] A. E. A. C. P., Vienne, 1809, vol. 382, folio 118, Bulletin de Vienne, March 10, 1809.

[4] Ibid.

[5] A. E. A. C. P., Vienne, 1809, vol. 382, folio 358, Dodun to Champagny from Vienna, April 13, 1809.

Not content with general orders to writers, the government specifically appointed a number of people to help wage the campaign of propaganda. Soon the land " was flooded with proclamations drawn up by Gentzes, Schlegels, Hormayrs and Carpanis." [1] Among the appointees none rated higher than Friedrich Schlegel, the Hanoverian romanticist. In the summer of 1808, Friedrich Schlegel followed his brother, August Wilhelm Schlegel, to Vienna from Cologne. Through the influence of friends he was appointed to the court chancery, and on March 28, 1809, he was made military secretary to Archduke Charles.[2] It so happened that several years before he came to Vienna, Schlegel had framed a theory of the nation in which he held that

a nation is, as it were, a large, all-inclusive family, in which numerous smaller families and tribes are united by community of constitutions, customs, usages, language and interests. . . . The concept of the nation implies that all of its members shall form only one individual. In order that this may be brought about, all the members must at least be descended from the same race. The older, purer and less mixed this race is, the more customs it has. And the more customs it has, and the more constancy and attachment to these customs it shows, the more

[1] *A. E. A. C. P., Vienne, 1809*, vol. 382, folio 279, Dodun to Champagny from Vienna, April 10, 1809. Gentz drew up a remarkable " Manifesto " which, issued in Francis' name, summed up French "misdeeds" since the Treaty of Pressburg, and justified a reopening of hostilities on Austria's part. Cold, logical and concise this manifesto was addressed "not to the people, but to the cabinets, statesmen and diplomats " of Europe; *cf.* Guglia, E., *Friedrich von Gentz*, p. 223. It remained for the military intendants or secretaries to make the official appeals to the people: Fr. Schlegel with the main body of troops under Charles; M. von Collin with Archduke Ferdinand and the Poles; the poet G. Carpani with John in northern Italy; and the inevitable Hormayr with Fieldmarshal von Chasteler in the Tyrol.

[2] Raich, J., *Dorothea Schlegel und deren Söhne... Briefwechsel* (Mainz, 1881), vol. i, p. 331.

of a nation will the race be. A common language is of the greatest importance in this connection, for it is the unexceptionable proof of common ancestry, and the most fervent and natural tie. Together with community of custom, language is the strongest and most likely guarantee that the nation will continue to exist for many centuries in indissoluble unity.[1]

This exposition alone, of course, should have been sufficient recommendation to secure for Schlegel an appointment to what we would call the official press bureau of the Austrian Government. Certainly so at a time when it was worth any price to emphasize the community of interests of the Germans of the North and the Germans of the South. It was through Schlegel's proclamations that Austria " spoke German, and German in more than one sense of the word." [2]

He wrote perhaps half a dozen or more of the powerful appeals which appeared in rapid succession beginning with March, 1809. The Army Order of April 6, which was signed by Charles, though written by Schlegel, has been referred to.[3] Two days later, on April 8, there appeared another proclamation, again signed by Charles, addressed "To the German Nation." [4] It announced that the Austrians were fighting " to regain for Germany its independence and national honor." " Our cause ", it continued, " is the cause of Germany. United with Austria, Germany was free and happy. Only through Austria can Germany again attain that state of bliss. . . . The Austrian troops regard you as their brothers. . . . Only the German who forgets his identity is our enemy." [5]

[1] *Friedrich Schlegel's Philosophische Vorlesungen aus den Jahren 1804 bis 1806*, edited by C. I. H. Windischmann (Bonn, 1846), pp. 357-358.

[2] Goedecke, vol. vi, p. 18.

[3] See *supra*, p. 43.

[4] *Vat. Bl.*, 1809, p. 159 and *Wiener Zeitung*, no. 30, April 15, 1809.

[5] Copies of the proclamation were distributed by the Austrian soldiers

In an "Appeal to the Bavarians", Schlegel [1] spoke in an even clearer German fashion: "You are beginning to realize that we [Austrians] are Germans every bit as much as you are. You are beginning to see how much closer to your welfare are the common interests of all the Germans, rather than those of a foreign, destroying people. It is gradually dawning upon you that only united and cooperative action can once more raise the Germans to their former level of grandeur." Further,

Mark well, ye Bavarians! All those who are imbued with a true German patriotism will be powerfully supported, and, if they so deserve, richly rewarded, by their former emperor, who did not resign his German heart along with his German crown. On the other hand, punishment and shame will fall upon those who, forgetting their German name, disregard the proffered assistance, and prefer to serve the common enemy rather than the native liberator.

Schlegel also wrote an anonymous tract entitled: "To the Germans: A German's Appeal for the Breaking of the Heavy Chains that Bind Us!" [2] It begins:

Germans! How much longer will you suffer the foreign yoke? How much longer will you be crushed beneath the

as they advanced into Bavaria. According to the Second Daily Report from Army Headquarters, April 12, 1809, the inhabitants of the Bavarian city of Passau ordered the printing of two thousand copies of this proclamation which would then "be distributed among the country folk, so that they, too, might develop a feeling for the independence of Germany."

[1] *Aufruf an die Bayern.* This and the succeeding proclamation are ascribed to Fr. Schlegel by Arnold and Wagner in *Achtzehnhundertneun*, pp. 306 *et seq.*

[2] *An die Deutschen. Aufruf eines Deutschen zum Zerbrechen drückender Fesseln* (Vienna?, 1809).

heels of a proud conqueror? How much longer will Hermann [1]
have to mourn his degenerated progeny? Was it for this that
the Cherusci fought in the Teutoburg Forest? Was it for this
that the Germans triumphed at Hochstädt, Blenheim and
Minden? Was it for this that Austria's great Charles won his
glorious victories? Has every spark of German courage been
extinguished? Is the olive wreath no longer a fitting adorn-
ment for the brow of German citizens? Does the clanging of
chains sound pleasing to you? Do you consider it nobler and
worthier of a man to slay guiltless people in distant lands, than
to die in unison with his compatriots for the welfare of his
own land? Awaken! Awaken, Germans, from the stupor of
shame and ignominy! Awaken and act for the sake of German
honor! There is still time! Austria's powerful forces are
approaching, imbued with a spirit of courage and faithfulness
They are led by Charles . . . [and so on for another page and
a half].

Poetically, Schlegel's chief contribution came in the re-
printing of the poems which he had published in Berlin early
in 1809. The best of these poems was his " Vow ". This
was removed from the volume of *Poems,* however, by the
Berlin censors because of its marked anti-French tone.
Fortunately, it was available in other editions, too, and therefore could be utilized in Austria:

> My heart and blood be consecrate
> Thee, Fatherland, to save.
> Indeed, that thou be free and great
> We'll raise thee from the grave!
> No longer shall the sorry fact
> Of alien's trick and wicked pact
> Be suffered to deprave.

[1] Hermann or Arminius, the Cheruscan (17 B. C.–A. D. 21) destroyed
the legions of Varus in 9 A. D. in the famous battle of the Teutoburg
Forest.

[2] Goedecke, vol. vi, p. 24. See Appendix, p. 199 for the German
version of this poem.

Who holds not dear whose heart beats free
Thy portrait beauteous fair?
As potent nature past degree
Breathes through thy forest air,
So thrive the life upon thy downs,
And in thy fine and thriving towns
The arts, beyond compare.

The German race is old and strong
With lofty faith imbued;
To truth its honor marks belong,
They stood when storms ensued.
A nobler sense it doth impart
Of such high pride in every heart
As no mere foe can wrong.

In spite of every danger new,
Liberty calls us all;
So wills the Right, and it stays true
Howe'er the dice may fall.
Yea, if we sink, o'erborne by might,
Yet will we close our mortal fight
With glory worth recall.

Original compositions did not complete the round of
Schlegel's contributions.   He was also one of the translators
of the famous " Collected Documents regarding the Change
of Dynasty in Spain ".[1]   The Austrian Government realized
that the heroic resistance offered by the Spaniards to
Napoleon would serve as an inspiring example to its own subjects,[2] and the " Documents " really did cause a " great sensa-

[1] *Sammlung der Aktenstücke über die spanische Thronveränderung,*
2 vols., 4 pts. (Germanien [Vienna] 1808). For Schlegel's appointment
cf. *Akten des Wiener Polizeiarchivs, J. 1809, Fasz. 2012/b und 3687/a.*

[2] *Beobachtungen und historische Sammlung wichtiger Ereignisse aus
dem Kriege zwischen Frankreich, dessen Verbündeten und Österreich
im Jahre 1809,* 5 vols. (Weimar, 1809), vol. i, p. 9 (pro-Bavarian). The
move was all the shrewder since it reminded the people that almost a
century earlier they had fought against France over the question of
the Spanish Succession.

tion ".[1]   They were read eagerly by everyone, including the
troops.[2]   The French Foreign Minister was led to complain
that the " libelous " documents were being " distributed with
profusion ", and that the police were allowing them to be
advertised and sold openly in Vienna.[3]   Apparently he did
not know that they were also being printed in great quantities
for distribution in the other areas of Austria by the " parish
priests, elders and officers of the militia ".[4]

The story of the " Spanish Documents " is as follows: In
the summer of 1808 the Spanish consul at Venice, Mexino,
while traveling through Graz in Styria, handed a series of
documents in Spanish and Italian to Archduke John.[5]   These
documents included: a description of events in Spain from
the outbreak of troubles at Aranjuez to the close of the Junta
at Bayonne,[6] written by Don Pedro Cevallos, First Secretary
of State; a series of Spanish proclamations, manifestoes,

[1] Reichardt, *op. cit.*, vol. i, p. 242.

[2] *Eipeldauer*, 1809, 5. Heft, pp. 12-13: "A good friend of mine took
me over to the guardroom, and just as we entered, a sergeant was engaged in reading to his men from the second part of the ' Spanish Documents '.   The soldiers were gathered around him and listened attentively.
Dear Cousin, I can hardly express in words, how delighted I was to see
our militia reading useful books instead of playing cards, while off duty."

[3] *A. E. A. C. P. Vienne, 1809*, Suppl. vol. 29, folio 44: " Rapport de
M. le Comte de Champagny à Sa Majesté l'Empereur," March 2, 1808
from Paris.   In this report Champagny records a conversation that he
had with Metternich during the course of which he made the quoted
complaints.

[4] Erzherzog Johann, *Feldzugserzählung*, p. 22.

[5] Wagner in *Anno Neun*, pp. 90 *et seq.*

[6] The Spanish court had been moved from Madrid to Aranjuez early in
1808 as a preliminary step in the projected flight of Charles IV, the
queen and Minister Godoy to America.   The Junta at Bayonne consisted
of a group of Spanish nobles who had been ordered to that city for the
express purpose of offering the throne to Joseph Bonaparte (June, 1808).
Cf. Chapman, C. E., *A History of Spain* (New York, 1918), pp. 408
and 490.

reports, appeals, newspapers and newspaper articles, army reports, memoirs of English admirals, etc.; the constitution forced upon Spain by Napoleon's brother, Joseph; documents regarding the capture of the French fleet under Rosilly; a proclamation of the Governor of Cuba; regulations for the Spanish militia; and a " Citizen's Catechism for the Schools of the Provinces ".[1]

John had the documents copied, and then entrusted Baron Hormayr with the task of getting them translated and seeing them through the press. Anton Strauss, of Vienna, agreed to act as publisher.[2] Hormayr secured the assistance of a number of writers, among whom Friedrich Schlegel was one, to do the translating into German, and the documents soon appeared in print under the title indicated.

The documents contained a number of striking statements which could not fail to influence both the government and the people of Austria. Thus, one proclamation warned Napoleon that " other nations would rise against him while he was busy tearing Spain to pieces with his fangs." [3] Another manifesto pointed out that there was not much to fear, since, in addition to being relatively weak in numbers, the enemy's troops " consisted of members from different nations collected by force." [4] A third called on those who had to remain at home, to help support the dependents of those who enlisted against the faithless French.[5] The proclamation of the Governor of Cuba assured " the worthy sons of the noble Spaniards " that other nations would join them in the great work of saving humanity from the jaws of

[1] All included in the *Sammlung*.
[2] *Feldzugserzählung*, p. 22 and Wagner, *op. cit.*, p. 92.
   Sammlung, vol. i, pt. ii, p. 137.
[4] *Ibid.*, vol. ii, pt. iii, pp. 91 *et seq.*
[5] *Ibid.*, vol. ii, pt. iv, p. 70.

the monster.[1]   The "Citizen's Catechism" contained such questions and answers as these:

Quest.: Is it a sin to kill a Frenchman?

Ans.:   Yes, sir, excepting those who are fighting under Napoleon's standards.

Quest.: What thoughts must inspire us to engage in battle?

Ans.:   The weal of the fatherland; the defense of the State and of our brothers; and the undying glory of the Nation.[2]

Doubtless the Austrian authorities drew inspirations from such suggestions as those contained in the " General Regulations for the Spanish Armies and Militia ", which provided, in Article 9, that " it will therefore be advisable for the generals to distribute numerous proclamations among the people, to uphold their courage and faith "; and in Article 10, that " all educated persons in the provinces should be urged to write short addresses, and to have these printed and distributed in order to keep up the enthusiasm of the nation." [3] Charles' proclamation " To the Germans ", moreover, may very well have been influenced by the Supreme Junta's appeal " To the Portuguese ", in which we read the words: "ᵢCome hither, valiant Portuguese!   Ally yourselves with Spain, to rescue honor and fatherland, and, if fate so decrees, to die for honor and fatherland.   We await you and we will welcome you as brothers. . . . Have confidence in our troops, and join them.   Their desires and wishes are the same as yours." [4]

Now, while most of Schlegel's contributions were in prose, the Stadion government also took care to draft the services

---

[1] *Sammlung*, vol. ii, pt. iv, p. 228.

[2] *Ibid.*, vol. ii, pt. iv, pp. 109 and 111.

[3] *Ibid.*, vol. i, pt. ii, pp. 219-222.

[4] *Ibid.*, vol. i, pt. ii, p. 142.

of talented sons of the Muse of Poetry, in its attempt to sway the minds of the people. Thus, the dramatist Heinrich Joseph von Collin received an order " from high authority ", through his friend, Major Catinelli, " to compose fitting songs " that would adequately express the noble sentiments entertained by the members of the *Landwehr*.[1] Collin was delighted with the task and set about composing his *Lieder Österreichischer Wehrmänner* at once.[2] However, his songs give little or no evidence of a consciousness of German nationality. The word " German " does not appear at all in the *Lieder,* although it is used in some of his other poems, for example, in " My Friends ", written in the spring of 1809. This lack can be accounted for in several ways. First, although Collin had a considerable number of works to his credit at this time, he had only just begun to devote his attention to patriotic themes for his plays and poems. It required the combined influence of his brother, Matthias, of his friend, Hormayr, and of the Romantic School, along with the depressed condition of the fatherland in 1806 and 1807 to interest him in " national heroes " and " national subjects ". Naturally, Collin proceeded only slowly and cautiously in what was virtually a new field for him.[3] Secondly, as he himself wrote, the *Lieder* " were meant for any possible future war, with no particular enemy as target." [4] Or, as he noted in a later edition of the songs:

I request the reader to bear in mind when he judges these songs, that they were purposely composed in language intelligible to all classes of the population. Moreover, they were composed

[1] Collin, H. J. von, *Sämmtliche Werke* (Vienna, 1814), vol. vi, pp. 433-434.

[2] *Ibid.*

[3] Laban, Ferd., *Heinrich Joseph Collin* (Vienna, 1879), pp. 68-69.

[4] Preface to Collin's *Lieder Österreichischer Wehrmänner* (Vienna, 1809).

before the outbreak of the war, and hence lack the power and force which would have been present had they been directed against a definite enemy. At the time I wrote them I merely wanted to make the militiamen feel the importance of their station, and accustom them to singing [!].[1]

With the possible exception of his *Östreich über Alles*,[2] then, Collin's songs were patriotic and popular, but not nationalistic.

Nevertheless, by appointing Collin to write patriotic songs, the government opened a new field to dozens of other poets and writers who carried on where he left off, and who made a definite attempt to unite all the Germans against Napoleon as the common adversary. As a result, a veritable shower of broadsheets, verses and tracts poured down upon Austria on the eve of the war. " It is raining pamphlets " said Rosenbaum in March.[3] " It is raining pamphlets " repeated Aulic Councillor Hudelist in April.[4] Unfortunately, not all these pamphlets and tracts have been preserved. When the French approached the city, many of the pamphlets were thrown into Vienna's chief moat which happened to contain some water. The " Spanish Documents ", Collin's songs, numerous pamphlets and booklets were brought up " in bales " and destroyed, lest the French use them as evidence for one charge or another.[5] Many others that happened to escape this fate were later collected and destroyed by the police upon the command of Metternich, who, in 1810, wanted to wipe out all traces of the " unfortunate exalta-

[1] Collin, J., *Gedichte* (Vienna, 1812), p. 280 n.

[2] See Appendix, p. 200 for this poem.

[3] Rosenbaum's *Tagebuch*, entry for March 13, 1809.

[4] *W. S. A., Staatskanzlei Korresp., Fasz. 73,* Hudelist to Stadion, Vienna, April 16, 1809.

[5] Rosenbaum's *Tagebuch*, entry for May 12, 1809.

tion ".[1] Yet, enough remained to serve as examples and
indicators of what the rest must have been like. A few of
these deserve closer consideration.

Adolf Bäuerle, then secretary of the Leopoldstädter
Theater, wrote a pamphlet entitled " Spain and Tyrol tolerate
no Foreign Fetters",[2] in which he tried to rouse all Germans
out of their lethargy.

Spain saved itself [he insisted] through its courage and
common spirit. The Tyrol, ever faithful and loyal, did likewise. They gave proof of what a people may accomplish when
actuated by common impulse, winning victories over huge
armies led by experienced generals and guided by military
strategy. Common spirit is the chief factor in a nation's victories. . . . Spain, too, was happy once; the Tyrol enjoyed a
happy existence. The rulers of these two areas acted like
fathers toward their subjects, and the children were joyous and
contented. And then there came a foreigner who tried to
separate the children from their fathers. These brave peoples,
however, refused to abide by such dispositions, and they freed
themselves.

O free and independent national existence, most beautiful
grace of life, why do so many of our German brothers regard
you as a stepmother? Why do your glorious rays penetrate
so rarely into the hearts of the oppressed people of Germany?
Why do the latter tolerate the yoke which is being fastened
upon them ever more terribly by a tyrannical conqueror?

German brothers, what has become of you! For centuries
you have maintained your ancient name, your ancient constitution,[3] your ancient glory against any and every enemy. And

[1] Metternich to Hager, Vienna, January 8, 1810, quoted in *A. f. o. G.*,
vol. civ, p. 386.

[2] *Spanien und Tyrol tragen keine fremden Fesseln* (Vienna, 1809).

[3] Bäuerle actually used the word *Konstitution*. What a change came
over the spirit and attitude of the government when, a few years later,
Francis became angry at the remark of his physician, Baron Stifft, that
the emperor had a healthy constitution!

now would you allow yourselves to be crushed by one people,
by one man, who has no more claim to the rights of citizenship
in your land than has a Tunguse[1] who comes from the far
corners of the earth? . . .

O brothers! . . . Look at Spain and Tyrol, and see what
nations can do, if they so desire. Let us not turn our swords
against one another. Let us turn them against the Franks,
those people who, from the dawn of history, have never been
upright in their dealings with the Germans.

Similar in spirit to this summons, were two others, entitled
respectively, "Austria in 1809",[2] and "An Appeal to
Austria's People".[3] The latter lamented the formation of
the Confederation of the Rhine (July 12, 1806) and the
subsequent dissolution of the Holy Roman Empire (August
6, 1806) in words such as these:

Our monarch was forced to see the dearly-purchased Peace
of Pressburg violated in every article. In this treaty the
majesty and dignity of the Holy Roman Emperor were recognized, and all his rights and privileges guaranteed. Hardly
was peace concluded, however, when a large group of the
German princes were induced to join a Confederation, loyalty
to which was incompatible with their sworn duties to the German Emperor. Half of Germany was thus made absolutely
subject to the French Emperor. Many German princes, on the
other hand, could not be seduced nor made to deny their imperial sovereign. In order that this obstacle to duty might be
removed, the German Emperor was now threatened with
immediate war if he did not renounce the crown. The Emperor
was confronted with the question of retaining or losing the
position of first rank among the monarchs of Europe. The

[1] The Tunguses are inhabitants of eastern Siberia.

[2] *Östreich im Jahre 1809* (Germanien, 1809?).

[3] *Aufruf an Österreichs Völker* (Vienna, 1809), anonymous, but according to a note of Hudelist, April 18, 1809 to Stadion, it is by Aulic
Councillor Lehmann. *Cf. W. S. A., Staatskanzlei Korresp., Fasz. 73.*

crown which had been worn by Habsburgs for almost 400 years [1] was at stake. The unity of the German nation depended on this decision, for the crown, as a bond of union, was very important in the event that some day the Germans might again realize the honor attaching to their name, and the need for acting in concert. It never has been fully appreciated, perhaps, how much our ruler sacrificed by giving up the crown in order that his hereditary possessions might have peace. The direct result of his abdication was the ousting of several of the reigning princes in northern Germany who were now left without any bond of union or protection. . . .

Further, one of the longest, and from our point of view, one of the best, pamphlets was entitled: " What does Germany owe the Habsburgs? " [2] Liberally interspersed with typographical and historical errors, this twenty-one page survey of Germanic prowess through the ages ended with a warm plea for harmony and union among the descendants of Hermann:

Gauls and Spaniards, Thracians and Greeks, the sensuous Asiatic and the distant African were forced to submit to the iron rule of the land-hungry Romans.

Emboldened by their victories over these peoples, the Romans then began to harass German soil. But the German hero Hermann defeated the Roman general Varus. For the first time in history someone succeeded in making himself terrible to the proud, wanton Romans, and this someone was a German! Eventually, the hitherto universally victorious Romans were completely overwhelmed by the fearless Germans.

Then the grim horde of Huns under the leadership of the

---

[1] From 1438 to 1806 the crown of the Holy Roman Empire was bestowed exclusively upon members of the Habsburg family with the exception of Charles VII of Bavaria (1742-1745) and Francis I of Lorraine (1745-1760).

[2] *Was verdankt Deutschland seit Jahrhunderten dem Hause Habsburg?* (Vienna, 1813?).

butcher Attila came to Germany, too, from Pannonia. Several hundred thousand strong, they threatened the Germans with destruction.

The German Emperor Otto and his Germans,[1] accompanied by Saint Ulrich,[2] however, hurried to the Lechfield near Augsburg, where Attila was encamped with four hundred thousand Huns. Confident in the assistance of Providence, Otto attacked the vicious foe, who twice outnumbered him. On August 10, 955, he was victorious, having won a victory such as the world had never witnessed previously.

'As a matter of fact, the Germans have made it a point to remain free from any foreign yoke. They have been quite adept at getting rid of any shackles which might have been placed upon them, and have always quickly reasserted their German freedom and independence. They have never been happy except when ruled by a German. They have never attained greater renown than when ruled by a Habsburg. Under the rule of this venerable House, Germany has covered itself with glamor and glory. And Germany would ever have remained in this state if the contrary interests of a *few* Germans had not loosened the bonds that have held *all* Germans together. . . . [3]

Once our German forefathers discovered the blessings of the just and mild sceptre of the Habsburgs, they never faltered in their allegiance to this House down to our own times. They remained loyal until that insatiable brute who rose upon the ruins of the French Revolution by dint of ceaseless disturbances and machinations was able to induce Francis the Good, Francis the German, to resign the diadem of the German Emperor.

---

[1] In his enthusiasm, or ignorance, the pamphleteer made a mess of his history. He confused the invasions of the Huns under Attila (d. 453) with the invasions of the Magyars or Hungarians five centuries later. In 955 Otto defeated the Magyars, and not the Huns, on the Lechfeld. The error hardly affects the importance of the German spirit expressed in the paragraph.

[2] Saint Ulrich, later Bishop of Augsburg, d. 973.

[3] *Was verdankt Deutschland* . . . , pp. 3-6.

. . . Oh! How safe and well off Germany was under the
sceptre of the Habsburg princes! German patriots still bless
the memory of Frederick the Peaceable, Maximilian the Brave,
the immortal Theresa, Leopold the Wise and certainly also
Francis the Good. . . . [1]

The Germans are well aware that they are fighting a common enemy of all Germans (when they fight Napoleon). They
know that only a common spirit can save them from the chains
of vilest servitude which are being forged for them in Gaul.
They realize that they must fight against those two most despic-
able of vices: lust of power and covetousness. They know
that only the Habsburgs are true, and that the promises of that
islander [Napoleon] are as fleeting as bubbles of air. . . .

A desire for innovation can come only upon cowardly souls,
mean begrudgers and voluptuous sybarites. Only these beings,
too, can sit back quietly and await their shameful fate. The
brave, honor-loving German, like the unpretentious, honest
Tyrolese, joyously follows the lead of Hermann, that great
German hero. Relying upon wise Providence, this German
courageously smites proud Varus and Attila's mercenaries.

Charles, the Germanic Hermann, never yet stood at the head
of so spirited an army as he does now. Nevertheless, he was
the victor at Würzburg and Ostrach, at Liptingen and Zürich,
at Verona, Trebbia and Novi. . . . [2]

It rests with the Germans now to uphold their ancient inte-
grity by deeds. Now is the time to give the world straightforward proof of their upright German character. Otherwise
they are doomed to dissipate their existence in abject thralldom,
and to condemn their children to live under the iron rod of a
despot. It is entirely for the Germans to choose between

[1] *Was verdankt Deutschland...*, pp. 8-9.

[2] *Ibid.*, pp. 13-15. The dates of the battles cited are as follows:
Würzburg, Sept. 3, 1796 *v.* Jourdan; Ostrach, March 21, 1799 *v.*
Jourdan; Liptingen, March 25-26, 1799; Zürich, June 4, 1799 *v.* Massena;
Verona, March 26, 1799; Trebbia, June 18-19, 1799 and Novi, Aug. 15,
1799 both *v.* Macdonald and Jourdan while Charles was under the orders
of Suvarov. *Cf. Österreichs Kriege seit 1495* (Vienna, 1878).

remaining the slaves of a wanton conqueror and returning to their state of ancient and honorable freedom.

For centuries Germany has owed its peace and harmony, its happiness and welfare, to the swords of the Habsburgs. Francis' subjects are bravely and willingly rallying around his eagles to restore to normal the unsettled conditions in Germany. Let our contemporaries as well as posterity judge whether or not Francis' people have resorted to arms in the fulfilment of a sacred trust: to keep a tyrannical foreigner remote from Germany's soil, and to restore peace and quiet to their German brothers.

Oh! May the sturdy Germans be successful in this noble enterprise! How happy and contented will future generations be under the aegis of the Habsburgs, of Austria's rulers! Then Germany will once again occupy its proper rank among the nations of the world. Then the many-headed hydra of discord, that one pit-fall of the Germans, will be shunned by all good citizens. Then the Germans will once again know how to appreciate good and glorious rulers.[1]

Finally, it is interesting at this point to read the explanation given of the lack of unity among the Germans by the editor of a volume on the occupation of Vienna by the French troops in 1805:[2]

The German princes have so often and so vainly been urged and summoned to form a general and powerful union against Germany's arch enemy, that the humble author, who, as a true German patriot, honors all the decisions of Germany's noble rulers, is convinced that unknown and perhaps even supernatural causes are responsible for the laxness and indifference with which the German people eye the approaching fate that is being prepared for them by foreigners. . . . Every German who sincerely loves his fatherland must perceive that nothing short of absolute union among all the German-speaking people

[1] *Was verdankt Deutschland* . . . , pp. 18-21.
[2] *Die Franzosen zu Wien*, pp. iii-iv.

can possibly save Germania from the slavery with which it is threatened.

Leaving for the next chapter the popular poems and songs which appeared parallel with the tracts, we turn now to a brief survey of the trend of the prose and dramatic literature of the period. One might have expected to find in this general literature something of the same spirit that pervaded the numerous tracts and pamphlets. Nationalistic romanticism had secured a footing in the north and central Germanies by the latter part of the eighteenth century, and therefore might well be expected to have had some influence in Austria, too—especially since Austria presented an environment which was thoroughly Catholic, and which was constantly envisaging war with " Napoleon the Leveler ", with the man who was bent upon erasing all national distinctions. Yet, curiously enough, this was not the case. Romanticism was practically a new phenomenon in Austria in 1808.[1] What few examples of romanticism had found their way into Vienna were ridiculed and satirized.[2] Unquestionably this was due to the fact that the reactionary censorship under Francis practically isolated Austria from the rest of Europe in the matter of intellectual fellowship and the exchange of ideas. The Chinese Wall of police restrictions resulted in a virtual paralysis of literary productivity in the leading city of the Germanies. Before long the intellectual outlook of the Vienna salons became as reactionary as the political outlook of the authorities. It seemed that only Baron Hormayr, to whose intense patriotism the romantic glorification of national heroes and folk-lore appealed tremendously, viewed the new development in a favorable light. He wanted everyone to become familiar with the rich heritage of glory sur-

[1] Nagl, *op. cit.*, vol. ii, pp. 840 *et seq.*
[2] *A. f. o. G.*, vol. civ, pp. 204 *et seq.*

rounding the growth of the fatherland through the centuries. Doubtless the beginning of a correspondence between Hormayr and the Swiss national historian, Johannes von Müller, in 1799,[1] had much to do with turning the thoughts of the young Tyrolese to the history of his own land. From 1802 to 1805 he edited a Tyrolese Almanach. In 1802 and 1803 he published a two-volume *Diplomatic History of Tyrol in the Middle Ages.* In 1805 appeared his *Frederick of Austria,* a play which was presented in the Burgtheater in Vienna in October of that year.[2] Five months later, in March, 1806, the same theatre produced his *Leopold the Handsome.*[3] His twenty-volume *Austrian Plutarch,* containing biographical sketches of famous Austrians, began to appear in 1807. Throughout 1804 and 1805 he propagandized his cause in the salon of Caroline Pichler. It was here that he met and influenced the Collin brothers, Joseph von Hammer-Purgstall and many other promising writers.[4] It was here, too, that Hormayr developed an interest for national history both in his hostess and in the younger members of her charming circle. And it was in Pichler's home, also, that he gave the impetus to a movement for utilizing the arts in the portrayal of events of national significance and interest.[5]

---

[1] Müller's *Sämmtliche Werke,* vol. xxxviii, pp. 239 *et seq.*

[2] Wlassack, Ed., *Chronik des k. k. Hofburgtheaters* (Vienna, 1876), p. 95.

[3] *Ibid.*

[4] Pichler, C., *Denkwürdigkeiten aus meinem Leben,* 4 vols. (Vienna, 1844), vol. ii, pp. 53 *et seq.,* 98, 109 *et seq.,* 115.

[5] Wihan, *op. cit.,* p. 115. In 1808 Pichler wrote a poem *"In das Stammbuch des Freyherrn von Hormayr"* in which she spoke of the *Deutsche Kraft und Deutschem Willen* in his heart, and expressed the hope

> *Möchte deine Gluth fürs Vaterland*
> *Heiss in alle deutschen Herzen dringen.*

Cf. Pichler, C., *Sämmtliche Werke* (Vienna, 1814), vol. xiv, pp. 93-94.

Then, with the year 1808, the idea of romanticism actually began to establish itself in Austria. In that year there arrived in Vienna August Wilhelm von Schlegel, brother of Friedrich, who, as we saw, followed him a year later. And other romanticists followed in due time. Despite the presence of these leaders, however, romanticism was forced to wage an up-hill battle before it triumphed. Led by Joseph Schreyvogel and his famous literary paper, the *Sonntagsblatt,* the Viennese press, whose circulation depended upon the maintenance of the type of literature of the " good old days ", fiercely attacked the " *klingklang* " of the newcomers.[1] For lack of a friendly journal the romanticists finally founded their own organ, *Prometheus* (1808), edited by Stoll and Seckendorff.[2]

What made some of the Viennese all the more bitter against the romanticists was the fact that the Austrian Government now suddenly took the lead in a movement for intellectual reform and actually smiled benevolently upon the " outsiders "—appointing them to official positions and giving them other tokens of its good-will.[3] The government, apparently, was quicker to realize the value of romanticism as a weapon against Napoleon than were the newspaper editors and the litterateurs. By emphasizing themes of a national character the romanticists were playing directly into the hands of the authorities, who were trying to make the impending war a " national one ". That is why the German visitors were so well received by Viennese officialdom. Indeed, August Wilhelm Schlegel was accorded a privilege which had hitherto been granted only to the most highly favored of native savants. He was allowed to deliver a

[1] Wagner, K., " Der Einzug der Romantiker in Wien ", in *Die Kultur* (Vienna, 1908), vol. ix, pp. 323 *et seq.*

[2] *A. f. o. G.,* vol. civ, p. 204.

[3] Wagner, *op. cit.,* p. 323.

series of private lectures. Even so, it required all the influence of the popular and shrewd Mme. de Staël, and the perseverance of the emperor's intimate, Count Summerau, to secure the necessary permission from Francis.[1]   Schlegel was permitted to deliver fifteen lectures on the general topic of " Dramatic Art and Literature ", but a police official was to be present at every one of them.   The lectures were attended by about three hundred men and women, including the leading figures in government, court, army, scholastic and artistic circles.[2]   It was Schlegel's purpose to win over some of the younger dramatists to national German themes in order that the contemporary generation might see reflected in these works the glorious position once occupied by their German ancestors.   He hoped that the Germans of his day might then be spurred on to try to regain that high position.   He held up Shakespeare as the " most perfect historical dramatist ", and went as far as he dared in showing the political implications of such " German " uses of art and literature.[3] " A general emotion was manifest during the last lecture ", he wrote later on, " aroused by so much that I could not mention, but over which the hearts understood each other." [4]

Unfortunately, Schlegel's hopes were not fulfilled before the outbreak of the war.   The time was too short, the inertia to be overcome too great, to allow of the immediate appearance of an Austrian Shakespeare — though Matthias von Collin was soon to have the ambition of becoming one.[5] But in a number of fields the influence, direct or indirect, of

---

[1] Wagner, *op. cit.*, p. 324.

[2] Perthes, *op. cit.*, vol. ii, p. 316.

[3] Minor, J., " August Wilhelm von Schlegel in den Jahren 1804-1815 ", in *Zeitschrift für die österreichischen Gymnasien* (Vienna, 1887), vol. xxxviii, p. 599.

[4] *Ibid.*

[5] *Cf.* Wihan, *op. cit., passim.*

romanticism was apparent. The *Vaterländische Blätter,* for instance, wondered why it was that " so many great people squander thousands in their English gardens by building Greek temples and Chinese summer houses and so on, while there is nowhere to be found an obelisk which names the deeds of our heroic countrymen." [1] Then it carried a series of articles entitled " Sketches and Anecdotes of Austria's Heroes, with a Background of their Times." [2] This series included German heroes chiefly, but not exclusively. In addition to Hormayr's *Plutarch,* and doubtless often based upon it, there were also published a number of pamphlets and booklets, of greater or less merit, devoted to brief biographies of Austrian heroes. One which was widely advertised bore the title " Attempts at Historical Discourses concerning Austria and its Heroes." [3] Moreover, there was a relatively great activity in the production of historical works.[4] A few of the more important books published were: Friedrich Fröhlich, *Arminius or the Struggle between the Germans and the Romans* (1808); Carl Franz Suntinger, *History of Lower Austria from the Ancient Days to the Time of the Union of the Various Provinces under the Sceptre of the Habsburgs* (1808); Franz Kurz, *Contributions to the History of Upper Austria* (4 volumes, 1805-1809); J. A. Kumar, *Attempts at a National History of Ottocar VI, First Duke of Styria* (1808); A. G. von Bergenstamm, *Materials for the History of National Defense in Austria, in particular*

---

[1] *Vat. Bl.,* July 19, 1808, p. 180.

[2] *Vat. Bl.,* 1808: nos. 42, 44, 50, 51; 1809: nos. 23, 24.

[3] Advertised in the *Wiener Zeitung,* no. 31, April 19, 1809: *Versuch einiger historischen Reden über Österreich und seine Helden, von I. J. von C.* (Vienna, 1809).

[4] Pichler, *Denkwürdigkeiten,* vol. ii, p. 109: " *Das Studium der Geschichte fing an bei der damaligen Generation ein lebhaftes Interesse zu erregen. Viele Gelehrte verlegten sich darauf, und man suchte Halt und Trost in der Betrachtung der Vergangenheit.*"

*of the Militia, down to the present Day. For the Patriot
and Historian* (1809); *Monument to heroically performed
Duties in the History of the Citizens and Inhabitants of
Vienna* (2 volumes, 1806); Johann Pezzl, *New Sketch of
Vienna* (1805); Hormayr's *Historical Handbooks* (1806-
1807); and Joseph Rohrer, *Essay on the German Inhabitants
of the Austrian Monarchy* (2 volumes, 1804).[1]

Although none of these titles sounds particularly " German " in spirit, most of the volumes contain expressions of
a decidedly German nature. Bergenstamm, for instance,
going back to medieval times, when Austria was only a German duchy, remarks:

How difficult it was, after the heroic Hermann, Margrave
of Baden [and therefore a German] died, for Ottocar, King of
Bohemia [that is, a Slav—a non-German], to wedge his way
into Austria and Styria.[2] It was only by force that he was
able to maintain himself here temporarily [1251-1273]. Even
when the Austrians accompanied Ottocar as far as Pressburg
in 1271 in his campaign against the Hungarians, they did so,
not so much for his sake, as to save themselves and the fatherland. The proof of this lies in the warm welcome which they
extended in 1273 to Rudolph, Count of Habsburg, when he
became emperor. They quickly demonstrated their displeasure
at being ruled by a foreign dynasty and readily joined Rudolph
in ousting a non-German who had forced himself upon them
by deceit and violence. They voluntarily offered blood and

[1] See Bibliography under the various authors' names for German titles.

[2] Hermann, Margrave of Baden, had a claim to Austria through his
wife, Gertrude, and secured control of a large part of the duchy of
Austria during the Interregnum of the thirteenth century. He died in
1250, and in 1251, Ottocar, son of the king of Bohemia, occupied Vienna.
In 1253 Ottocar became King of Bohemia himself, and in 1260 he conquered Styria. When Rudolph of Habsburg became emperor in 1273,
Ottocar refused to recognize him. Several wars resulted and Ottocar
was defeated in 1276 and 1278. In the latter year Ottocar met his death
on the Marchfeld. *Cf.* Brockhaus, vol. xii, p. 732.

goods to the savior of Germany and thus hastened their own deliverance from foreign domination.[1]

Further on in the same book Bergenstamm also takes special occasion to contrast the " candidness and honesty " of the Germans, with the character of " enemies [the French] who have ever been accustomed to violate their sacred promises." [2]

Then Pezzl, in his sketch of Vienna, says: " We have several journals which supply us with information and news of various foreign capitals. . . . Now, if the Germans are interested enough in those distant places to want to know more about them, then perhaps they will also be willing to spend a few spare hours in reading about some of the points of interest in the leading city of their own fatherland." [3]

Again, Baron Gaheis,[4] in a book of memorabilia of the war of 1805, published in 1808, lamented the constantly diminishing strength of mind of Germany's rulers, and the decrease of civic virtues among Germany's citizens. " The nobler members of the nation," he said, " are forced to grieve over the death of that love of the fatherland which once burned so brightly in the hearts of all Germans. They are sorrow-stricken over the foreign atmosphere which has been permeating the innermost crevices of the national body, and has been leading us further and further away from the strength and simplicity which have ever been Germany's most splendid heritage." [5]

[1] Bergenstamm, A. von, *Materialien zur Geschichte der österreichischen Landesvertheidigung*, pp. 11-12.

[2] *Ibid.*, p. 45.

[3] Pezzl, *Neue Skizze von Wien*, p. ii.

[4] Franz Freiherr von Gaheis was born in 1763 in Krems, and died in 1811 in Vienna. He was a prolific writer on all subjects, and at one time was a member of the Municipal Council of Vienna. *Cf.* Goedecke, vol. vi, pp. 545-548.

[5] Gaheis, *Denkwürdigkeiten Wiens*, p. 15.

And Rohrer maintained, with Pezzl:

We have kept our gaze fixed abroad long enough. It is high time that we direct it back into the heart of our own fatherland. Long enough have hotheaded scribblers dished out to us in their novels and political writings what we ought to be like, according to their caprices. Let us go to work in a calmer, more natural fashion. Let us first see and ponder over what we *are* like, and then decide whether or not anything should be changed. Proceeding on this basis, it should be fairly easy for us to pass judgment on what we must strengthen or weaken, learn or forget, do or avoid, in order to render ourselves more worthy of humanity in general, and of the fatherland in particular.[1]

Naturally, the romantic movement might also be expected to have had some influence on the study or appreciation of the German language in Austria. Here again, however, the incidence of the romanticists was too late to have any widespread effect before 1809. On the other hand, there was considerable agitation prior to 1809 for a purification of the German language for reasons of national pride and national self-esteem. Pezzl, for instance, though he does not directly advocate the expulsion of all French-speaking people from Austria, relates with significance: " Sullen old Cato drove all Greek teachers out of Rome in his day. The Greek language and Greek customs stood in about the same relation to the Roman language and customs of the time, as the French language and customs have been standing in relation to the language and customs of Germany for the past century." [2]

[1] Rohrer, J., *Versuch über die deutschen Bewohner* ..., vol. i, Preface, pp. iv-v. Rohrer is fairly well satisfied with conditions, but also decries the trend away from the days of German hegemony and glory.

[2] Pezzl, *op. cit.*, vol. ii, p. 266.

Gaheis distinguished himself in this line of endeavor, too. In 1808 he published an ode to the newly-married imperial couple, which he entitled *Hochgesang*, using this German designation in preference to the commonly-used Latin *Ode*. Throughout the song he employed words of strictly German origin wherever possible, and then added two pages of " Notes " explaining his procedure. Following is an extract from these notes, giving the word he is explaining and its possible alternative in italics :

Hochgesang. Today, if ever, it is necessary for Germans to be zealous about the preservation of their language in pure form. Campe [1] already has made some wise and patriotic remarks concerning this subject. Germany should be grateful to him. I believe I am doing my share to pay him homage by hereby acknowledging his principles. Your indulgence for this trial attempt! To be sure, Campe maintains that the word *Ode* has as yet no German equivalent, and that therefore it might well be retained as a necessary substitute. It seems to me, however, that *Hochgesang* or *hohes Lied* are completely expressive of what we mean when we combine the words *Ode* and *lyrisch.—Apostolische Majestät.* I retain this foreign phrase, not so much because it is exceedingly difficult to render into German, but rather because it has been sanctioned as honorable and inviolable by virtue of the common consent of all civilized peoples, and of the supreme executive power. — *Franziskus,* must be left in its original, unique, though foreign form. The customary shortening of this name in the vernacular [to Franz] is contrary to the lofty spirit of the song and to the dignity of the one who is being praised.—*Tiefblau oder Heitre* instead of

[1] Joachim Heinrich Campe (1746-1818) was born in Brunswick. He was a famous lexicographer, educator and author of children's books. His child's edition of *Robinson Crusoe* was translated into all European languages, including English. He agitated for a purification of the German language, especially in his *Wörterbuch der Erklärung und Verdeutschung der unserer Sprache aufgedrungenen fremden Ausdrücke* (Brunswick, 1801, 2 ed., 1813). *Cf.* Brockhaus, vol. iii, pp. 841-842.

Äther, after Klopstock, is explained by this notation. I did not think it proper to use Kinderling's *Feinluft* nor Campe's *Luftgeist.—Orion, Leyer, Wage, Jungfrau, Kranz, Rose, etc.* are well-known constellations.—*Aldebaran* in place of *Ochsenauge.* It was necessary to use this oriental designation in order to avoid ambiguity.—*Wonnemond* rather than the Latin *Mai.* It would probably be more difficult to Germanize the names of some of the other months.—*Nordens Gauen* instead of *mitternächtliches Deutschland* is more in the spirit of the *Hochgesang.* Moreover, there are plenty of first-rate authorities among the Germans who hold that *Nordens Gauen* is German.[1]

Going even further than Gaheis, the Baron Rothkirch, in 1808, wrote a poem "To the German Language".[2] This cannot possibly be rendered into English without taking it out of its proper setting and implications.:

An die deutsche Sprache

Sprache, die im Eichenhain geboren,
  Jetzt ein Sturm mit Donnerstimme schallt,
Jetzt, zu süsser Liebe laut erkoren,
  Sanft ein West durch junge Bäume wallt:
Lass mein Lied, dich würdig zu begrüssen,
Zürnend gleich dem Bergstrom sich ergiessen,
  Klagend aus der Hoffnung schöner Höh'n
  Mild ein Blütenregen niederweh'n!

Von des Beltes eisigen Gestaden
  Zum Gebirg, das in die Wolken strebt,
Wo der Wand'rer von den Felsenpfaden
  In des Rheines Abgrund blickend bebt,

---

[1] Gaheis, F., *Hochgesang* (Vienna, 1808).

[2] Leonhard Graf von Rothkirch und Panthen, *Gedichte* (Vienna, 1848), pp. 149-154. Rothkirch was born in Hungary but wrote in German, and was a personal friend of Archduke Charles and of J. von Collin. He fought with distinction in 1793, 1797, 1799, 1800, 1809 and 1813. He died in 1842. *Cf.* Goedecke, vol. vii, p. 123.

Herrschest du voll Anmuth, Kraft und Würde,
Unser Stolz und uns're letzte Zierde,
  Schlingst der Eintracht letztes heil'ges Band
  Um's besiegt zerrissne Vaterland.

Kannst du noch dies Vaterland erkennen,
  Das den Feind in seiner Mitte schaut?
Kannst du dein noch jene Fluren nennen,
  Die der Sklav' für fremde Herrscher baut?—
Nicht zur Klage darffst du dich erheben,
Nur in todten Zeichen sollst du leben;
  Aus Thuiskons weiten Reichen fort
  Floh die Kraft und das beseelte Wort.

Wandelnd arm und schmucklos durch die Wälder
  Riefst du einst Cherusker auf zur Schlacht,
Jubeltest durch Teutoburgens Felder,
  Als gebrochen lag der Römer Macht.
Reich geschmückt mit hoher Dichtung Gaben,
Kann dich nie der Freudebecher laben,
  Stürmst du nie auf hehrer Siegesbahn
  Kühn mit Pindars Fluge himmelan.

Mächtig tönt, der Ahnen Geist zu wecken,
  Deiner Barden kühner Hochgesang,
Doch den Enkel träger Ruh' entschrecken
  Kann auch nicht der Feinde Waffenklang;
Fühllos, von der Knechtschaft Band umschlungen,
Folgt er dumpfgehorchend fremden Zungen,
  Noch beglückt, dass seine Hürde steht,
  Wenn Gesetz und Freiheit untergeht.

Selbst bereitend sich die schweren Ketten,
  Stolz allein auf schnöden Flittertand
Eilt, von inn'rer Leere sich zu retten,
  Er bewundernd an der *Seine* Strand.
Gallisch darf den Lippen nur enttönen,
Deine Laute wagt er zu verhöhnen,
  Weil zum Spiel verlarvter Lüsternheit
  Nie dein Mund sich doppelzüngig beut.

Und so sieht die Abkunft der Heroen,
  Deren kühnes, unbezwinglich Schwert
Gallier und Römer zitternd flohen,
  Umgestürzt den heimatlichen Herd;
Und so musst du Deutschlands schönste Auen
Abgetrennt vom Vaterlande schauen,
  Sehen, wie in's fremde Joch gebeugt
  Bald dein Laut auf deutschen Fluren schweigt.

Lass in Schmach das feige Volk versinken,
  Seufzen unter fremdem Machtgeboth!
Soll der Stern der Freiheit siegend blinken,
  Muss ein Glück erscheinen ihm der Tod.
Wenn des Elends Schrecken es umdrängen,
Dann erst wird es seine Ketten sprengen;
  Was in träger Üppigkeit erschlafft,
  Weckt Verzweiflung nur zur Riesenkraft.

Ja du wirst, Teutonia, erwachen,
  Der Begeist'rung heilig hehre Wuth
Wird zur hohen Himmelsflamme fachen
  Deinen tief in Staub gebeugten Muth;
Kämpfend werden Tausende erliegen,
Deutsche Kraft und deutsche Treu' wird siegen,
  Aus Verderben, Untergang, Ruin
  Wird der Freiheit Leben neu erblüh'n.

Nur die bess're Nachwelt wird dich sehen,
  Schöne Zeit, für uns erscheinst du nicht!
Winde werden unsern Staub verwehen,
  Eh' hervor die neue Sonne bricht.
Uns wird nie ein Tag der Sonne glänzen,
Unser Haupt kein Siegeslorbeer kränzen;
  Jeder Keim des Grossen ist erstickt,
  Wo das Joch den feigen Nacken drückt.

Doch du wirst zu bessern Enkeln wallen,
  Ewige, die froh mein Lied begrüsst!
Unter Freien wirst du mächtig schallen,
  Wenn verstummt lang' meine Klage ist.

Seh'n wirst du das Vaterland verbunden,
Und geheilt erblicken seine Wunden,
  Seh'n ein fest verbrüdertes Geschlecht,
  Teilen gleich Gesetz und gleiches Recht.

Weit wird dich ein siegend Volk verbreiten,
  Und der Weisen Stimme wirst du sein;
Hören wird entzückt in deinen Saiten
  Hellas Klang Apollo's Lorbeerhain.
Nur dein Tod wird deutsche Frauen rühren,
Fremder Laut nie ihren Mund entzieren;
  Von der Töchter edler Schaar umkreist
  Sieht vollendet dich mein trunk'ner Geist.

Wird dies Lied zu bessern Enkeln dringen,
  Das, in Wehmuthsthränen eingetaucht,
Schwebend auf der Klage dunkeln Schwingen
  Tiefen Schmerz und heisse Liebe haucht?
Süsser Früchte Labung zu gebären,
Muss die Zeit der Blüthen Reiz zerstören;
  Aus dem Keim, den deutsche Nacht begräbt,
  Spriesst der Baum, der durch Äonen lebt.

Such, then, were the preparatory measures of the government and its assistants for the coming struggle. Salvation seemed to lie in the closest spiritual cooperation between all members of the German nationality. Hence all the stops were released, and every lever was put into motion, to produce the desired tones of devotion and death-defying determination.

CHAPTER IV

GERMAN NATIONALISM AMONG THE PEOPLE

No people could be so adamant as to remain unmoved amidst such preparations and doings. The Austrians were no exception. The wave of enthusiasm caught nearly all, high and low, noble and burgher alike, even the peasants to a lesser degree. Noblemen entered the ranks and wealthy citizens who were unable personally to do military service, volunteered to support the wives and children of those of their fellow-citizens who would enlist.[1] Still others valiantly wielded the pen if not the sword.[2] Of parades and processions there was no end.[3] The overpowering force of the spirit that prevailed may be gauged from the fact that one patriot committed suicide when fate destined him to remain behind in Vienna to help guard the supply depots while his comrades of the Fourth Battalion of Vienna Volunteers went out to engage the foe.[4] More cheerful was the

[1] *Vat. Bl.*, April 1809, p. 160. Also " Steuermarkisch-Grätzerisches Tagebuch ", a contemporary diary published in *Mitt. des Hist. Ver. für Steiermark* (Graz, 1887), vol. xxxv, pp. 38-39, 44. The *Tagebuch* is continued in vol. xxxvi.

[2] Thus I. F. Castelli: " ... *und da ich mit dem Schwerte für dasselbe [das Vaterland] nicht kämpfen konnte, so that ich mit der Feder was in meinen Kräften lag.*" Castelli, I. F., *Aus dem Leben eines Wiener Phäaken, 1781-1862* (Stuttgart, 1912), p. 157.

[3] Rosenbaum's *Tagebuch*, entry of April 19, 1809 and others.

[4] The stay-at-home lot naturally fell to the smallest and weakest of the recruits, of whom George Kräsemann, a shoemaker, happened to be one. His friends were unable to convince him that the one service was as honorable as the other, and after two days of brooding he shot himself. *Cf.* Hormayr, J. von, *Wien, Seine Geschichte und Denkwürdigkeiten* (Vienna, 1824), vol. v, pt. ii, p. 23.

Viennese Matthias Franz Perthes who rejoicingly wrote:
" The present epoch remains the most beautiful in all of
Austrian history. Everyone is contributing for all he is
worth. Class vies with class for the best of the German
fatherland. Never was there such enthusiasm as. now." [1]

The French chargé was astounded at the display of activity
and intense excitement.

> I am hardly able to portray [he reported to Paris] the extra-
> ordinary appearance which the capital presents. The embank-
> ments of the city are crowded with carts and picketted horses;
> the suburbs are filled with peasants and their transport wagons.
> Within the city itself there is the spectacle of soldiers and offi-
> cers making hurried purchases. Young people they are, and
> all of them wear the symbol of enlistment in their caps. The
> theatres present only timely plays which excite the spectators.
> The newspapers contain nothing but tirades directed against
> France, and advertisements of patriotic works and accounts
> of the prowess of Austrian heroes.[2]

The patriotic zeal of the entire populace increased from day
to day,[3] and the nation countenanced the energetic measures
taken by the government with " unprecedented enthusiasm
and good-will ".[4] M. Dodun found it " impossible to picture
the almost universal aversion " which was exhibited toward
all individuals connected in any way with Napoleon or the
princes who were his allies. " We were regarded like
plague-stricken individuals," he wrote. " The people would
have nothing to do with us, and it was only in the presence

---

[1] Perthes, M. F., " Tagebuch eines Wieners ", contributed by K. Glossy
to *Wiener Neujahrsalmanach* (Vienna, 1900), entry of March 9, 1809.

[2] *A. E. A. C. P., Vienne, 1809*, vol. 382, folio 152, Dodun to Champagny,
Vienna, March 23, 1809.

[3] Reichardt, *op. cit.*, vol. ii, p. 154, letter of March 14, 1809.

[4] *Publicationen aus den königl. Preuss. Staatsarchiven*, vol. vi, p. 521,
Finkenstein to the king from Vienna, July 9, 1808.

of witnesses that anyone dared come near us." [1]   More than one poet was so absorbed in the trend of events that his literary output suffered serious curtailment for some time.[2] As early as September, 1808, people placed bets on the outbreak of the war.[3]   The musician Reichardt marveled at the demonstrations of energy and the joyous mood of the people. He complimented himself upon having been present at a spectacle than which there could be none more pleasing or inspiring.[4]

That the famous Vienna cafés should become seething craters adding their share to the general upheaval was to be expected.   They were more crowded than ever, and the patrons loudly discussed the latest news, or boastfully predicted the hour of victory.   The *Bulletin de Vienne*, containing the reports of an official French observer in Vienna, complained that " frightful remarks " were being passed against the French.   The habitués criticized the newspapers unmercifully and denied the accuracy of the reports concerning Napoleon's successes in Spain.   " *Il ne serait pas prudent de montrer un doute sur les oracles prononcés dans ces temples de la raison,*" concluded the French report.[5]

Naturally not everyone in Austria was enthusiastic about

[1] *A. E. A. C. P., Vienne, 1809*, vol. 382, folio 138, Dodun to Champagny, Vienna, March 18, 1809.

[2] H. J. von Collin: " *Die politischen Eräugnisse* [sic] *nehmen mir den Kopf so ein, dass ich wohl noch längere Zeit zu aller poetischen Arbeit unfähig sein werde.*" Letter dated October 30, 1806, in Laban, F., *op. cit.*, Appendix Ia, p. 211. Similarly Pichler: " *Das folgende Jahr* [*1809*] *war zu stürmisch für mein Vaterland und daher zu schmerzlich für mich, als dass es irgend etwas von Bedeutung hätte in mir hervorbringen sollen*", quoted in Schindel, C. W. O. A., *Die deutschen Schriftstellerinnen des 19. Jahrhunderts* (Leipzig, 1825), vol. ii, p. 111.

[3] Rosenbaum's *Tagebuch*, entry for September 6, 1808.

[4] Reichardt, *op. cit.*, letters of January to March, 1809.

[5] *A. E. A. C. P., Vienne, 1809*, vol. 382, folio 151, *Bulletin de Vienne*, March 23, 1809.

the war. In addition to some opposition from official circles there was also fear in the heart of many a lukewarm patriot. Lulu Thürheim detected timid misgivings and much uneasiness in the midst of the general enthusiasm.[1] Joseph Carl Rosenbaum, in the service of Count Esterhazy in Vienna, and a well-known theatre habitué, thought the old Peace of Pressburg (signed December 26, 1805) was so good, that in celebration of its third anniversary he made his wife, Theresa, a present of " three pair of white silk stockings ".[2] When he realized how many people were dissatisfied with the terms of the treaty he consoled himself with the remark that he " never thought there were so many stupid people around Vienna." [3] Three weeks later he feared that the political structure of the monarchy was in danger. " One really cannot be calm," he wrote in his effeminate script, " for the thought as to how it all will end simply upsets one completely." [4]

The army, however, was " grander, prouder, stronger than ever before, and imbued with a spirit and enthusiasm hitherto unknown within its ranks." [5] The prevailing sentiment among the people was for death rather than for life under a foreign yoke. " *Nous périrons tous plustôt que de soubir un joug étranger. Ces derniers mots . . . sont dans toutes les bouches,"* wrote Dodum.[6] " *Der Krieg war im höchsten*

---

[1] Thürheim, *op. cit.,* vol. i, p. 265, entry for January 27, 1809 in her *Tagebuch.*

[2] Rosenbaum's *Tagebuch,* entry for December 28, 1808.

[3] *Ibid.*

[4] *Ibid.,* entry for January 17, 1809.

[5] General Grünne, *Politisches Journal, 1810,* p. 509, quoted in Droysen, *op. cit.,* vol. ii, p. 323.

[6] The *Bulletin de Vienne* of March 10, 1809 (*A. E. A. C. P., Vienne, 1809,* vol. 382, folio 120) also reported that the Austrians, when reminded that the great Napoleon himself, with his invincible troops and terrible vengeance, was the prospective enemy, replied: " *Plûtot mourier* [sic] *que de vivre sans être Autrichien."*

Grade volkstümlich," recorded Kübeck in his diary.[1]   The
editor of a popular Vienna news sheet growled threaten-
ingly: " It seems to me that these Parisians are ignorant of
the fact that we Austrians still possess our old German
courage, and that we would rather battle to the point of death
than submit to a foreign yoke." [2]

The theatres quickly catered to the popular demand for
patriotic performances.   Naturally, all references to current
conditions, in particular references to the " independence of
Germany," were greeted by the audiences with thunderous
applause [3]—or " immoderate applause," to use the words of
the *Bulletin de Vienne*.[4]   In such moments any unfortunate
individual who showed signs of dissent from the popular
attitude, either because of his official position or for any other
reason, was likely to experience some rough treatment at the
hands of the crowd.[5]   Productions that failed to take
cognizance of the burning issues of the day were foredoomed
to failure.   Thus, early in 1809, a young playwright found
to his dismay that a tragedy which he had completed three
years previously met with little success.   In his despair he
sought an interview with the celebrated dramatic critic, Count
Esterhazy.   The latter told him to revise the conclusion of
his tragedy.   " But how shall I revise it? " asked the author.
" At present it conforms to history."   " History nothing! "
replied the Count.   " The tyrant must fall!   Your play must
be made to conform to the spirit of the day." [6]

---

1 Kübeck's *Tagebücher*, vol. i, pt. i, p. 264, fragment dated March 23,
1809.

2 *Eipeldauer*, 1809, 5. Heft, p. 32.

3 *Sammler*, no. 39, 1809, *Notizen*.

4 March 23, 1809 in *A. E. A. C. P., Vienne, 1809*, vol. 382, folio 150.

5 *Ibid.*

6 *A. E. A. C. P., Vienne, 1809*, vol. 382, folios 117-118, *Bulletin de
Vienne*, March 10, 1809.

A typical, popular, patriotic play was Alois Gleich's *Unter-tanenliebe.*[1] It was first presented in the theatre in the Leopoldstadt, on April 20, 1809. The price of admission to this performance was twice the ordinary charge, and the proceeds were donated as a fund for the families of the soldiers.[2] The plot is as follows: William, who supports his aged father and himself by painting, is in love with Theresa, the daughter of the innkeeper Jacob Reinberg. The latter, however, plans to have Theresa marry a wealthy wine merchant, named Silbersack. To further his ends, Reinberg orders William and his father to quit the inn, so that the artist may find it more difficult to see his beloved. Now another factor enters. William would join the *Landwehr* but cannot do so because he must support his father. This consideration makes Reinberg relent, and he permits his daughter to marry William. Hereupon the latter enlists, and the innkeeper takes care of both his newly-married daughter and her father-in-law. Albeit the story is not yet ended. Franz, the son of the village magistrate, Christopher, wishes to marry Nanerl, Reinberg's cook. The magistrate fears that his son's anxiety to wed is in part caused by the youth's desire to escape military service. He therefore withdraws the consent which he had already given, until Franz promises to heed the call to the colors.

More important than the plot itself is the constant recurrence of allusions reflecting the spirit of the times. The old people, unable themselves to fight, do their best to help the cause in an indirect way. Veit, the village cobbler, for instance, is engaged in making shoes for the army, and he determines to work just as long as there is a breath left in him. Every time he strikes a blow with his hammer, he says, he will imagine the nail to represent one of the enemy.

[1] Jos. Alois Gleich (1772-1841) wrote about 200 plays and 300 terrible novels, *cf. A. f. o. G.*, vol. civ, p. 228 n.

[2] *Sammler*, no. 48, April 22, 1809, *Notizen*.

" *Und so lang' die Welt steht, soll noch kein Schuhnagel so fest gehalten haben.*" [1]   There is also an abundance of references to the splendid spirit of the Austrians, to their love for the reigning dynasty, to their admiration for the Archduke Charles, and to the ceremonies attending the consecration of the new colors of the *Landwehr*. Whenever possible, and often at other times as well, there are introduced duets, arias and choruses which afford the opportunity for special patriotic plaudits. A fitting climax is provided by concluding the play with one of the best-liked songs of the day, Collin's *Östreich über Alles!*

Another play that was popular in the critical days of 1808 and 1809 was one called simply *German Family*. In a performance of this play on September 23, 1808, in the Karl Theater in Vienna, the famous German actor, Iffland, played his part so well that the audience was moved to tears, and insisted on calling him before the curtain. He responded, and with one brief but powerful sentence called forth renewed and deafening applause: " You are moved at the portrayal of a German family," he said, " because you yourselves are sturdy, honorable Germans." [2]

The performances in the Hoftheater, next to the Imperial Burg, had a semi-official character, and were chosen with a view toward making the populace eager for the approaching war. On March 25, 1809, for example, there was presented a special musical program, which, though not particularly well received that evening, was repeated several times during the following weeks with great success. [3]   The official notice announced the following selections :

[1] Gleich, J. A., *Untertanenliebe* (Vienna, 1809), Act One, Scene Eleven.

[2] Rosenbaum's *Tagebuch*, entry for September 23, 1808.

[3] *Tagebuch eines Wieners*, entry for April 16, 1809, p. 52.

PART ONE

1. *A Military Symphony*, by Joseph Haydn
2. *The War-Oath*, one of H. J. von Collin's *Wehrmänncr* songs, set to music by Joseph Weigl, imperial bandmaster
3. *The Prayer*, by H. J. von Collin, set to music by Gyrowetz, imperial bandmaster
4. A brand new *Concerto* for the *Clarinet*, by Pösinger
5. *The Graybeard*, by H. J. von Collin, set to music by Gyrowetz
6. *The March*, by H. J. von Collin

PART TWO

1. *A Spanish Rondo* for violoncello, by Romberg
2. *The Bride-Groom*, by H. J. von Collin, set to music by Joseph Weigl
3. *Austria's Genius*, by Castelli, set to music by the late bandmaster Süssmayr
4. *The Militiaman's Farewell to his Parents*, by Castelli, set to music by Joseph Weigl
5. *Östreich über Alles*, by von Collin, chorus by Joseph Weigl [1]

The French report of this performance comments upon the noteworthy fact that the program consisted largely of Collin's war songs and war poems, and that these were set to music by the *" maître de chapelle de la cour! "* Moreover, it continues, " the enthusiasm of the audience was unbounded. Few selections were not called for a second time, and the patriotic listeners could not restrain themselves from joining their voices to those of the regular chorus in singing the refrains." [2]

[1] Original copy of the official program as found in *A. E. A. C. P., Vienne, 1809*, vol. 382, folio 156. A somewhat different program is reproduced in *Achtzehnhundertneun*, pp. 334-335.

[2] *A. E. A. C. P., Vienne, 1809*, vol. 382, folio 211, *Bulletin de Vienne*, March 28, 1809.

Referring to another performance of this same program, a contemporary Viennese diary contains the following entry, dated April 7, 1809: " When in one of the verses the line: *Österreich über Alles, wenn es nur will,* was reached, there resounded from the boxes, the parterre and the galleries just one cry: *Es will, es will!* " [1]   On another occasion M. Dodun's ire was aroused in the Hoftheater when an actor in the rôle of a valet pronounced the following eulogy over his master: " In combat he was as brave as a German.   In his dealings with his fellow-men he was as noble as a Spaniard. In his relations with women he was as amiable as a Frenchman."   After these last words, says Dodun, the valet " expectorated with affectation, and the audience applauded this indecency." [2]

As representative of the activities of some of Austria's women in the events of 1809, we may take the contributions of Caroline Pichler.   Born in Vienna, in 1769, she developed into a staunch patriot at the courts of Maria Theresa and Joseph II.   As a result of numerous short excursions into the beautiful mountain regions of Upper Austria and Styria, she became well acquainted with some of the country outside Vienna.   Her love of the fatherland grew with her increased knowledge of its characteristics. [3]   After her marriage her home became the gathering place for the outstanding German

---

[1] *Tagebuch eines Wieners,* entry for April 7, 1809. On another occasion the strains of the stirring *Östreich über Alles* drove a crowd into a frenzy of acclamation. As described by the German musician Reichardt who was present at the time, "there was a burst of applause, calls, loud outcries, jubilation and sobbing that extended from the imperial boxes down into the very pit. Never have I experienced a greater sensation." Reichardt, *op. cit.,* vol. ii, pp. 105-106, letter of March 31, 1809 from Vienna.

[2] *A. E. A. C. P., Vienne, 1809,* Suppl. vol. 29, folio 125, Dodun to Champagny, Vienna, April 17, 1809.

[3] Wurzbach, vol. xxii, p. 254.

litterateurs of the day. She gave evidence of considerable literary ability herself, and wrote patriotic poems and articles, as well as plays and short stories, over a number of years. She was also a leader in the movement to have the women of Germany change their mode of life and dress to conform more nearly to that of the Teutonic women of old.[1] Similarly, she pointed out that among the ancient Germans no one was considered a " complete man " who could not wield the sword as well as he could use the plow. " Every citizen a soldier, and every soldier a citizen " was the slogan she advanced in praising the *Landwehr*.[2] She liked to allude to herself as a " German-feeling soul," [3] and anything reprehensible or cowardly or objectionable was summed up by her in the word " un-German." [4] Although her most important literary work, at least from our point of view, came in the days of 1813 and 1814, she did contribute to the literature of 1809. In addition to the articles referred to above, her chief composition at this time was a poem on " Emperor Ferdinand II ". She was inspired to write these verses by the appearance of the Hohenzollern cavalry regiment in Vienna on March 8, 1809.[5] This regiment became famous

---

[1] She contributed an article on this subject to the *Vat. Bl.* in January, 1810, pp. 191-194, entitled "Über die Bildung des weiblichen Geschlechts." German men and women in Austria and elsewhere took the movement for a *Nationaltracht* seriously, the women going back to a sort of *Gretchentracht*. See Hottenroth, F., *Handbuch der deutschen Tracht*, p. 873.

[2] Pichler, C., "Über den Volksausdruck in unserer Sprache: Ein ganzer Mann," in *Vat. Bl.*, April, 1809, pp. 175-178.

[3] In the Dedication of her play *Germanicus* to Charles, 1813. The Swedish poet Atterborn once remarked: "Pichler and the tower of St. Stephen's are the two curiosities of Vienna", quoted in Nagl, *op. cit.*, vol. ii, p. 736. Some of Pichler's other writings will be considered later —in the chapter dealing with the period 1813-1815.

[4] Thus, she used this term in speaking of Bavaria's conduct, *cf.* her *Denkwürdigkeiten*, vol. ii, p. 164.

[5] Pichler, *Denkwürdigkeiten*, vol. ii, p. 140.

when it rescued the Catholic Emperor Ferdinand from some of his rebellious Protestant subjects in 1619. As a reward for its service it was given the unique privilege of passing through the Imperial Burg, and of setting up its recruiting stand in the Burgplatz, every time it came to Vienna.[1] The spirit of Pichler's poem, or " romance," as she called it, is given in these two lines of stanza sixteen:

> *Die Vaterlandslieb' ist ein heiliges Feuer—*
> *Kein Opfer zu gross—kein Blut ihr zu teuer!*

Now, the writing of patriotic songs was, as has been said, no monopoly of official scribes. All classes and all sections contributed to the new literature. The nobility was represented, among others, by Count Rothkirch and Baron Enzenberg; the clergy by Haschka; the army by Dorian, Fellinger and Reissig; the professions by Binder and Kumpf; journalism by Bäuerle and Richter; and the stage by Perinet and Sannens. Caroline Pichler represented her sex.[2] Castelli, Posch, Schleifer and Lehne were other outstanding names. Anonymous works were legion.

A fair proportion of the mass of verse that emanated from the hearts and pens of these people gives evidence of a consciousness of German nationality and of German nationalism. Battle songs, of course, formed the chief vehicle of expression of this nationalism in lyrics. They provided ample opportunity for praise of the German fatherland; for protestations of pride in the possession of a German name and a German heritage; for comparing Francis, Charles and John to ancient German heroes; for exhorting the people to uphold the Germanic traditions; for praising the Habsburg dynasty; for pleading for unity among the Germans; for

---

[1] Pichler, *Denkwürdigkeiten*, vol. ii, p. 140.

[2] *Achtzehnhundertneun*, p. xvi.

defending the German language; for glorifying the *Land-wehr;* for reassuring a groaning humanity; and for giving vent to some opinions about Napoleon and the French. It may be of interest to analyze in some detail a few of the more strongly nationalistic poems and songs. Many of the bards tried to spur their German brethren on to the war of liberation by recalling the struggle of the ancient Germans against Rome. Thus, one poet tried to make clear [1] that it was only by sowing dissension among the Germans that treacherous Rome had been able to defeat them. Indeed, he wrote, as soon as the Germans were united under Hermann and Marbod [2] the Romans began to tremble for fear. Next, the poet proceeded to draw an analogy, pointing out that now a French Romulus, aping the Romans, also was trying to spread discord in the camp of the Germans. Needless to say, he continued, Napoleon, too, would find Flavii,[3] who, for the sake of some promised German soil, would willingly forget their membership in the great German brotherhood. As a matter of fact, chided the patriot, foreign boards already were settling German disputes,[4] while the French tongue, so reminiscent of the fetters of Rome, already was replacing the German in some localities.[5] But the poet was optimistic of the future. " Sorrow fled his heart " as he watched the

---

[1] *Aufstehen zum Freyheitskampfe* (Vienna, March, 1809). See Appendix p. 201 for the poem in German.

[2] Marbod was a chief of the Marcomanni. After a period of friendship Marbod fought with Hermann for the supremacy in Germany but was defeated by the *liberator Germaniae. Cf. Cambridge Medieval History* (New York, 1911-1926), vol. i, p. 196.

[3] Flavius, a brother of Hermann, went over to the side of the Romans. The reference here is to the rulers of Bavaria, Württemberg and the members of the Confederation of the Rhine.

[4] Between members of the Confederation.

[5] Refers particularly to the Kingdom of Westphalia, where King Jerome Bonaparte fostered French.

Styrians, Carinthians, Tyrolese and other Germans rallying around Austria's standards for what was to be a " sacred, beautiful struggle—for our own customs, our own rulers, our own language." He felt certain that Germany would be liberated from the snares of the new Rome and the new Caesar. He knew that the Germans would beat Napoleon on the Rhine, as the freedom-loving Spaniards had beaten him on the Tagus.[1]

Another patriot, a " noble sharpshooter," appealed to his German brothers to uphold the traditions of Hermann.[2] He urged his countrymen to fight for German freedom, to keep alive Germania's name, and to help recreate the powerful German fatherland of old by rallying to Austria's standards. A second Hermann, he said, had been created by God to be the savior of Germany. Let all men of German blood, then, follow the lead of Charles. Let them live and die as Germans should—for the greater glory of emperor and fatherland! Let their joyous battle-cry be: To conquer or to die!

Among the more powerful of anti-Napoleonic poems was the " Voice from the Desert " by Matthias Leopold Schleifer. Schleifer was one of the most popular German poets of the period. He hated the French, and continued to sing the events of 1809 and 1814 twenty and more years after they had transpired.[3] In the " Voice from the Desert " Napoleon was warned that his fatal hour was approaching, and that he would not be permitted to make of Europe a land of slaves condemned to silence and despair. The men of Germany,

---

[1] Refers to the struggles of the Spaniards in July and August, 1808.

[2] *An meine deutschen Brüder. Von einem ritterlich-bürgerlichen Scharfschützen aus der 8ten Compagnie* (1809). See Appendix p. 204 for the poem.

[3] Goedecke, vol. vi, pp. 552-554. " Die Stimme aus der Wüste ", pp. 147 *et seq.* of *Poetische Versuche von Matthias Leopold Schleifer* (Vienna, 1830).

said Schleifer, would not sit by impotently and watch the new Caesar place a yoke about their neck. No! Germania was not orphaned, nor had the spirit of Hermann departed from his descendants. The sacred flame of patriotism, of German loyalty, cried the poet, still burned within the breast of every staunch defender of the fatherland. The same swords that drove the Roman and the Hun into a bloody retreat would cut the new Genghis Khan to pieces. " Men of Germany, unite!" pleaded Schleifer, and he swore that Germania would not fall until the very earth did crumble!

Johann Gustav Fellinger (1781-1816), the " Styrian Theodore Körner," also composed some stirring songs and marches in 1808 and 1809.[1] Fellinger enlisted in a Styrian *Landwehr* battalion in 1808, simultaneously with his aged father and two of his brothers. Then, finding that the *Landwehr* was meant for service on domestic soil only, Fellinger applied for a commission in the regular army. He wanted to go out and meet the foe as quickly as possible, rather than sit back and wait to help repel an invasion. His request was granted, and in 1809 he was commissioned a lieutenant. By the time he received the notice of his new assignment, however, the regiment which he was to join had begun campaigning. He was forced, therefore, to remain with the *Landwehr,* which now, to his delight, was also ordered to duty across the frontier — in northern Italy.[2] Meanwhile, in 1808, he had composed a " March for the Styrian *Landwehr*" beginning with the stanza:[3]

[1] Ilwof, F., " Johann Georg Fellinger der ' steirische Theodor Körner '", in *Jahrbuch der Grillparzer Gesellschaft*, vol. xix, pp. 164-182. Also Goedecke, vol. vi, pp. 644 *et seq*. According to Goedecke and to Arnold and Wagner in *Achtzehnhundertneun*, p. 304, Fellinger's second name was Gustav.

[2] Ilwof, *op. cit., passim*.

[3] Fellinger, J. G., *Marsch für die Steyermärkische Landwehr* (Grätz, 1808).

> Rise, brothers, rise!   The flags are waving,
> Gather for the clash of arms.
> In battle we will stand as men,
> Like Germans in the war's alarms.
> Formed in well-drilled battle hosts,
> First in danger must we be.
> And if we fight with German might,
> Ours will be the victory.

In 1809 Fellinger added a " Call of the Styrian *Landwehr* "
the first stanza of which reads: [1]

> Come along!   Come along!
> Whoever still can carry arms,
> Whoever has German blood in his veins,
> Whoever is possessed of noble strains.
> In Styria let the cry ring out:
> Come along and join in the glorious bout!
> Come along!   Come along!

Finally, Joseph Fridolin Lehne's " Song of a German "
may serve as the concluding example.[2]   In this poem Lehne
praised God that he could revel in the thought of being a
German.   No matter what evils Germany may have had to
suffer, or what cursed happenings it may have had to witness,
Lehne vowed that he would ever remain a loyal son of the
fatherland.   As a German, he boasted, he could live in peace
on the fruits of his labor, unvexed by any foreign king, and
undisturbed by foreign hirelings, for the German nation
would never submit to slavery.   Happy he who could join
in the refrain: Well for me, I am a German!

The public received both the official proclamations and the

---

[1] Fellinger, J. G., *Heeresruf der Steyermärkischen Landwehr* (Grätz, 1809).

[2] " Lied eines Deutschen Mannes ", dated 1809 in Lehne, J. F., *Gedichte* (Vienna, 1817), vol. i, pp. 92-94.

patriotic songs and pamphlets kindly.   On April 14, 1809, it
was reported from Vienna that " everyone there spoke of
nothing but the Manifesto " that had been drawn up by
Gentz.[1]   Moreover, the simultaneous demand for the proclamation " To the German Nation " was so great that the government found it necessary to order a second printing.[2]
Again, when it was rumored, toward the end of March, 1809,
that Baron vom Stein's memoirs were soon to appear in
print, the bookshop that was indicated as the publishing house
" was literally stormed by the crowds for several days in
succession." [3]   Adolf Bäuerle had the satisfaction of seeing
25,000 copies of his work on Spain and the Tyrol sold.[4]
Schlegel's *Armeebefehl,* too, was immensely popular.   Allowing for pardonable exaggeration, there still remains much
significance in the words which Dorothea Schlegel wrote her
husband from Vienna:

The people are going into ecstasies over the Army Order.
They all but engage in fisticuffs to secure copies of it.   Persons
are paying a ten-fold price so as to get possession of it at the
earliest possible moment.   Several copies that were sold sur-
reptitiously yesterday [April 5, instead of April 6, the date that
appeared at the head of the order] brought five florins [about
$2.41] · apiece.   Everyone is speaking of the proclamation.
People are both laughing and crying with joy.   Everyone is
congratulating his neighbors.   It is a most remarkable demonstration.[5]

Of the numerous *Landwehrlieder* that appeared in print,
the *Eipeldauer* wrote: " These songs are being sold by the

---

[1] *W. S. A., Staatskanzlei Korresp., Fasz. 73,* note of Hudelist to
Stadion, April 14, 1809.

[2] *Ibid.*

[3] Reichardt, *op. cit.,* vol. ii, p. 54 and Pertz, *Stein,* vol. ii, p. 358.

[4] Wurzbach, vol. i, p. 118.

[5] Raich, *Dorothea's Briefwechsel,* vol. i, p. 334.

dozen." [1]   The letters of the *Tulbinger Resel* [2] similarly announced that the entire first edition of the anonymous poem " We know Thee ", addressed to Charles, was sold out within two days.   In this instance it is well to note, however, that the editor of Resel's letters, Joachim Perinet, was really the author of the poem, and consequently had a " vested interest " in publicity for it.   But he was modest enough to ascribe the large sale to the popular esteem in which the famous savior of his country was held. [3]   The *Eipeldauer* also reported a gratifying sale of the *Volkslieder,* and expressed the wish that all musicians might stop playing silly love songs, and instead carry the new patriotic tunes into the cafés—a proceeding much more honorable in the opinion of all lovers of their fatherland.   " My good cousin has no idea," the *Eipeldauer* wrote, " of the great impression which such a patriotic song, accompanied by good music, makes upon the heart of the listener. . . . Many a young man has rushed from a café to the nearest recruiting station after listening to a few of the inspiring verses." [4]   Castelli, in his memoirs, relates in one place that his " War-Song " appeared in an edition of 300,000 copies.   On another page he speaks of an edition of only 100,000.   The discrepancy looks suspicious, and doubtless even the latter figure is an exaggeration, but it may serve as an indication that the song really was very popular. [5]

[1] *Eipeldauer*, 1809, 4. Heft, p. 21.

[2] *Briefe der Tulbinger Resel*, edited by Joachim Perinet in imitation of Richter's *Eipeldauer*. Perinet (1763-1813), who was a Viennese actor and author, was more cautious and less satirical than Richter. *Cf. A. f. o. G.*, vol. civ, pp. 225 n. and 228 n.   See Appendix p. 210 for the poem *Wir kennen Dich.*

[3] *Briefe der Tulbinger Resel*, 1809, 3. Heft, p. 26.

[4] *Eipeldauer*, 1809, 4. Heft, p. 21.

[5] *Achtzehnhundertneun*, pp. 350-351.   See Appendix p. 212 for the *Kriegslied.*

The extraordinary popularity of Collin's songs has been remarked upon in connection with the enthusiasm displayed by theatre audiences when his verses appeared on the program. In addition, newspapers like the *Eipeldauer* and the *Tulbinger Resel* showered praises upon them. Said *Resel:* " Herrn von Kolin's [*sic*] *Landwehrlieder* are really lovely, and if all those who bought copies of them were assembled together there would be militiamen a-plenty." [1] A note in the handwriting of Vice-President of Police von Hager confirms the great volume of sales by pointing out that Anton Strauss, who undertook to publish the songs in a cheap edition at his own risk, was selling them at two groschen (two cents) per booklet and was suffering no financial loss whatever.[2] Perhaps the best gauge of the effectiveness of Collin's songs is the negative tribute paid by the *Morgenbote,* a pro-French sheet published in Vienna while the city was in the hands of Napoleon. " These songs," it says, " are a perfect example of how war songs ought not to be." [3]

The popular interest in Spain and the Spaniards is attested to by the appearance of a number of works dealing with Spanish history or heroes. Thus, under the title *Miscellanies for Newspaper Readers* there was published a book whose frontispiece was a portrait of the Prince of Asturias (later Ferdinand VII), and which contained articles on the Spanish militia, the Sierra Morena mountains in Spain, reminiscences of the Spanish-French War of 1808, highlights in the history of Brazil, Prince Ferdinand, and other similar subjects.[4]

While some people busied themselves writing songs and poems, others went so far as to issue proclamations and

---

[1] *Briefe der Tulbinger Resel,* 1809, 15. Heft, p. 26.

[2] Note of March 11, 1809, quoted in *Achtzehnhundertneun,* p. 328.

[3] *Morgenbote,* vol. i, pp. 102 *et seq.,* quoted in *ibid.,* p. 327.

[4] Advertised in the *Wiener Zeitung,* no. 14, February 18, 1809.

manifestoes on their own account. These proclamations
were, of course, unofficial, at least in the sense that they did
not bear the stamp of the central government at Vienna. In
some cases it was probably the local authorities who were
responsible for their appearance. Perhaps the best of these
appeals was one made public in various parts of Austria on
the eve of Archduke Charles' campaign in 1809: [1]
People of Germany! [2]

The hour of deliverance has come! Once again Austria
comes to your aid, ready to save you. Do not imagine for a
moment that Austria ever withdrew its protecting gaze from
you—you who in happier days were so closely united with it.
Austria was distressed to see you bound with chains forged
long ago across the Rhine; to see your independence mocked,
and the rights of your rulers crushed under foot by a wilful
tyrant. Austria was aware of the forcible revocation of the
most fundamental and century-old principles of your constitutions—principles which breathed the soul and spirit of ancient
Germania—principles which so often afforded you and your
forefathers protection against autocracy and arbitrariness.
Austria also saw the foreigners carry off priceless German
treasures and belongings. It witnessed the dethronement of two
of the leading German families so that—to the insult of all German people—a monarchy might be created for a foreign youth. [3]
Austria saw foreign military leaders rewarded with German

[1] Unsigned proclamation dated April 8, 1809 (in library of Univ. of
Vienna). Wagner and Arnold in their *Achtzehnhundertneun* (pp. 314-
317) think the proclamation may be one of Schlegel's, but even that
would not change its unofficial character since the government could
not assume responsibility for so truculent a message.

[2] Though the author of the proclamation addresses it to the *Völker
Deutschlands* he uses the word *Völker* in the sense of "people". Thus
he speaks later on of "*die schändliche Unterjochung von Millionen
einst freyer deutscher Völker.*"

[3] Brunswick and Hesse-Cassel were incorporated in the Kingdom of
Westphalia, of which Napoleon's youngest brother, Jerome, became king,
all by the Treaty of Tilsit, July 7, 1807.

lands for deeds of oppression carried out on German soil. Austria saw you forced to accept a foreign code of laws—every German heart bled at the sight. And Austria beheld your sons, German youths, led off to battle against other Germans who were not yet conquered, or carried across the Pyrenees to bleed in Spain in support of the unjust cause of a rapacious foreigner.

However, it was necessary for things to come to such a pass. The shameful subjugation of millions of formerly free Germans had to be completed within the space of a few years in order to call forth still further pretensions on the part of the enemy. This success heightened his arrogance to the point where it finally threatened to destroy even the independence and national honor of the only remaining free German people, the Austrians, and of the other nations so happily united with Austria under one monarch.[1] Thus these groups have become convinced that the hour finally has struck when the despotic foreigner plans to subject even them to his iron sceptre. This realization has caused them to draw closer than ever to their legitimate ruler—your former emperor, Germans!—in an attempt to ward off the impending disaster. They are now literally burning with a zeal to fight for their own and for your salvation.

People of Germany! These are not ordinary troops that are hastening to your rescue. No! They are inflamed with love for the fatherland, and filled with a horror of foreign subjugation and tyranny. They are fighting for themselves and their possessions, for freedom, for national existence, for national honor, for fatherland and justice, and for their beloved princes. The very masses have arisen in righteous indignation and have armed themselves for the fray. They offer you their hands as brothers. They encourage you to raise your bowed necks and to tear asunder the chains that bind you fast. They are ready to form a league with you such as is usual among independent peoples.

[1] "*Des einzigen noch freyen deutschen Volkes, und [der] mit ihm unter einem Monarchen glücklich vereinten Nationen....*"

Do not let the present opportunity slip by you. Follow Spain's inspiring example. The Spaniards courageously took up arms in defense of their rights even after numerous enemy legions already had swarmed over Spanish soil. Now give proof that you, too, cherish your fatherland and that you want an independent German régime. Show that you are determined and able to save the fatherland from this threatening slavery. Leave your fatherland to your children free from any foreign yoke. Do not fear the bloody battle for it will end in victory. He who begins courageously, finishes honorably.

Germans! Hearken to the voice from Austria's happy regions. It calls upon you to rally around the standards of a German general—a general who has led you to victory so often. Charles is hastening to you for the final conflict. He is determined to save you. He *will* save you!

Much popular enthusiasm also centered in the activities of that " national institution," [1] the *Landwehr*. To begin with, the ceremonies connected with the blessing of the battalion flags afforded the opportunity for the delivery of a number of sermons of more or less patriotic content.[2] Then, the *Landwehr* system offered an equal chance to the members of all classes to come to the aid of their country. Rich and poor, noble and peasant, professional and artisan, all could join and add strength to the cause. According to a contemporary account

members of the oldest and wealthiest noble families are proving themselves worthy citizens. Many of the princes and counts are organizing and leading battalions. Moreover, a number of them actually are marching along as subalterns in battalions organized and led by members of the so-called lower nobility and even by commoners. . . . On the other hand, some of the largest commercial houses are suffering from a shortage of

---

[1] So referred to in an article in the semi-official *Wiener Zeitung,* no. 24, March 25, 1809.

[2] *Achtzehnhundertneun*, pp. 367 and 285.

clerks and assistants as well as of bookkeepers, cashiers and copyists, since everyone is leaving to enlist. . . . Even the stage is badly crippled by the loss of patriotic extras and supers.[1]

Wrote another observer: " Fathers left their families, while manufacturers, artists and professionals left their callings to enlist. Verily, this was no artificially aroused enthusiasm such as would vanish as suddenly as it appeared." [2]

Both officers and men strove to improve themselves in the arts of war. They drilled with vigor and fervor regardless of cold or slush throughout the winter of 1808 and 1809.[3] Those officers who lacked actual military experience formed themselves into special groups around nuclei of seasoned veterans who taught them all they could of military strategy and tactics.[4] Furthermore, the officers made special efforts to be friendly in their relations with the troops, so that the latter were ready to do their duty with joy and alacrity,[5] while their military ardor increased from day to day.[6] The rest of the people, those who for physical or other reasons could not join the ranks, contributed their share by voluntarily supporting the families and dependents of the uniformed heroes. A special campaign in Vienna alone netted 56,000 guldens (about \$26,880) within five days, and 140,000 guldens (about \$67,200) at the end of ten days.[7]

---

[1] Reichardt, *op. cit.*, vol. ii, pp. 55-56, letter of March 14, 1809.

[2] *Tagebuch eines Wieners*, entry for March 9, 1809.

[3] *A. E. A. C. P., Vienne, 1809*, Suppl. vol. 29, folio 19: *Rapport de Son Excellence le Ministre des Relations éxterieurs à Sa Majesté l'Empereur et Roi*, April 12, 1809. The minister in this case was Champagny. Also Reichardt, *op. cit.*, vol. ii, pp. 55-56.

[4] Reichardt, *op. cit.*, vol. i, pp. 242-244, letter of January 8, 1809.

[5] *Eipeldauer*, 1809, 9. Heft, pp. 20-21.

[6] Reichardt, *op. cit.*, vol i, p. 243.

[7] *Achtzehnhundertneun*, p. 366. Also *Eipeldauer*, 1809, 5. Heft, pp. 8-9, and *A. E. A. C. P., Vienne, 1809*, vol. 382, folio 117, *Bulletin de Vienne*, March 10, 1809.

In the crisis of 1809, as in so many other instances, the students of German Austria played a conspicuous rôle. In most of the larger cities enough students from the universities and academies volunteered so that they could be formed into companies and battalions of their own.[1] The rector of the Theresianum (Maria Theresa Academy) in Vienna appeared before the emperor on March 10, 1809, and complained that the students of the two highest grades were so bent upon joining the army that he was at a loss as to how to restrain them and keep them in school. Upon being informed that the " young gentlemen " in question were between the ages of sixteen and eighteen, Francis replied to the rector: " All right, then let them join; I need them. The war is not yet a certainty, but it looks as though it might, come." [2]

In Carinthia, Styria and parts of Lower Austria outside Vienna, however, the tendency for students to enlist was discouraged by the authorities. In Klagenfurt in Carinthia, for example, an entire company of students was sent back to school by order of Archduke John. The prince said he took this step in order that the culture of the future might be safeguarded.[3] Similarly, Stadion upheld the decision of the recruiting officers in Lower Austria to prohibit the formation of a student corps in the rural sections of that province.[4] The military fervor, nevertheless, seemed also to infect the youngest generation in Austria, judging by a report of the French

[1] They were thus " aping the example of the Spanish students " according to various French papers of March 15 and 16, 1809 as reported by the *Wiener Zeitung*, no. 25, March 29, 1809.

[2] *A. E. A. C. P., Vienne, 1809*, vol. 382, folio 118, *Bulletin de Vienne,* March 10, 1809.

[3] Hamberger, *Die französischen Invasionen*, p. 8. John issued a similar order, couched in flattering terms, regarding two companies of students in Styrian Graz, *cf. Wiener Zeitung*, no. 29, April 12, 1809.

[4] *W. S. A., Kabinets Akten 1809*, Prot. 2380.

Ambassador rendered in August, 1808, in which he said: " Even the children in the cities and villages are organized into groups and are drilling with wooden guns and with sticks." [1]

Incidentally, it would seem that the authorities did wisely in restraining the ardor of at least the younger students. Those who were allowed to participate, such as the Viennese students, did not prove to be particularly useful when it came to actual combat. They looked brave enough as they fiercely paraded around on the bastion before the palace of Archduke Albert—while the French army was still far away. But when the French approached the city, valor gave way to discretionary inactivity. We read in Rosenbaum's diary for May 10, 1809: " A few Frenchmen ventured through the city gates and were fired upon by the guard. This encouraged the students on the ramparts to fire, too, whereby they killed and wounded a number of their own comrades." Perhaps this marksmanship on the part of the students was due to the circumstance, as one of their contemporaries sarcastically remarked, that " *die meisten dieser Musensöhne hatten vorher kein Gewehr in der Hand gehabt und hatten in ihrer ganzen Lebenszeit nichts anderes geschossen als—Böcke.*" [2] At any rate, in the words of the poet Grillparzer, who was one of the volunteers, most of the students were " neither particularly courageous nor particularly frightened," but they " were all rather glad to get home again " when the fireworks were ended.[3]

One other possible aspect of popular activity in 1809 de-

[1] *A. E. A. C. P., Vienne, 1808*, vol. 381, folio 345, Andréossy to Champagny, Vienna, August 24, 1808.

[2] *Das bedrängte und befreite Österreich im Jahre 1809* (Vienna, 1809), pp. 6-7.

[3] Grillparzer, F., *Sämmtliche Werke*, edited by a A. Sauer, 20 vols. (Stuttgart, 1893), vol. xix, pp. 45 *et seq.*

serves mention: the formation of secret patriotic societies.
The evidence, chiefly negative, on this point would seem to
indicate that such societies did not exist within the boundaries
of German Austria at the time.[1]   There were at least three
of them in Prague and several more in other parts of
Bohemia during the war, and according to Francis' own
testimony, they served a useful purpose.[2]   But no reference
is made in the available official correspondence and reports
of the period to any similar organizations in Austria.   Indeed, early in 1810, the emperor requested the opinion of
Baron Hager on the advisability of encouraging the formation of such societies.   Hager, however, discouraged the
idea on the grounds that the conditions of wartime emergency, which had warranted a benevolent attitude toward such
manifestations as those in Prague, were now past; that the
aims of the government might easily be misinterpreted; and
that it lay in the very nature of such secret societies to " de-
generate ".   These arguments convinced Francis that secret
societies were dangerous, and he forthwith dropped the
matter.[3]   The *Tugendverein* or League of Virtue of northern Germany may have had some influence within the Habsburg domains in 1809, but this was confined chiefly to the
area in and around Prague, the city in which many of the
North German exiles, like Baron vom Stein, lived.

As the fateful April 9, 1809, the day on which war was
declared on France, approached, the country was filled with

[1] The logical source for materials on secret societies is, of course, the
police records. These, however, are not available at present, since they
were stored in the Palace of Justice which was partially destroyed in
the Vienna riots of July, 1927. Many valuable documents were lost
or destroyed, and those that were saved have not yet been reassorted
or made accessible.

[2] *W. S. A., Kabinets Akten 1809*, Prot. 2287 and *Kabinets Akten 1810*,
Prot. 998.

[3] *W. S. A., Kabinets Akten 1810*, Prot. 998 and 2918.

an eager anticipation of victory. The salons of Vienna in 1808 and 1809 bore a striking resemblance to those of Berlin in 1806.[1] Toasts to German freedom became more frequent, as did also jests aimed at Napoleon.[2] The zeal of the people to save their country, and their determination to defend themselves at all odds against the encroachments of a greedy foreigner grew from day to day.[3] " Everyone capable of carrying a gun wants to rush off to the war," wrote the admiring Reichardt. " It is indeed a glorious and inspiring sight." [4]

THE TYROLESE IN 1809

Though the Tyrol belonged to Bavaria in 1809, it is necessary to say a few additional words about the events of 1806 to 1809 in this Austrian province. When the Tyrol was ceded to Bavaria by Austria in 1805 under the terms of the Treaty of Pressburg, the Bavarians faced the difficult task of governing a people as conservative, as courageous, as proud of their own institutions, and as loyal to their former ruling dynasty, as could be found anywhere in the world. Perhaps, if the Bavarians had attempted to deal with their newly-acquired subjects in a conciliatory and reasonable manner, they might have accomplished something in time. However, it almost seems as though they set out deliberately to see how much mistreatment and goading the Tyrolese would endure before revolting. King Maximilian's government " introduced new officials, new laws and new institutions; tried to obliterate the ancient and venerable name of

---

[1] *A. E. A. C. P., Vienne, 1808,* vol. 381, folio 524, Andréossy to Champagny, Vienna, December 3, 1808.

[2] Rosenbaum's *Tagebuch*, entry for March 30, 1809.

[3] *W. S. A., Staatskanzlei Korresp., Fasz. 73,* Hudelist to Stadion, April 28, 1809.

[4] Reichardt, *op. cit.*, vol. ii, p. 54.

the land; and did away with nearly everything that the Tyrolese had considered to be characteristically their own." [1] The use of the name Tyrol was forbidden, and the area was split up into three administrative " circles "—the Inn-Kreis, the Eisack-Kreis and the Etsch-Kreis—named after three rivers. Religious grievances increased the discontent. The Bavarians abolished some of the holidays, forbade the telling of rosary beads on Sunday afternoons, made the distribution of benefices a governmental affair, forbade appeals to Rome, and, when the Tyrolese bishops objected to these changes, persecuted the latter and drove them out.[2] Then the name of the *Kaiserturm* or Emperor's Tower in Kuffstein was changed to *Königsturm* or King's Tower, because the Wittelsbachs were only regal and not imperial. Similarly, the famous *Kaiserbirnen* became *Königsbirnen,* and so on.[3] Certainly Archduke John was correct when he wrote that Bavaria was awakening the " slumbering common spirit " of the people.[4] This " common spirit ", however, could hardly take the form of unmistakable German nationalism since the Tyrolese were simply striving to throw off the yoke of *one* German people, the Bavarians, in order to come back into the fold with *another* German people, the Austrians. The emphasis perforce was on dynasty rather than nationality, else there could not have been a preference.

The Austrians let slip no opportunity to maintain contact with the discontented Tyrolese. The spiritual ties between the Tyrol and Austria, particularly Vienna, were never

---

[1] Venturini, *Chronik des neunz. Jahrhunderts,* pp. 160-161.

[2] Mayer, *Geschichte Österreichs,* vol. ii, p. 540.

[3] The "old fox" Montgelas, Bavarian Minister, was responsible for this attempt to make Bavarians out of the Tyrolese. *Cf.* Häusser, L., *Deutsche Geschichte vom Tode Friedrichs des Grossen bis zur Gründung des deutschen Bundes,* 4 ed., 4 vols. (Berlin, 1869), vol. iii, p. 286.

[4] Erzherzog Johann, *Feldzugserzählung,* p. 20.

severed—much to the disgust and chagrin of the Bavarians.
In 1806 a Bavarian official in Vienna reported and commented upon the remarkably friendly and ceremonious receptions which Tyrolese visitors were accorded there.   They
were received at court and were invited to dine with the
nobility.   It seemed to be the style to entertain Tyrolers at
one's home.[1]

The chief links in the chain of communications were
Archduke John and Baron Hormayr, as also one Andreas
Dipauli.   Dipauli was a native of Tyrol who entered the
service of Bavaria after the Treaty of Pressburg, but who
remained, first and last, a Tyrolese patriot.   Though he
served his king and new master faithfully, he felt constrained
to do something that would redound to the glory of the
province whose very name, he knew, was soon to be
eradicated from the map of Europe.   The result of his endeavors was a five-volume collection of materials relating to
the *History and Statistics of Tyrol*.   One of the leading
contributors to this work was Archduke John.   He depicted
the events of the year 1805 at length, pointing out that it
was Mack's defeat at Ulm that made further resistance on
the part of the courageous mountain folk futile.   Wherever
possible, he stressed the evidences of Tyrolese attachment to
the Habsburgs and to the land's ancient rights, customs and
traditions, which had never been violated by Austria.   Since
the book in which these articles appeared was published in a
Bavarian province, John's authorship naturally was kept
secret.   Moreover, Dipauli edited the narrative in such a
way as to make identification of the author, whom he simply
labelled " a well-informed Austrian ", unlikely, or at least
difficult.   He also injected numerous allusions to the mutual

---

[1] Hirn, J., *Literarische Vorläufer des Tiroler Aufstandes 1809, passim*.
This convenient study has been drawn on heavily for this and the
following paragraphs.

love and esteem between John and the Tyrolese. Doubtless everything in the undertaking served to form a train of memories that reminded the people of their affection for the House of Austria.[1]

Concretely, John and Hormayr conspired together, without the authorization of either the emperor or Count Stadion, to prepare the Tyrol for an insurrection to take place simultaneously with the expected outbreak of war between Austria and France. Hormayr spared no amount of flattery to keep John warm in the cause. In their correspondence he contrasted the Archduke with the Prince of Asturias, the weakling heir to the Spanish throne, who, together with his father Charles IV, was so easily though treacherously put out of the way by Napoleon. Then he compared John to " the two Leopolds ", and professed to see in him a reawakening of the " spirit of Theuerdank ", of the great Maximilian of three centuries earlier.[2]

The two men supervised the preparation and distribution of proclamations, declarations and war-songs which were widely circulated in the Tyrol by trusted messengers.[3] A

[1] In spite of all precautions and attempts at camouflage, the Bavarian authorities soon became suspicious of Dipauli and his historical *Collections*. Some officials probably even guessed at John's connection with this enterprise which was threatening to nullify all their efforts to wipe out the traces of past affiliations. Events moved too swiftly, however, for any definite counter-steps to be taken. *Cf.* Hirn, *op. cit., passim.*

[2] Leopold I (1658-1705), persistent enemy of Louis XIV, and Leopold II (1790-1792), who had become famous as the enlightened despot of Tuscany, and who induced Frederick William II of Prussia to sign the Declaration of Pillnitz with him in 1792. *Theuerdank* is an allegorical poem written in 1517 in Nürnberg, in which *Theuerdank* (Emperor Maximilian) embarks upon a journey during the course of which he meets and overcomes such enemies as *Fürwittig* (the follies of youth), *Unfalo* (obstacles met in early manhood), and *Neidelhart* (the political and other enemies of older men). The idea of the poem came from Maximilian himself, but it was completed by Sigismund von Dietrichstein and Marx Treizsaurwein. *Cf.* Brockhaus, vol. xv, p. 771.

[3] *Feldzugserzählung*, p. 22. In order to overcome the scruples which

regular correspondence in secret code was kept up between Vienna and the Tyrol. In this code John was referred to as the " bridegroom ", who was planning to call for and carry home his " bride ", the Tyrol, with the assistance of the " bearded one ", Andreas Hofer.[1] Apparently this propaganda work was effective. It actually became necessary, as 1809 approached, to exercise great caution lest the Tyrolese should break into open revolt prematurely and before Austria was ready to lend support.[2] Beginning with January, 1809, then, delegations from the South Tyrol frequently visited John at his residence in Vienna. Among the deputies were Andreas Hofer from the Passeier valley,[3] Franz Anton Nessing from Bozen, and Kreiter Peter from Bruneck, all of whom were to become famous as heroic insurgent leaders. These men were promised military and financial aid, were instructed as to how to conduct themselves in the near future, and were cautioned to wait patiently for the opportune moment to strike. Early in March came similar delegations from the North Tyrol. They received identical encouragements and instructions.[4]

made some of the more conservative Tyrolese feel that once Providence had decreed their subjection to Bavaria they had no right to break away, the Austrians (at Hormayr's suggestion) explained in the proclamations that Bavaria had violated the terms of Pressburg which said that the Tyrol was to go to Bavaria just as it came from Austria, with its existing laws, institutions and so on, " *et non autrement* ". Now, the Austrians explained, since Bavaria violated this clause by overthrowing the old Tyrolese laws and institutions, therefore the Tyrolese could revolt without any moral compunctions. *Cf.* John's proclamation of April 13, 1809.

[1] *Cf. Die Männer des Volks in der Zeit des deutschen Elends, 1805-1813* (Berlin, 1864), *passim.*

[2] *Feldzugserzählung,* p. 20.

[3] Called by Walter Savage Landor " the greatest man that Europe has produced in our days."

[4] *Feldzugserzählung,* p. 20.

Another aspect of Tyrolese activity, of course, was the writing and singing of folk- and war-songs, which, if lacking in polish, betray the existence of an embryo German nationalism expressed in crude dialect and hearty invective.   Many of the songs of 1797, and even of 1703, so reminiscent of struggles against the Bavarians and the French, became popular again.   The fact that a fair proportion of the new songs was tinged with traces of German nationalism was probably due, in some degree, to the activities of the Austrian Government.   Once the Vienna authorities became sure of themselves in 1809, they made a special effort to spread the same type of German nationalist literature in the Tyrol as they did in the other German-speaking provinces.   Then, the Austrian troops that marched into the Tyrol after the war was on, brought much of a German spirit, as well as many proclamations and war-songs, with them.   The last stanza of one of their favorite songs, for example, emphasized the point that many an enemy had found to his cost that the Germans still were the brave and courageous lot that they always had been.[1]   Naturally, many of the Tyrolese songs were directed primarily against the Bavarians and only secondarily against the French, yet there was ample opportunity for extolling such German heroes as Archduke John, Andreas Hofer and Count Lehrbach.[2]

[1] Quoted from a Swiss paper (Bamberg) of June 12, 1809, in *Interessante Beyträge zu einer Geschichte der Ereignisse in Tyrol vom 10. April, 1809 bis zum 20. Februar, 1810* (n. p., 1810), p. 133. This anonymous collection was probably made by a Bavarian official named Müller, according to Bartholdy, L. S., *Der Krieg der Tiroler Landleute im Jahre 1809* (1814), p. 393.

[2] Count Lehrbach (1750-1805) came from an old Hessian family. In 1792 he became Austrian minister at Munich, and used his influence to arouse the smaller German states against France. Later on he became Austrian minister at Berlin, Regensburg and Basel. Returning to Vienna he soon acquired a reputation as a hater of Napoleon, and in 1796 he was sent to the Tyrol by the emperor to organize the resist-

John's appearance in the Tyrol at the head of his troops was preceded by a proclamation, signed by himself, but written by Hormayr, assuring the Tyrolese that

never yet has Austria entered the lists with such overwhelming might. The emperor's presence in the field steels the courage of the soldiers. They are led by the victor of Wurzbach and Stockach—by the man [Charles] whom all Germans know, love and trust. Encouraged by the knowledge of our united strength, supported by the knowledge that this is the most righteous of causes for which the sword has ever been unsheathed, I hereby once again raise the Austrian eagle over the Tyrolese soil in which the sacred remains of so many of my glorious ancestors repose![1]

The Austrian General von Kolb, and others, distributed additional proclamations written in the same spirit. They recalled to the Tyrolese the beloved name of their province " now proscribed like the name of an accursed criminal." They called attention to the gradual destruction of all the Tyrolese customs, laws and liberties, " aye, the very marrow and blood of the land." They declared that the purpose of all this was simply to make the Tyrol " approach the more quickly that same position of subjection to which Bavaria herself has been reduced."[2]

Hormayr, because of his knowledge of the Tyrol and Tyrolese affairs, was appointed intendant to accompany the Army of Inner Austria which was led by John.   This action

ance against the French. In 1798 and 1799 he was one of the Austrian delegates to the Congress of Rastatt, where he was implicated in the murder of several of the French delegates. He returned to Vienna again and remained until after the signing of the Peace of Lunéville in 1801, when, upon Napoleon's request, he was asked to quit Austria. He went to Switzerland, where he died in 1805. Wurzbach, vol. xiv, pp. 318-319.

[1] *Interessante Beyträge*, p. 9.

[2] *Ibid.*, p. 4.

brought forth a vote of thanks to Emperor Francis from the
" Four Estates of Tyrol ", expressing their appreciation to
him for giving them as intendant " the chronicler of our
history, and the favorite of his fatherland, Baron
Hormayr." [1] Incidentally, while acting in his designated
capacity in the Tyrol, Hormayr received a letter from a
native who had accepted service under Bavaria, and who felt
that the cause both of his province and of Germany could
best be served by a reconciliation between the Tyrol and
Bavaria.   The letter ran, in part: " It is because the fate of
Tyrol, your native land, hangs in the balance, that I turn to
you.   Like you I am a German, and therefore I love candor.
I have read all of your works with great admiration, and I
am happy in the thought that Germany has found in you a
second Johannes von Müller, a second Plutarch."   Utz-
schneider, for this was the correspondent's name, then urged
Hormayr to quit the Austrians and take service under the
King of Bavaria.   He could not convince Hormayr, however, of the superiority of the Wittelsbachs over the Habsburgs as German princes.[2]

When war finally was declared, the Tyrolese were ready.
A number of ingenious devices, such as " chalkfires " on the
hilltops, and the casting of flour, blood or sawdust into the
rivers and brooks, quickly spread the news that the time for
revolt was at hand.[3]   Soon the bullets began to fly *" Für
Gott, Kaiser und Vaterland."*

[1] *W. S. A., Kabinets Akten 1809*, Prot. 1761, letter of May 11, 1809
to Francis from Innsbruck.

[2] *Ibid.*, letter of June 22, 1809 from Innsbruck, as enclosure with
Hormayr's complete report of his activities as intendant in the Tyrol
to Count Zichy, August 20, 1809.

[3] Mailath, J. von, *Geschichte des österreichischen Kaiserstaats* (Hamburg, 1850), vol. v, p. 288.

CHAPTER V

1809 to 1812: The War and After

THERE is no need for undertaking a thorough analysis of the causes of the war of 1809 between France and Austria. The blame has variously been placed upon the wounded pride of the ex-imperial knights and the mediatized princes of the Rhine and North German regions; upon the greed of financiers and money-brokers; upon the thirst for glory among the younger Austrian princes, and upon the desire of the majority of Austrian army officers to wipe out the stains of past defeats at the hands of the French by new victories; upon a general desire to reestablish Austria's position of leadership among the European powers; upon the corruption of Stadion by English gold; upon the hypocrisy and machinations of Ambassador Count Metternich; upon chagrin over an apparent Russo-French reconciliation; and upon the intrigues of men like Gentz, Rasumowskij and Pozzo di Borgo.[1]   All these reasons, however, though they

[1] Andrej Rasumowskij (1752-1836), Russian ambassador at Stockholm, Naples and Vienna, who hated Napoleon and was active in agitating for war upon him.   Karl Andreas Pozzo di Borgo (1764-1842) was known as one of Napoleon's bitterest and most persistent enemies.   Born in Corsica, he joined the Paoli faction in its feud with the Bonapartes. He worked for the formation of the coalition against Napoleon in 1797 and 1798, and entered Russian diplomatic services soon thereafter.   When Russia and France became friendly after Tilsit, Pozzo left Russia and spent the years 1809 and 1810 agitating in Austria, England and Turkey against Napoleon.   Beginning with 1812 he was even more active, working in Sweden, and influencing both Alexander and Bernadotte. In January, 1814, he went to England to urge a last supreme effort. From 1815 to 1839 he served as Russian ambassador at Paris and London. From 1839 to 1842 he lived as a private citizen in Paris.   Brockhaus, vol. xiii, pp. 631 and 344.

might have been, and probably were, factors in bringing on the conflict, were only secondary. The fundamental cause was this: The Austrians believed they, too, would be engulfed in the swirl of conquests unless the ogre were overthrown. Napoleon did not hesitate to oust the ancient Bourbons from Spain. He annexed nominally independent Italian states, like Tuscany, by mere imperial decree. He blithely announced that certain parts of the Papal dominions were thenceforth to be considered parts of his Kingdom of Italy. What might he not do next? Might not the terms of Pressburg have been an earnest of what he meant to do later on? The ever-threatening menace had to be removed. And the present opportunity, during which Napoleon was being harassed by the Spaniards, might never return.

Austria searched for allies to help her, but failed to find any. Frederick William III of Prussia would do nothing without the support of Russia. And Alexander of Russia, so far from fighting Napoleon, actually assisted him by sending an army corps into Austrian Galicia.[1] But if Austria could obtain no allies, then Austria would fight Napoleon alone. *Austria Erit in Orbe Ultima*—ran a version of an ancient prophecy—Austria will endure on earth forever. Three times had Austria met disaster at Napoleon's hands. Three times had she survived.[2] The time for the supreme effort was at hand.

Napoleon, for his part, was glad to fight Austria again. The constant military preparations and the " ceaseless

[1] England did provide large subsidies, and agreed to land an army in the Netherlands to divert some of Napoleon's troops from Austria. Such a diversion was attempted at Walcheren (July-Dec. 1809), but disease and mismanagement frustrated the attack. *The Cambridge Modern History*, 13 vols. (New York, 1903-1912), vol. ix, pp. 238-239 and 357 *et seq.*

[2] The three treaties were Campo Formio, 1797, Lunéville, 1801 and Pressburg, 1805.

machinations and intrigues" of the Austrians ever since Pressburg made him uneasy and vexed him. Moreover, he needed victories to offset his failures in Spain; and he needed money. When, therefore, Austria proclaimed war on April 9, Napoleon confidently left Spain, saying: "I am leaving my best troops with Joseph, and am starting along for Vienna with my little conscripts, my name and my long boots."[1] He did not mention the thousands of additional troops that he had assigned to himself from the states of the Confederation.

Austria's black double eagle screamed defiance at Napoleon. The people of Austria, excited to the highest pitch of enthusiasm, were up in arms to defend their national existence against a second Genghis Khan and his hordes.[2] They were supported only by their confidence and by the other peoples of the Habsburg monarchy. Who would win?

An ill-fated, inexplicable, last-minute change of plan of campaign; lack of cooperation among Austria's generals; excessive caution and even sluggishness where cool audacity should have prevailed, to say nothing of Napoleon's superior genius, decided the issue against the Habsburg forces. April 19 to 23 Napoleon won the campaign of Ratisbon. The middle of May had not arrived when the French troops entered Vienna in triumph. *"Ils sont sur le Danube comme s'ils étaient sur le Rhin!"* groaned Gentz.[3] "My God, my God, all is lost!" cried Stadion.[4] Yet all was not lost. Had not Austria's masses vowed to die rather than submit?

[1] Quoted in Gottschalk, L., *The Era of the French Revolution* (New York, 1929), p. 383.

[2] So referred to in stanza six of Schleifer's "Voice from the Desert" (1809).

[3] *Gentz' Tagebücher*, p. 78, entry in *Journal Politique* dated June 18, 1809.

[4] Quoted in Droysen, *op. cit.*, vol. ii, p. 330.

Was not Charles the " greatest of the generals who yet had faced Napoleon? "

On May 21 and 22 Charles defeated Napoleon in open battle at the villages of Aspern and Essling, on the Danube, and forced the beaten Corsican to withdraw to the island of Lobau, there to wait idly until the arrival of reenforcements from Italy. Why, it may be asked, did not other states lend their support now? Why did Charles play the piano [1] and sit back contentedly and hope for an immediate peace offer all through the month of June, when he should have starved out and routed Napoleon's army on Lobau? Why, as long as Napoleon was destined to be overthrown, was he not overthrown then and there so that Europe might be spared another six years of strife and bloodshed? Why?

At any rate, Napoleon was given a precious breathing spell, and on July 5 and 6, with an army now larger than that of Charles, he crossed the Danube and won a bloody and fateful contest at Deutsch-Wagram. The Austrians were not routed. They amazed Napoleon with their courage and obstinacy. But they finally withdrew. By this time, Francis the Good was tired of the war. Charles, moreover, wanted a breathing spell—as Napoleon had had. Accordingly an armistice was signed at Znaim on July 12. Francis remained with his army. Napoleon settled down in the palace and gardens of Schönbrunn.

The dismay of the Viennese over the outcome of the war can easily be imagined. It was only four years since they had been subjected to a similar humiliation. But though the reception to the French in 1805 was marked by curiosity and even by genuine interest on the part of the inhabitants, the attitude of the latter in 1809 was decidedly unfriendly and hostile. [2] In the first place, the citizens of Vienna were really

---

[1] Springer, *op. cit.*, vol. i, p. 96.

[2] Boguth, W., " Die Okkupation Wiens," p. 300, and Hoen, M. von, " Der Fall von Wien ", in *Die Kultur* (Vienna, 1908), vol. ix, p. 321.

ready to defend the city with their lives this time, if necessary.[1] On one occasion, for example, Herr Wurth, gold-
smith to the court, and characterized as a "violent man and
warm patriot," repaired to the headquarters of the emperor
and offered Francis the services of the entire citizenry of
Vienna. He depicted in detail the possibilities of a successful defense and graphically described the advantages in
numbers which the Viennese possessed over the French
forces. The latter, he said, would inevitably be annihilated.
He then demanded arms for the people of the suburbs and
proposed a variety of means for the massacre of the invaders. "He left, thoroughly satisfied with the audience
that was accorded him."[2] Then, following Archduke Maximilian's call of May 7 for volunteers to help defend the city,
young and old rushed to the arsenal to secure arms. "The
enthusiasm of the mob was so great that even disinterested
passers-by were forced to accept weapons and man the
walls."[3] Further, "women and children seized spears and
halberds, while little boys ran around with guns."[4] It was

[1] Of course there were exceptions to this attitude. Rosenbaum, for
example, has these two entries in his diaries for April 26 and 27, respectively: "The empress has ordered her things to be packed. What
horrible prospects! The effects [of Davoust's advance] are incalculable.
What will become of us!" "We have fallen back on the defensive
for the moment. It is impossible to portray the extent to which this has
upset everyone and crushed every hope to earth. Our last days will
be made miserable by penury, distress and subjugation."

[2] *A. E. A. C. P., Vienne, 1809*, vol. 383, folio 27, *Bulletin de Vienne*,
May 4, 1809.

[3] Geusau, *Historisches Taschenbuch*, p. 99.

[4] Rosenbaum's *Tagebuch*, entry for May 10, 1809. Military victories
seem to have had a medicinal value in the Rosenbaum family. An entry
in the diary, dated April 24, 1809, reads: "Remained at the Count's
[Esterhazy] until after six o'clock. Presently messenger after messenger arrived with the news that Charles had defeated Napoleon at Ingol-
stadt. I rushed home to tell Theresa [his wife] the joyful news. She
was so delighted that she lost completely a headache from which she
had been suffering."

all to no avail. The French occupied Vienna without much
ado.[1] Once they were in the city, however, they were made
to feel in a number of ways that they were unwanted guests.
The Austrians welcomed every opportunity to side with the
German Rhenish allies of the French in the numerous alter-
cations which ensued between these two groups. On the
evening of September 2, for instance, there was a pitched
battle in the Prater[2] between the French troops on the one
hand, and their Hessian and Württemberg allies supported
by a Viennese mob, on the other.[3] Incidentally, the fact that
the French used German troops in this campaign seems to
have done much to arouse the Austrians, too. They felt that
Napoleon was forcing brother to fight against brother, and
it made them all the angrier—and perhaps also all the more
conscious that they were of an identic nationality with the
Germans. The government apparently realized this fact and
made the most of it, especially in the daily army reports that
were sent to Vienna from Headquarters. Thus, the fifth
report, dated Landshut, April 13, indicated that in Bavaria,
too, " French craft had successfully corrupted foreign blood
and turned the weapons of our German brothers against their
liberators." [4]

[1] Years later Archduke John wrote down his disgust at the submis-
siveness of the Viennese in 1809. He could understand their surrender-
ing the city, but he felt that they should have retained their arms and
refused all French requisitions. This would have made it necessary
for Napoleon to keep twenty or thirty thousand troops in Vienna, instead of using them at Aspern and Wagram. Zwiedeneck-Südenhorst,
Erzherzog Johann, p. 20.

[2] The Prater is the famous park and playground, the " Coney Island ",
of Vienna.

[3] *Tagebuch eines Wieners*, pp. 126 et seq.

[4] *Fünfter Tagesbericht von der k. k. Armee, Hauptquartier Landshut,
den 17ten April, 1809.* Since the *Wiener Zeitung* came into the hands
of the French when they occupied Vienna, the Austrian Government
continued its newspaper propaganda campaign during the war by the

Interesting also were the activities of Viennese citizens like Dr. Wenzel Grillparzer, father of the poet. The sight of a Frenchman " was like the thrust of a dagger to him ". Yet he spent every evening during the Occupation walking through the streets—in order to be able to take sides with such of his compatriots as might have become embroiled with the swaggering foreigners. Truly a dangerous undertaking in a dangerous environment! [1] The humiliating terms of the peace treaty that finally replaced the armistic affected this devoted patriot to such an extent that he died broken-hearted soon after its signing.[2]

While in Vienna, Napoleon took it into his head to have his birthday, August 15, celebrated with great pomp and splendor. He was treated to some rather unexpected results. The French, of course, did their share to make the affair as brilliant as possible; but measures approaching closely to force had to be resorted to in order to make some of the more obstreperous natives comply with orders.[3] Even so, the day passed rather tranquilly. Cries of *Vivat Napoleon* were conspicuously scattered and weak. According to Marie Louise, the daughter of Emperor Francis, people did not even bother looking out of their windows to watch the parades.[4] This lack of attention was more than compen-

publication of a special *Österreichische Zeitung* or *Armeezeitung*. This was edited by Fr. Schlegel who remained at army headquarters for the purpose. According to special orders from the emperor, Count Fr. Stadion was to supervise Schlegel's work, and to indicate the tone of the paper. *W. S. A.*, Francis' reply from Wolkersdorf to a proposal of Fr. Stadion concerning the establishment of a military, political paper, to be issued from army headquarters. Submitted to the emperor by Ph. Stadion, June 5, 1809.

[1] Grillparzer, *Werke*, vol. xix, p. 47.

[2] Bücher, *Grillparzer's Verhältniss zur Politik seiner Zeit*, p. 23.

[3] Varnhagen's *Ausgewählte Schriften*, vol. ii, p. 255.

[4] *Correspondance de Marie Louise, 1799-1847* (Vienna, 1887), pp. 113 et seq.

sated for, however, by a variety of trick signs and transparent pictures displayed in the evening.   There was one reading: " Long live the Emperor " — without saying which emperor.   Another read:

> Since I'm ordered so to do
> I put a light in my window, too.

A third carried the words:

> O, Napoleon, how great is thy fame!
> But we prefer Francis just the same.

One of the illuminated transparent pictures simply quoted the words of the French decree ordering the display.   Perhaps the prize belonged to the following illuminated acrostic:

> **Z**ur
> **W**eihe
> **A**n
> **N**apoleons
> **G**eburtstag

The initial letter in each case was in red, thus bringing clearly into the foreground the word *Zwang* (compulsion).[1]

There were other occasions, too, when the French troops were treated to disagreeable surprises in Vienna.   On September 13, for example, there was a performance, in the Theater an der Wien, of Heinrich Zschokke's *Der Unbegreifliche*.   When one of the actors came to the part which runs: " All is not yet lost; every good citizen is willing to offer his last drop of blood in the service of his sovereign ", there arose so vehement a burst of applause and cheering that the actors had to wait several minutes before continuing, while the French officers who were present gazed about them

---

[1] Rosenbaum's *Tagebuch*, entry for August 18, 1809, and *Correspondance de Marie Louise*, pp. 113 *passim*.

in amazement and wonder.[1]   Or again, late in July or early
in August, the following burlesque on Napoleon " was discovered in all public places " : [2]

> Once there were two German men
> Fighting over Bonaparte;
> Each thought he knew the Corsican
> Better than his counterpart.
> The one did praise his gallant deeds
> And called him a towering genius.
> The other decried these laurel wreaths
> And called him an ignoramus.
> The one said surely he is great,
> The other called him small.
> And each was sure that what he said
> Contained the truth withal.
> Along now comes a third, and gives
> Advice to set them right:
> Both great and small are adjectives
> That modify, he cried.
> I gen'rally let them call him great
> But always add (though on the sly)
> When others him so designate
> A noun for " great " to qualify.

Some of the Viennese women, sad to say, could not long
withstand the attentions of the gallant French military.   The
Chevalier de Gassicourt, who took part in the campaign,
wrote: "During the first few days after our arrival, the
Viennese girls did not dare to associate with us.   They were
afraid to be seen walking with a French soldier.   But little
by little they weakened and pretty soon there wasn't a single
female in the city who had not made a choice either of a lover

[1] *Tagebuch eines Wieners*, p. 132.
[2] *Ibid.*, p. 105.

or a cicisbeo, for cicisbeism still exists in certain parts of Germany." [1]

That the good chevalier, however, must have been flattering himself and his comrades to the point of gross exaggeration, when he wrote these words, need hardly be stated.

After three months had passed in tedious diplomatic negotiations, the booming of guns on October 14 finally announced the signing of the Treaty of Schönbrunn or Vienna. The news was greeted with great demonstrations of joy and elation.[2] But when the harsh peace terms were made public the general resentment against the French increased even further. The Austrian emperor gave up Galicia, the maritime provinces and much of German Austria. He lost about 3,500,000 subjects, and agreed to pay a heavy war indemnity. He promised to limit his army to 150,000 men, and to adhere to the Continental System against England. German Austria was diminished in size and strength by the cession of Salzburg and the Inn Quarter in Upper Austria to Bavaria, and of the greater part of Carinthia to the French Empire. Bavaria's control over the Tyrol was confirmed.

Not long after the terms were published in the *Wiener Zeitung* (October 25), copies of a fiery proclamation were scattered in several public places in Vienna. Unsigned and undated, it aimed to arouse the natives to a pitch of fury that would spend itself in the slaughter of the French soldiers who were not yet withdrawn:[3]

Germans and inhabitants of Vienna! Cast your eyes over

[1] Gassicourt, C. L. Cadet de, *Voyage en Autriche, en Moravie et en Bavière fait à la suite de l'armée française pendant la campagne de 1809* (Paris, 1818), p. 288.

[2] Rosenbaum's *Tagebuch*, entry for October 14, 1809.

[3] *A. E. A. C. P., Vienne, 1809*, vol. 383, folio 297: *Traduction d'une proclamation répandue dans quelques lieux publics à Vienne, peu de jours avant le 20 Novembre.*

this beloved natal city of yours, this century-old cradle of your children. Gaze with sorrow upon the ruins which surround it. See how you have been surprised and defeated by a horde of brigands. See what misfortunes you have brought upon yourselves by your culpable negligence. Viennese and Germans, seize knives, secure firearms and other murderous weapons. Everyone who is at all capable of moving should rush to assassinate, first, Andréossy [the governor-general during the Occupation] and the rest of the French governors, and then all others who are in any way affiliated with this horde of French brigands. That is the least a citizen can do to render himself worthy of his State and of the love of his fatherland. Brothers and sisters of mine, hasten and seize them all. Kill them after the example of the heroic Prussians and Spaniards. Carry their heads on pikes. For the love of your rulers annihilate this infamous French nation. Look at the brave Tyrolese. What love, what fidelity to their Emperor Francis! And you, on the other hand, would you quietly do the bidding of a corrupt nation? No, never! Vengeance, vengeance against the French!

On the whole, the people of Vienna had but little time to worry about their nationality during the Occupation. The secret police report of May 31 to June 1 comments upon the circumstance that "the people were completely preoccupied by the task of securing the necessary foodstuffs which were becoming scantier every day."[1] Not until the French withdrew and Francis reentered his capital city, did the spirits of the burghers rise again. Then they became almost delirious with joy as Francis appeared in a coach-and-six, accompanied only by Count Wrbna. Festivities were held three consecutive days and nights, and the police interfered as little as possible with the hilarity and boisterousness of the people.[2]

[1] Starzer, A., "Aus den Polizei-Rapporten des Jahres 1809", in *Mitt. des k. k. Archivs für Niederösterreich* (Vienna, 1909), vol. ii, p. 125.

[2] *A. E. A. C. P., Vienne, 1809*, vol. 383, folios 312 and 303. Also Rosenbaum's *Tagebuch*, entry for November 27, 1809, and Varnhagen's *Ausgewählte Schriften*, vol. ii, p. 307.

Unfortunately, the course of the war again had been such as to make the most heroic efforts on the part of the Tyrolese futile. They were panic-stricken when the news reached them that the Austrian troops would be withdrawn from the Tyrol so that the Bavarians could reoccupy it. The fear of reprisals was now added to the hatred of Bavarian tyranny and misrule in general. At first Hofer would not believe the rumors. He was certain that Francis would not forsake these people whose loyalty had been so frequently proven under trying circumstances. He sent the emperor a message of thanks for the gift of a gold medal and chain and 3000 ducats which had been bestowed upon him, and at the same time hastened to assure Francis that *Gott, Kaiser und Vaterland* were still the watchwords of all Tyrolers.[1] Similarly, he told John that " every Tyrolese heart lived and beat solely for the House of Austria." [2] But Napoleon was the victor, and Francis loved peace. The Austrians withdrew and the Bavarians reappeared. On February 20, 1810, Hofer faced a French firing squad. Napoleon insisted upon the execution.[3]

The unfortunate outcome of the war reacted unfavorably upon both the men and the means that had brought it on in 1809. The Treaty of Schönbrunn convinced Francis of a number of things : that Napoleon still was invincible and that therefore conciliation was to be preferred to further opposition; that the whole group of Gentzes, Steins and Pozzos were trouble-making foreigners who were willing to

[1] *W. S. A., Kaiser Franz Akten, Fasz. 78d*, letter of Hofer dated October 5, 1809 at Innsbruck.

[2] *Ibid.*, letter of Hofer to John, October 4, 1809 from Innsbruck.

[3] Emperor Francis tried to save Hofer from death. He ordered Metternich to intercede for the innkeeper and to insist on his release as an earnest of the newly-cemented friendship between France and Austria in 1810. *W. S. A.*, Francis to Metternich, Vienna, February 12, 1810.

sacrifice Austria so that their personal grudges against Bonaparte might be satisfied; that the policies of Stadion and Archduke Charles were directly opposed to the best interests of his remaining possessions; and that the venerable "system" of the former century was still the best, and certainly much better than a lot of new-fangled reforms which lately had been introduced for no good reason at all.[1] There always had been a pro-French, anti-Stadion clique at court, and this group now secured influence and power. Stadion resigned. Archduke Charles was retired. The old-fashioned bureaucracy was restored. "There is a much calmer spirit here than I had dared to hope" reported Count Otto, the new French Ambassador at Vienna, to his chief, Talleyrand.[2] But men like Baron Stein were sad. He compared the Austria of 1810 with that of 1809, and wrote: "Everything here terminates in slothfulness or bureaucracy. The innumerable bureaus concern themselves solely with the application of a system of clumsy, intricate formalities which are a constant delay to any form of free activity, and which substitute for it masses of paper and empty stupidity and laziness."[3]

For the next thirty-nine years the actual head of the government was Count Clemens Wenzel Lothar von Metternich-Winneburg. Francis, and the Ferdinand who followed him, merely remained as titular heads.

Metternich,[4] the scion of a distinguished Rhenish family,

[1] Weiss, *Geschichte der Stadt Wien*, vol. ii, pp. 272 *et seq.*, and Bücher *op. cit.*, pp. 24-25.

[2] *A. E. A. C. P., Vienne, 1810*, vol. 385, folio 49, Otto to Talleyrand, February 10, 1810.

[3] Pertz, *Stein*, vol. ii, pp. 433.

[4] Srbik, H. von, *Metternich, der Staatsmann und der Mensch*, 2 vols. (Munich, 1925), *passim*. This recent and thorough-going biography does much to change long-standing opinions regarding the purposes and policies of Metternich.

was remarkably good-looking, clever, and an experienced and subtle diplomat. He hated revolution and he disliked change of any form. He was witty and cynical, not a great mind, but shrewd on occasion, and unscrupulous when necessary. He married the granddaughter of the famous Count Kaunitz in 1795. Thenceforth he rose rapidly in the diplomatic service of Austria. Now, at thirty-six, he practically ruled the Habsburg Empire. His motto was: "Everything for the people, nothing through the people." [1]

Realizing that Austria must take a few years to recuperate from the blows she had just been dealt, Metternich proceeded to adopt a policy of apparent friendship with France, while secretly scheming the overthrow of Napoleon through craft and diplomacy. "We must confine our system to tacking, and turning, and flattering," he said to Francis upon assuming office. "There remains but one expedient, to increase our strength for better days and to work out our preservation by gentle means." [2] He was as much afraid of a super-Russia as he was of a Napoleonic France, and he knew that Austria's salvation lay in playing off the Tsar and the Corsican against each other. He was quite ready to sacrifice the happiness of his sovereign's daughter to win this salvation.

On March 11, 1810, Emperor Francis' eighteen-year-old daughter, Marie Louise, was wedded to Napoleon in Vienna by proxy. Her uncle, Archduke Charles, took her hand for Bonaparte. On March 13, the young empress left Vienna to meet her husband. The real wedding took place on April 1, in Paris, amid the greatest pomp and splendor. Napoleon was happy. No longer could he be sneered at as an upstart. He was now allied by marriage to Europe's oldest and proud-

---

[1] Mailath, *op. cit.*, vol. v, p. 371. Mailath knew Metternich personally.

[2] Rose, J. H., *The Revolutionary and Napoleonic Era 1789-1815*, 6 ed. (New York, 1913), p. 211.

est dynasty.   Moreover, it was to be expected that his new wife would present him with the longed-for legitimate heir. Metternich was happy, too.   He knew that Habsburg marriages were more successful than Habsburg wars.   He knew that Austria now was sure of peace for some time to come. He knew that Austria would occupy a pivotal position in the approaching conflict between France and Russia.   And Marie Louise?   She hated the " Antichrist ", and she cried a bit, but she did as she was told.   After all, Napoleon's wife was the first lady of the Continent!

The Viennese naturally viewed the marriage with mixed feelings.   Many were delighted at the prospect of a lasting peace.   Marshal Berthier, who came to Vienna to woo the archduchess for Napoleon, wrote home that the people were " delirious with joy ".[1]   The French Ambassador Otto described to Talleyrand the effect of the announcement of the marriage, saying: " The bourse is always the best indicator of the state of public opinion.   In less than two hours [after the announcement], securities rose in value by as much as thirty per cent." [2]   On the other hand, many people were saddened at the sight of the Tricolor decorating the walls and ceiling of the imperial ballrooms during the festival held there on the evening of March 11.   As Caroline Pichler remarked, these were the very rooms in which, less than a year previously, enthusiastic crowds had sung Collin's *Landwehrlieder,* and where " every German breast had been enflamed with hatred against the French, and filled with a determination to resist their power and wantonness to the utmost." [3]   The police, moreover, were horrified at the spiteful pranks that were perpetrated, and the satirical

[1] Mayer, *Geschichte Österreichs*, vol. ii, p. 552.

[2] *A. E. A. C. P., Vienne, 1810*, vol. 385, folio 79, Otto to Talleyrand, February 19, 1810.

[3] Pichler, *Denkwürdigkeiten*, vol. ii, p. 187.

pictures and inscriptions that were displayed. In the window
of a pastry shop, for instance, there was exhibited a coarse
legend to the effect that the wedding cake looked good
enough, but it was to be hoped the offspring would not turn
out to be a dumpling.[1]   And those who passed by a certain
tailor shop could read the ditty:

> Louise's skirts and Napoleon's pants
> Now unite Austria and France.[2]

However, in order to secure the proper atmosphere for the
newly-established relationship between Austria and France,
the Habsburg emperor and Metternich set out at once to
quiet the few remaining reverberations of the excitement of
1809.   Metternich drafted the following note which he urged
Francis to have distributed to all the provincial authorities:

November 3, 1809

My dear A. B.—
In view of the pacific relations which now have been established with France and her allies, it becomes necessary to have
all newspapers adopt a tone and language analogous to those
relations. You will see to it that nothing which may in any
way serve as a reminder of the past events appears in print in
the area within your jurisdiction.[3]

Three months later the French ambassador wrote that, so
far as he could tell, this order was being carried out with
" much exactitude ".[4]   With regard to the *Wiener Zeitung,*
Francis asked Metternich to be particularly careful to see
that it printed " no articles which might give occasion for

[1]   *Die Pastete sieht gut aus,*
Wenn nur kein Dalken wird daraus.

[2] Weiss, *op. cit.,* vol. ii, p. 275.

[3] *W. S. A., Vortrag Metternichs,* November 2, 1809.

[4] *A. E. A. C. P., Vienne, 1810,* vol. 385, folio 33, Otto to Talleyrand,
February 7, 1810.

ambiguous interpretations."[1] In one case Metternich actually denied the renewal of the right to publish one of the papers which had its origins in the period just prior to the outbreak of the war.[2] In another, he ordered the immediate and complete suppression of an issue of the *Allgemeine Zeitung* because it contained "an insulting article on the previous year's events in the Tyrol."[3]

The new minister was equally strict regarding other phases of literary work, and regarding the stage.[4] He told Hager that it was essential that all pamphlets and writings of 1809 which were in any way directed against France be withdrawn from circulation at once, and that all publishers and booksellers be notified immediately that the further sale of such works was prohibited under severe penalty. "For greater safety, it is also advisable that Your Excellency have the existing stocks put under official seal and into official custody, until their complete destruction can be consummated."[5] Anton Strauss, the publisher, was even forbidden to issue a collected edition of the daily army reports that had been drawn up at Army Headquarters during the war. The reason was simply that Metternich preferred not to bring up "reminiscences" which might better be forgotten.[6] In August, 1811, Metternich forbade the printing of an article on the renewed warfare in Spain, and on the British blockade of Cadiz.[7]

[1] *W. S. A.*, Francis to Metternich, Prague, May 27, 1810.

[2] *W. S. A., Pol. Corresp. 1811-1812, Fasz. 3*, Metternich to Hager, February 27, 1812. The paper was J. M. Armbruster's *Wanderer*.

[3] *W. S. A., Pol. Corresp. 1807-1810. Noten an die Pol. Hofstelle, Fasz. 2*, Metternich to Hager, February 1, 1810.

[4] Thus, on April 11, 1810, he prohibited a performance of *Frederick the Warlike*. *Ibid.*

[5] *Ibid.*, Metternich to Hager, January 8, 1810.

[6] *Ibid.*, Metternich to Hager, January 15, 1810.

[7] *W. S. A., Pol. Corresp. 1811-1812, Fasz. 3*, Metternich to Hager, August 27, 1811.

Metternich also kept a watchful eye over activities in northern Germany and in the Tyrol. Writing to Francis, he said that if certain reports concerning the *Tugendbund* (namely that it was working for a united Germany) were true, then the *Bund* would certainly have a subversive influence in Austria, and would bear very close observation on the part of the police. But he was confident that the reports were untrue, and he " doubted very much the possibility of carrying out such a system which aimed at a unified Germany, since there was so little common spirit among the Germans ".[1] It seems, however, that the authorities tried to keep the loyalty of the Tyrolese, and to make them forget Austria's desertion of their cause, through the generous dispensation of pensions to all those who had participated in the fighting of 1809. Even the widows and orphans of fallen participants were taken care of. On the other hand, everyone was cautioned against singing or reciting any of the songs which bore relation to the war. " Hofer is as much taboo as Bonaparte," one of the natives is reported to have told a traveler.[2]

Under these conditions it is hardly surprising that even good patriots began to wonder whether, after all, there was anything to the pre-war talk about a " German nation " and about the identity of the traditions, customs and interests of all the German brothers. Grillparzer, to cite just one instance, became so doubtful of the existence of distinct nationalities, after noting Metternich's policies, that he once wrote:

[1] *W. S. A., Kabinets Akten 1811*, Prot. 2104. December 1810–January 1811.

[2] Quoted in Arnold, *Achtzehnhundertneuner Nachlese*, p. 11, with the remark: " *Diese Notiz stammt aus 1833 und Innsbruck; ob oder inwieweit sie auf Wahrheit beruhen mag?* "

A vantage that from us can ne'er be torn
Is called our nationality.
It holds that somewhere all of us were born,
Which is, in truth, no novelty.[1]

No wonder, too, that there was much distrust of the ministry in the public mind. Popular opinion in 1812 felt that the Metternich régime was totally inferior to the Stadion régime of 1806-1809. According to a secret summary of the state of public opinion on the question of faith in the ministry, sent by Hager to Francis on April 28, 1812, the people considered " Metternich to be a senile old man, already approaching his second childhood [he was thirty-nine at the time], and one who had always, even in his earlier diplomatic career, been regarded as an imbecile." [2]

A further effect of the reaction is reflected in these lines, taken from the third volume of Pezzl's *New Sketch of Vienna,* which appeared in 1812 : [3]

The Viennese seem to have lost their love for reading since the last war. The enormously high price of books, and the other results of the political exertions have turned the attention and expenditures of the public to other things. Even the best authors have difficulty in securing proper *emolumenta laborum.* About the only books that are being put through the press now-adays are those that are practically indispensable for general family use. . . . Would to Heaven I were mistaken, but I am filled with a sad foreboding that all Germany is on the brink of a marked cultural relapse. Let no one suppose that the public institutions of learning can forestall this relapse unaided. They

[1] Quoted in Bernatzik, E., *Die Ausgestaltung des Nationalgefühls im 19. Jahrhundert* (Hannover, 1912), p. 15.

[2] *W. S. A., Kaiser Franz Akten, Fasz. 80.* Perhaps it should be added here that Hager may have had a grudge against Metternich, for the latter had frequently criticized the inaccuracy and unreliability of the police reports, e. g., in a *Vortrag* of August 4, 1810, *W. S. A.*

[3] Pezzl, J., *Neue Skizze von Wien* (Vienna, 1812), vol. iii, pp. 88, *et seq.*

must be supported and supplemented by a widespread national literature and by widespread reading, if the tragedy is to be averted.

Yet it was not really a straight drop from zenith to nadir in Austria. A man who knew the value of newspapers as Metternich did, would not destroy them.[1] Moreover, none other than Baron Hormayr was elevated to the rank of chief censor, and it was not to be expected that he would allow the intellectual darkness of the first few years of the nineteenth century to return to his fatherland. Again, the Viennese had enjoyed relative freedom from censorship regulations during the French Occupation.[2] Hence the announcement that the government intended to " steer back the unbridled freedom of the press into its proper, restricted channels ",[3] and to punish all those printers and publishers who had taken advantage of the occasion to sell hitherto forbidden books, created " bitter feelings " in all circles.[4] Now that they had been permitted to peer into the works of Goethe, Schiller and Wieland, the people seriously objected to any system which once more banned these gems of German literature. Hormayr pointed this out to Metternich and condemned any regulations which tended to keep out of Austria the works of literary geniuses, upon which works the " pride of a great

[1] *Cf.* a valuable article by E. Wertheimer, "Metternich und die Presse", in *Neue Freie Presse*, Vienna, July 13, 1899, pp. 1-4. Also various notes of Metternich in *W. S. A.*, e. g. to Hager, July (no day), 1811, and April 22, 1811, in *Pol. Corresp. Noten an die Pol. Hofstelle 1811-1812, Fass. 3.*

[2] "Enjoyed" in the literal sense of the word. They purchased as many of the previously forbidden works as they could afford, *cf. A. f. o. G.*, vol. civ, p. 310. Grillparzer, e. g., when he heard that an edition of Goethe's works would be put on sale, "ordered a set just as quickly as he could". *Ibid.*

[3] *W. S. A., Kabinets Akten* 1809, no. 485.

[4] *Note of Hager to Francis*, quoted in *A. f. o. G.*, vol. civ, p. 310 n. 1.

nation rested." He further called attention to the bad re-
pute into which Austria had fallen intellectually, and quoted
from Bavarian papers which sarcastically commented upon
the circumstance that not until the advent of a foreign invasion could the Austrian people properly educate themselves.[1] Obviously, Hormayr would not censor Goethe,
Schiller and Wieland. And Metternich declared himself
" in complete accord " with these views.[2]

The relatively liberal-minded Hager, who was now President of Police, went even further. In a report of March 14,
1810, he complained that the fear aroused by the French
Revolution turned Austrian censorship not only against the
" abuse " of literary talent, but against the talent itself, and
against science and culture as a whole. This tendency, he
said, not only caused a scarcity of capable teachers in Austria,
but it actually frightened most of the Germans away from the
thought of an *Anschluss* with Austria because they feared
" a successful Austria might found an empire of darkness
and would hinder all further intellectual progress." The
Peace of Vienna, he continued, ushered in a new epoch which
made it essential for Austria to keep step with the neighbor-
ing states in intellectual developments. He then presented a
draft of instructions for censors, involving great liberality
for works of a " religious, social and classical nature ".[3]
Unfortunately, Hager's suggestions were only partially incorporated in the new censorship law of 1810, and even here
the spirit of execution served to counteract the apparently
liberal wording.[4]

[1] Wertheimer, *Metternich und die Presse*, and *A. f. o. G.*, vol. civ, p.
310 n. 2.

[2] Wertheimer, *ibid.*

[3] *Vortrag Hagers vom 14. März, 1810*, quoted in *A. f. o. G.*, vol. civ,
p. 310 n. 2.

[4] Wiesner, A., *Denkwürdigkeiten der österreichischen Zensur vom
Zeitalter der Reformation bis auf die Gegenwart* (Stuttgart, 1847), pp.
220-240.

As a result of this relatively liberal attitude on the part of the authorities, and perhaps, also, because the government was deeply involved in questions of financial rehabilitation and in watching the turbulent events in the Balkans,[1] the years 1810 to 1812 were not utterly devoid of expressions of anti-French sentiment and of German nationalism. In April, 1810, Count Otto observed that beneath a superficial attitude of good-will, many of the officials and a large part of "society" still retained their anti-French prejudices.[2] And in December of the same year he thought he saw increased symptoms "of animosity" among the upper classes. The manifestations of hatred were called forth by the momentary retreat of the French Army of Portugal, and by the annexation to the French Empire of all the lands between the Lower Rhine and the Free City of Lübeck, as well as of the Canton Valais (December).[3]

The *Vaterländische Blätter,* which naturally had suspended publication during the Occupation, came back with renewed vigor in 1810. Its reappearance was announced in the *Annals of Literature and Art* [4] with the notice: " The course of the war interrupted the continuation of the *Blätter,* for its tendency was incompatible with the influence of a foreign spirit." A list of contributors, including H. J. von Collin, Hormayr and Pichler, was announced at the same time. Only gradually did the *Blätter* give evidence of the old spirit, but as early as March it let fall hints of its attitude. An issue of that month contained an article commenting upon the exodus from the land of various writers, after the Peace

---

[1] *A. E. A. C. P., Vienne, 1810,* vol. 385 *passim.*

[2] *A. E. A. C. P., Vienne, 1810,* vol. 385, folio 206, Otto to Talleyrand, April 13, 1810.

[3] *Ibid.,* vol. 385 *bis,* folio 338, Otto to Talleyrand, December 26, 1810.

[4] *Annalen der Literatur und Kunst des In- und Auslandes* (Vienna, 1810), vol. ii, pp. 148-154.

of Vienna: " After the last war, several foreign newspapers remarked upon the fact that prominent authors were leaving the Austrian states. They pointed out that these authors attached themselves to a foreign cause during the war [i. e. to Napoleon during the Occupation], and that they therefore found it expedient to quit the fatherland upon the restoration of peace." The *Blätter* then proved at length that not a single one of these emigrants was a " leading author ", and furthermore, that not one of them was a German Austrian. This latter is made clear rather adroitly by the *Blätter's* listing those who did leave the country as " a Bohemian ", " a Hungarian ", and so on.[1]

The year 1810, too, saw Hormayr in the field with another publication. "Ought we not be enflamed to similar attempts," he queried of his public, " when we notice what Shakespeare's gigantic spirit did for the self-consciousness of Old England; what its ballads did for Spain? "[2] To provide a vehicle of expression for such attempts he founded his *Archiv für Geographie, Historie, Staats- und Kriegskunst,* a periodical which appeared regularly down to 1828. Materials of a *vaterländisch* nature were assured the *Archiv,* since it counted among its contributors, Hormayr, the Collins, Pichler, Armbruster, Hammer, Sartori, Weissenbach, Count Moritz von Dietrichstein and the Prussian Varnhagen. Before long any patriot who was at all interested in the story of his fatherland need only turn to the *Archiv* to find numerous poems, plays and essays upon such heroic figures as Empress Cunigunda, Emperors Albert I, Henry II and Maximilian I, Philippine Welser, Count Guido Starhemberg, the " iron duke " Ernest and many others.[8]

[1] *Vat. Bl.*, March 1810, pp. 293-294.

[2] *Archiv für Geographie, Historie, Staats- und Kriegskunst,* 1810, no. 53, pp. 237 *et seq.*

[8] St. Cunigunda, empress of Henry II (Duke of Bavaria and emperor 1002-1024). She retired to a convent after the death of Henry, and

The *Archiv* was influential in another way, too.   The second volume contained an essay by Matthias von Collin on " The National Substance of Art." [1] In this paper Collin maintained that " art should encompass the entire globe within its purview; but the focal point from which it must make its all-inclusive survey lies within the confines of the fatherland."   He believed it to be the duty of the state to further art.   The best way in which this could be done was for the state to set up the glorification of the fatherland as the goal for which art must strive. Moreover, since a people's uniqueness and individuality is best reflected in its history, it is a duty of the state to guide art along the path of national history.   Hormayr himself, and the veteran romanticists, could not have expressed their ideas more clearly.   It was M. von Collin who finally supplied the " theoretical basis " for the new developments in German Austrian literature—for a patriotic and romantic trend that began with his brother, Joseph, and with Caroline Pichler, and that was continued by Castelli, Kalchberg, Weissenbach, Deinhardtstein, Hammer and others.   And many of the works of these poets and writers first saw the light of day in Hormayr's *Archiv*.[2]

was canonized by Innocent III in 1200. Albert I of Austria, emperor 1289-1308, was the second Habsburg emperor and a very capable man. Count Guido Starhemberg (1657-1737) was one of Austria's best field-marshals, and a cousin of the defender of Vienna against the Turks in 1683. He fought against Turks, Hungarians, Italians, Spaniards and French. Ernest (1377-1424), the "iron duke", was an archduke of Austria. Philippine Welser (1527-1580), niece of the famous Bartholomew Welser who was reported to have loaned twelve tons of gold to Charles V, secretly married Archduke Ferdinand, a son of Emperor Frederick I. She loved the Tyrol and spent much time and money in charitable work among its inhabitants. Her children were morganatic, and one of her sons became a cardinal and Bishop of Brixen. Brockhaus, *passim.*

[1] *Archiv für Geographie etc.*, nos. 122-124, October 11, 14, 16; 1811: " Über die nationale Wesenheit der Kunst."

[2] Wihan, *op. cit.*, pp. 140-142.

The years 1811 and 1812 were even more reminiscent of
1807 and 1808. Books began to appear on the history of the
Landwehr,[1] and on the events of the war of 1809.[2] In June,
1811, the city of Graz in Styria received as a gift from John,
the Joanneum, a museum to house historical relics of the
province. It was to be the center of the cultural and intel-
lecual life of the city and of Styria.[3] One of the three cur-
ators of the museum was Johann Kalchberg, a Styrian
dramatist, whose *Ulrich, Graf von Cilly*[4] was performed in
Graz on October 28, 1811. Fellinger's *Graf von Sella* was
presented in the same city on November 18.[5] In Vienna itself such plays as M. H. Mynart's *Rudolph von Habsburg*
became popular again. *Rudolph* was presented on October
11, 1812, in the Theater an der Wien,[6] which theatre, incidentally, was labelled " the best theatre in Germany at present " (1812).[7] In a series of soirées held at the Kärntnerthor Theater in Vienna H. J. von Collin's hero-worshipping
ballads provided the chief entertainment throughout these
two years.[8] Indeed, H. J. von Collin's death on July 28,
1811, due to a fever brought on by overwork, and the en-
suing funeral rites celebrated in the hall of the University on
December 15, 1811, and in the Hoftheater on April 3, 1812,
did much to remind the people of 1809. For it was as a
" national poet " that Collin was remembered and revered.[9]

[1] Such as Kurz' *Geschichte der Landwehr, op. cit.*

[2] Noted in *A. E. A. C. P., Vienne, 1811,* vol. 390, folio 96.

[3] Nagl, *op. cit.,* vol. ii, p. 933.

[4] Ulrich III, Graf von Cilly, d. 1456, one of the ablest and most powerful members of a famous family of rulers in Styria.

[5] Wihan, *op. cit.,* p. 135.

[6] Laban, *op. cit.,* p. 209.

[7] Pezzl, *op. cit.,* vol. iii, p. 143.

[8] Wihan, *op. cit.,* p. 135.

[9] *Ibid.*

The year of Collin's death saw the appearance in Vienna of that immortal soldier-poet of the Wars of Liberation, the young Saxon, Theodore Körner, and of Wilhelm von Humboldt, founder of the University of Berlin (1810).[1] In this same year Franz Sartori, from 1806 to 1810 editor of the *Annalen der Literatur des österreichischen Kaiserstaats,* and now a censor, announced his interest in two ambitious projects. The first, which he termed " an important national matter ", concerned the preparation of a German dictionary to include the vocabularies of all the German-speaking provinces of Austria.[2] The other was a proposal to present the public with a *Biographical Dictionary of the Great Men of the Austrian Monarchy.* Sartori observed that the monarchy had produced men of the highest calibre, and it was only fitting that a complete gallery of them be gotten together. He welcomed information and contributions from all who had knowledge of the life and work of any genius.[3] It seems that neither of these projects was ever completed.

The year 1812 brought into the foreground once more Friedrich Schlegel, whose activities in 1809 have been noted in detail, but who was without official employment for several years after 1809. With the express purpose of furthering the cause of romanticism in Vienna, Schlegel, in January, 1812, began publication of his well-known periodical, the *Deutsches Museum.* Although it lived only two years, since Schlegel was too busy in an official capacity at the Congress of Vienna to continue editing it, the *Museum* was an im-

---

[1] The presence of a large number of North Germans in Carlsbad at this time made that city a stronghold of the *Tugendbund.* The police, however, were careful to keep Austria pure of its influence. *Cf. A. E. A. C. P., Vienne, 1811,* vol. 390, folio 88, *Bulletin de Vienne,* August 3, 1811.

[2] *Vat. Bl.,* 1811, p. 586.

[3] *A. E. A. C. P., Vienne, 1811,* vol. 389, folio 303, *Bulletin de Vienne,* June 1, 1811, quoting an advertisement from the *Wiener Zeitung.*

portant influence.[1] Schlegel strove to uphold and strengthen the spirit and thought of the German nation. Hence his work would cover every field of national culture and civilization: history in the broadest sense of the term, the philosophy of life, and the literature and art of the people. In the preface to the first number of the *Museum* he wrote:

We use the term history in its widest sense. The historical attitude must prevail in the spheres of literature, philosophy and art. At present German literature is suffering from two opposing evils. The first of these evils is a certain esthetic-philosophic indifference, which tolerates no moral or religious bonds, but which bears with equanimity all other possible fetters and bonds, as long as it is permitted to shuffle indiscriminately, and to toy in pseudo-scientific fashion with all phases of human and inhuman knowledge. The other evil is the restraining and narrowing influence of the spirit of provincialism which still pervades German literature. Every literature must be national; that is its destiny. Only by being national can a literature realize its full worth and value. Indiscriminate, exclusive praise of national authors or of so-called indigenous themes is far from being conclusive proof of a patriotic mind.

The *Museum* could boast of an outstanding group of contributors. Schlegel himself, of course, contributed much, including fragments of his lectures on the history of literature which he delivered in Vienna in February, 1812, before a " brilliant audience ".[2] August Wilhelm Schlegel contributed a number of papers including a series on the Lay of the Nibelungs, and one on contemporary (i. e. thirteenth century) poems on Rudolph of Habsburg. Jacob Grimm, Joseph Görres, Pichler, Adam Müller, M. von Collin,[3] all participated, along with a host of others.[4]

[1] Nagl, *op. cit.*, vol. ii, pp. 877-878, 880.

[2] *Ibid.*, vol. ii, p. 879.

[3] E. g., in *Museum*, vol. ii, pp. 192-193, there is an article by M. von Collin " Über das historische Schauspiel."

[4] Nagl, *op. cit.*, vol. ii, p. 879.

In one other field did cultural nationalism become evident during these "quiet" years—in that of music. Emperor Joseph II had essayed a "Germanization" of the stage as early as the 1780's, but without much success. Among other efforts in this direction, he had founded a German *National-theater* which was to be devoted exclusively to German musical art. But, as Pezzl said, "pretty soon people began to yawn at this unvarying monotony". The voluptuous Italian music was more to the taste of the Viennese public.[1] At the opening of the nineteenth century a revival of the works of Christoph Willibald von Gluck (1714-1787) and George Frederick Händel (1685-1759) regained first place for the German opera for a short time. Gluck originally had broken with the Italian opera in his *Alceste* in 1767, and now the performance of his *Iphigenia at Aulis,* on January 1, 1807, in the Kärntnerthor Theater "inspired" the Viennese.[2] So cordially did they receive the opera that the imperial band-master Ignaz Franz von Mosel could write in their praise that they obviously recognized the superiority of German over Italian music—a superiority which lay in the striving for truth of feeling, correctness of expression and power of portrayal.[3] Mosel's joy was destined to be short-lived. The Viennese soon returned to their preference for Italian music, in spite of the attempts of various patriots to make the choice a matter of national pride.[4] By 1812 interest in German music had so far declined again, that the management of the Hoftheater in Vienna, on March 16, offered two prizes of one hundred ducats in gold each, for the best German tragic and comic opera scores.[5]

[1] Pezzl, *op. cit.*, vol. iii, p. 421.

[2] Collin, H. von, *Sämmtliche Werke,* vol. vi, p. 420.

[3] *Vat. Bl.*, 1808, p. 41.

[4] Batka, R., "Grillparzer und der Kampf gegen die deutsche Oper in Wien," in *Jahrbuch der Grillparzer Gesellschaft* (Vienna, 1894), vol. iv, p. 129.

[5] Wihan, *op. cit.*, p. 155.

And what happened in the rest of Europe during these years? Prussia was being "regenerated". Wellington was driving the French under Massena and Soult out of the Peninsula. The *Tugendbund* was becoming more powerful every day. Napoleon was trying to draw the meshes of the Continental System ever tighter. Alexander of Russia was becoming more and more exasperated over Napoleon's actions. By 1811 a break between France and Russia was obvious. Both sides prepared for war, and the year 1812 saw Napoleon once more facing a coalition—this time of Russia, England and Sweden. Prussia, however, was frightened into granting permission to Napoleon to march his troops through that land, and into promising the support of 20,000 men to protect his left flank. The Austrian Government assured Napoleon of its sympathy and promised 30,000 men to protect his right flank.

Prussia's action made the patriotic Scharnhorst, Gneisenau and von Boyen resign their offices. They had no desire " to serve under Napoleon " Prussia's and Austria's actions made the " hellishly blasé " Gentz, who had been living in retirement since 1810, write a stirring proclamation: " To the German Princes and to the Germans." " Has Germany, then, really sunk to its lowest depths? " he asked. And he warned his countrymen that the only way to consolidate all the political might of Germany was first to have only *one* national will predominate.[1] Such manifestations, however, meant but little to Napoleon. On June 24 he crossed the Niemen River into Russia. More than half a million men, of whom only about one-third were French, followed him. On December 14, about 20,000 haggard survivors recrossed the Niemen into Germany.[2] The cold and the snow, disease and starvation, swollen streams and broken bridges, Cossacks

[1] Kralick, *op. cit.*, p. 358.
[2] Rose, *op. cit.*, p. 262.

and cannons, General Kutusoff and a Russian winter had claimed the rest.

The magnitude of Napoleon's losses cannot be measured in terms of lives alone. His reputation for invincibility now was shattered. And on December 30, the Prussian commander, General Yorck, came to an agreement with the Russians at Tauroggen whereby the Prussian troops withdrew from the conflict. The Austrians under Prince Karl Schwarzenberg gradually withdrew from Russian and Polish territory, until they, too, ceased fighting after an armistice was signed on January 30, 1813. At the same time, both Prussia and Austria were increasing their armaments. On January 13, 1813, the Niemen was again crossed from East to West by a large body of troops—but this time they were led by Alexander, who proclaimed the liberation of Europe. On February 27, a Russo-Prussian treaty of alliance was signed at Kalisch, and the following month Prussia declared war against France. On March 17, Frederick William delivered his famous address *An Mein Volk*. The rest of northern and central Germany soon followed the lead of Prussia, and before long the Confederation of the Rhine began to crumble. Napoleon, however, returned to the field, and on May 2, 1813, defeated the Russians and Prussians at Lützen. On May 20 and 21, he defeated them again at Bautzen. But these victories were not like those of Austerlitz and Jena and Friedland. It was not long before both parties were glad to rest a while, and on June 4 an armistice was signed at Poischwitz, through the good offices of Austria, which, under the cool guidance of Metternich, had maintained an exasperating neutrality in the struggle. Provision was made for the calling of a peace congress to meet at Prague. On July 12 this congress convened.

CHAPTER VI

1813-1815: THE WARS OF LIBERATION

METTERNICH'S policy of " watchful waiting " during the
winter of 1812 and the spring of 1813 aroused great indignation among some of the Austrian people.   In spite of the Austrian Government's efforts to keep the news of Napoleon's
disasters in Russia from the public ear, and thereby to avoid
diplomatically embarassing outbreaks,[1] General Kutusoff's
health was drunk so frequently that the Viennese innkeepers
joyfully reported bumper profits.[2]   So absorbed were the
people in the trend of foreign affairs that matters of domestic
policy held little interest for them.[3]   When a rumor was
circulated, early in April, 1813, that Metternich had concluded a new alliance with Napoleon, the Viennese became so
restless and angry that the government became worried.[4]
While excited mobs asked " Where does that damned Count
Metternich live, anyway? " the troops intimated that they
would rather throw away their guns than fight for the
French.[5]   Not until special secret agents were employed by
the government to mix with the people on the Bourse, in the
salons, and in other places, and to suggest to them the pre-

---

[1] Horstenau, *Die Heimkehr Tirols*, p. 56.

[2] *Bericht, 21. November 1812 beiliegend dem Vortrage Hagers vom 24.
November, Min. d. Inn.*, quoted in Wertheimer, E., " Wien und das
Kriegsjahr 1813," in *A. f. o. G.*, vol. lxxix, p. 382.   In the future this
article will be cited *A. f. o. G.*, vol. lxxix.

[3] *Ibid.*

[4] *A. f. o. G.*, vol. lxxix, p. 366.

[5] *Ibid.*, p. 365.

posterousness of such an alliance, was comparative calm restored.[1] As a matter of fact, Metternich could not adopt a definite stand as yet.   He had no thought of joining Napoleon.   But he was not ready to attack him, either.

Naturally, there was considerable difference of opinion among the people as to the advisability of fighting Napoleon again.   While some Viennese, for example, demanded war in fiery and impetuous tones,[2] others were still fearful of Napoleon's might.[3]   While some were jubilant, in March, 1813, over the Prussian king's address *An Mein Volk*,[4] others preferred to conjure up the spectre of a third occupation of Vienna.[5]   A little later, while certain citizens kept the recruiting stations busy enlisting volunteers,[6] others remarked with awe upon the invincible genius of the French emperor.[7]   Eventually, lest timidity secure the upper hand over courage, one of the sturdier patriots took occasion to publish a pamphlet entitled: "A Timely Word by an Austrian to his Despondent Fellow-Citizens."   In this paper he tried to convince the despairing ones that their fears were groundless, since, in the event of war, all the chances inclined to victory.   Then, toward the close of his admonition, he addressed a few sentences to those " upright, honest, German fellow-citizens " of his who were not afraid, urging them to rally around the monarch in loyal fashion.[8]

---

[1] *A. f. o. G.*, vol. lxxix, p. 367.

[2] Kralick, *op. cit.*, p. 360.

[3] Pichler, *Denkwürdigkeiten*, vol. ii, p. 239.

[4] Kralick, *op. cit.*, p. 363.

[5] *A. f. o. G.*, vol. lxxix, p. 368.

[6] *A. E. A. C. P., Vienne, 1813*, vol. 396, folio 190: *Extrait du Conservateur impartial, No. 45, St. Petersbourg le 6/18 juin 1813*.

[7] *A. f. o. G.*, vol. lxxix, p. 370.

[8] Castelli, I. F., *Ein Wort zu rechter Zeit eines Österreichers an seine verzagten Mitbürger* (Vienna, 1813).

It is only fair to add that some of this mistrust and timidity evidenced in the summer of 1813 must be attributed to the disillusionment occasioned by the appointment of Prince Karl Schwarzenberg to the post of commander-in-chief of the imperial forces.[1] It had been confidently expected that the Archduke Charles would be reinvested with supreme command,[2] and in the general disappointment Schwarzenberg became the target of much unjust criticism and censure.

During the summer of 1813 the government finally decided to organize a definite campaign of propaganda to inflame the people to a last supreme effort against Napoleon, and to assure them that success was not only probable, but actually inevitable. Every influence must be used, said the emperor, " so that the memory of earlier failures may not lead to the conviction that similar misfortunes will follow this attempt " at liberation.[3] The plan was to have the papers carry regular items regarding, on the one hand, the actual strength of Napoleon's forces and the story of his losses in Spain, and on the other, the really great power of Austria, as well as the numerous safety and precautionary measures taken by the Habsburg government. Further, the foreign office was to prepare and hold in readiness a sheaf of pamphlets which could be distributed among the people immediately upon the outbreak of hostilities.[4] This time, however, in interesting contrast to the attitude it took in 1809, the government intended to " avoid all passionate outbursts; " to " make lasting rather than transitory impressions; " to " influence the reason rather than to inflame the imagination " of the public;

[1] *A. f. o. G.*, vol. lxxix, pp. 370 and 397.

[2] Pichler, *Denkwürdigkeiten*, vol. ii, p. 255.

[3] Quoted in *A. f. o. G.*, vol. lxxix, p. 371.

[4] *Ibid.*, p. 396.

and to "outline clearly and logically the necessity for war." [1]
Court Secretary Armbruster went so far as to list the following " guiding principles " for the government and for those
who might be employed to write pamphlets for the
authorities:

1. Never to outstep the bounds of urbanity in respect of
Napoleon's person, since, after all, he is the son-in-law of our
monarch; 2. Never to have recourse to vulgar expressions, nor
to taunt the enemy in an eccentric manner; 3. Not to permit the
flooding of the land with badly-written, insipid pamphlets, but
only to allow the appearance of the better and more appropriate
ones; 4. As long as our troops remain on *Austrian* soil, to
spread only *Austrian* patriotism, and to mention *Germanism* as
rarely as possible. To beware of saying anything that savors
of German liberty in the sense that the members of the *Tugendbund* use that phrase. [2]

How cold all this sounds when compared with the utterances
of 1809! Quite obviously this was the régime of Metternich, and not of Stadion. The latter tried to invoke the
spirit of a nationalist revolution. Metternich, however, was
more careful. He would not light any fires that he could not

---

[1] *A. f. o. G.*, vol. lxxix, p. 396.

[2] *Ibid.*, p. 399. Gentz, who now was in hearty sympathy with Metternich's policies, seems to have shared Armbruster's sentiments judging
by a letter he wrote Metternich from Prague on August 28, 1813: " Shall
we permit some of these miserable pamphleteers to disturb our peace?
One of them writes: ' A Timely Word by an Austrian to his Despondent
Fellow-Citizens'—a pamphlet which intrinsically would not be one of
the worst, if only some intelligent censor had cut out the title. Another
writer dares to advocate a general levy of the people, although the government has not given the slightest indication of intending to resort to
this. I am told that a number of tracts regarding the Tyrol are circulating in Vienna, which contain material diametrically opposed to the wise
policy which the ministerial council is adopting in its relations with
Bavaria." Quoted in *Österreichs Teilnahme an den Befreiungskriegen*,
edited by R. von Metternich (Vienna, 1887), p. 49.

later extinguish. Moreover, he was as much concerned with making Austria powerful in Italy as he was with making it dominant in Germany.[1]

It was not long before Metternich found that it was difficult to secure authors who could produce pamphlets that at one and the same time were " safe ", and yet would have the desired effect in arousing the people.[2] Moreover, many self-respecting writers became disgusted with the foreign office's policy of discarding whatever tracts it did not like, and so revising the rest as to make them unrecognizable to their own creators.[3] Nevertheless, a fairly long list might be made of pamphlets that were printed under these conditions. Some of the more widely-distributed ones were Armbruster's *Wer ist ein österreichischer Patriot im Geist und in der Wahrheit?;* Castelli's *Ein Wort zur rechten Zeit;* Enzenberg's *Das liebe Ich und das bedrohte Vaterland;* Wieland's son's *Was ist gegenwärtig das Eine, was Noth thut?;* Dr. Jenull's

[1] Bibl, *Metternich*, vol. i, p. 163. The foreign minister's attitude can be gleaned directly from a report rendered to Francis in May, 1813, regarding a pamphlet entitled: "On the Origin and Purpose of the German Legion." The report reads as follows: "This pamphlet summarizes the teachings of the *Tugendbund*, including all its infamous, subversive and destructive doctrines. It maintains that subjects are absolved from their obedience to their rulers, and that sovereigns lose their rights, whenever, in any given political situation, the government acts contrary to the views of any one of the members of the League. Further, that the fatherland has prior and more lasting claims to man's loyalty than has the sovereign ... etc., etc. At the present time northern Germany is being swamped with productions of this type. Unfortunately, many people there consider them a means toward the fulfilment of desirable ends. Hence it becomes all the more necessary to exercise great caution and to prevent the spreading of this stuff within the monarchy. This, of course, will necessitate the closest cooperation between the police, the secret service and the postal authorities." *W. S. A., Vortrag Metternich's*, May 3, 1813.

[2] *A. f. o. G.*, vol. lxxix, pp. 272-273.

[3] *Ibid.*

Wer soll sich im gegenwärtigen Kriege dem Soldatenstande widmen?; and Holler's *Das Jahr 1813, oder warum haben wir Krieg?* [1]

Despite this pliability on the part of some Viennese, and this attitude of indifference or even disfavor on the part of the government, the thought of German nationality did not disappear from Austria in the earlier half of 1813. The new French ambassador to Vienna, Count Narbonne, became quite excited over the general aspect of things in April, 1813. He clumsily described the situation in a note to Paris in these words: [2]

It is impossible to remain oblivious to the fermentation which is menacing Germany with the most violent and general explosion of its history. In every German land into which the Russian troops are setting foot, the necessary measures seem to have been taken beforehand to convert each German into an impassioned enemy of the French. I say each *German*, because they affect, above everything else, not to recognize any division of the German state, and because the timely literary productions, now, more than at any other time, are reiterating to the German the abjuration of everything that might weaken the common hatred which all those who live between the Rhine and the Niemen are expected to bear us. These writings are deluging the whole Austrian monarchy, and when I speak to the authorities here about checking the flood, they do not seem to be able to fathom the responsibility. They say that no papers are forbidden, and they even make a virtue of the fact that the semi-official *Beobachter*, edited by a government agent, presents nothing but official news from all parts of Germany without adding any of the nauseating diatribes which are current in other papers. They insist that an absolute silence, if it could be enforced, would only increase the ferment, and that coercive

[1] *A. f. o. G.*, vol. lxxix, pp. 272-273.

[2] *A. E. A. C. P., Vienne, 1813*, vol. 394, folio 338, Narbonne to the foreign minister, the Duke de Bassano, April 2, 1813.

measures would be exceedingly dangerous. In short, taking everything here [in Austria] together, it presents the same picture that Prussia did before Jena.

The theatres, moreover, still found it profitable to produce such plays as *The German House-Wife, German-Mindedness* and *German Loyalty*.[1] Commenting upon a performance of the latter play on June 11, 1813, in the Theater an der Wien, th *Eipeldauer* reproachfully wrote: " The play was received with much applause, even though it is called *German Loyalty*. This is remarkable in view of the fact that there are so many people in Vienna who, sorry to say, care not a fig about German loyalty." [2]

At this time, too, Caroline Pichler was completing a dramatic work entitled *Germanicus*.[3] She explained her choice of this Roman general as the hero on the basis of the resemblance he bore to Charles:

I saw in the Caesar Germanicus not only a great general and one of the noblest Romans of his time, but I also seemed to see in his characteristics and in his relations with others an even closer similarity between him and Archduke Charles. It seemed to me that the victor of Stockach and Würzburg had as much claim to the title of Germanicus, for having saved Germany, as had the Roman general because of his leadership in an attempted but uncompleted subjugation of Germany. Many things have happened in the German fatherland since then, but the old memories still linger on in every German-feeling soul. The

---

[1] Rosenbaum's *Tagebuch*, entries for June 15, June 19, etc., and *Eipeldauer*, 1813, 11. Heft, pp. 33 *et seq*. *Die deutsche Treue* was a one-act play written by Johanna Franul von Weissenthurn. It had its première in the Burgtheater on February 3, 1803.

[2] *Eipeldauer*, 1813, 8. Heft, pp. 29 *et seq*.

[3] Germanicus was a famous Roman general. He campaigned against the German tribes for years and finally defeated Arminius or Hermann. He died in 19 A. D. while on a mission to Syria.

days of Caldiero and Aspern have imbedded themselves in our minds more deeply and indelibly than ever.[1]

The play, which soon was performed in the Theater in Hietzing,[2] also afforded Pichler ample opportunities for discrediting prevailing foreign customs in Austria, by pointing them out as unwelcome signs in ancient Rome. Moreover, Pichler's home continued to be a rendezvous for patriots and poets, and her guests spent many an evening regaling themselves by singing songs of the fatherland. The company in 1813 included Hormayr, the Schlegels, Adam Müller, Theodore Körner, the Humboldts, the romanticist Clemens von Brentano, Johanna von Weissenthurn and others.[3] On one particular evening the enthusiasm was so great that the guests sang Körner's *Jägerlied*[4] in chorus, despite the presence of a member of the Westphalian legation, Baron von der Malsburg.[5]

Archduke John and Baron Hormayr, too, were destined to play leading, if secret, rôles in 1812 and 1813. It seems that early in January, 1812, John was approached by a representative of the London government who promised British financial support in the event that the archduke would be

[1] Dedication of *Germanicus*, written in March, 1813. Pichler, C., *Sämmtliche Werke*, 45 vols. (Vienna, 1813), vol. viii. Also *Denkwürdigkeiten*, vol. ii, pp. 217-218.

[2] *Eipeldauer*, 1813, 3. Heft, p. 16.

[3] Pichler, *Denkwürdigkeiten*, vol. ii, *passim*.

[4] See Appendix p. 215 for this poem.

[5] Pichler, from whose memoirs (vol. ii, p. 224) this notice is taken, erroneously writes that the group sang Körner's " *Auf, auf, ihr Brüder und seid stark* ", but Körner never wrote such a song. Rather, he composed the *Jägerlied* to the tune of Chr. F. D. Schubart's *Kaplied*, which was written in 1787 upon the departure of some Württemberg troops for service at the Cape of Good Hope in the interests of the Dutch East India Company. Schubart's song began with the line " *Auf, auf, ihr Brüder, etc.*"

willing " to place himself at the head of the mountain people
and to create a military diversion in the Tyrol." Although
averring that he " was ready to unsheath his sword at any
moment in which the people of the Alps . . . might rise in
revolt," John felt that German blood ought not to be squand-
ered in premature efforts at that time. Moreover, he preferred to see his fatherland liberated without the aid of English money. He thought a combined effort on the part of the
Tyrol and Switzerland to throw off the yoke would be much
more desirable, since, after all, it was the duty of the Germans
to complete the work of liberation themselves. Knowing that
this was the prince's attitude, it is easy to understand how
two other German patriots, Hormayr and Gagern, could have
won him over to become the leader of a wide-spread conspiracy known as the *Alpenbund* or Alpine League. But that
is a story in itself.[1]

It was hardly to be expected that Hormayr would remain
quiet while the Tyrol was in the hands of Bavaria. In truth,
he organized a revolutionary council, in 1811, which met on
his estate at Klosterneuburg, near Vienna, there to plot an
uprising of the Tyrolese, supported by the inhabitants of
Vorarlberg, Salzburg and the Illyrian Provinces. Hormayr's
chief lieutenants in the organization of this *Alpenbund* were
the Vorarlberger, Anton von Schneider, and the Rhinelander,
Hans von Gagern, the first volume of whose *National
History of the Germans* appeared in Vienna in 1813.[2] And
then there were dozens of Tyrolese, Viennese and Bavarians
like the Counts Reisach, who came and went to and from

---

[1] This section is based upon the third chapter of Horstenau's *Die
Heimkehr Tirols*. No sources are indicated in this volume, but the
appropriate documents upon which the story is based are in a collection
in the *W. S. A.* called *Geheime orig. Vorträge des Gr. Metternich, Staatskanzlei Vorträge, Fasz. 284*, March 1813 and *Fasz. 285*, April-May 1813.

[2] Pichler, *op. cit.*, vol. ii, p. 231.

the house suspiciously often.   The Swiss Count Johann Salis-Saglio came as the representative of such of his country-men as lived in Austria.   The Englishman, William King, was a frequent official visitor and abettor.   Archduke John soon joined the group and naturally became at least nominal head of the conspiracy.

So rapidly did the plans of these men mature that John drew up a daring, almost chimerical, plan of campaign in January, 1813.   His own comment upon the scheme is in-teresting: "Many will be astonished; many will call my undertaking a fool's trick; many will censure it; some will pity me as a lost being.   But why should that worry me? *Si deus nobiscum, qui contra nos?*" [1]

Supposedly, no outsider had knowledge of the plot.   The one possible exception was John's sister-in-law, the Empress Maria Ludovica, in whom he confided.   Although Maria advised John to cease being a "peasant incitor", and to think of marriage instead of conspiracies, she did not betray him. The initiates held their meetings at any and all conceivable places to escape the vigilance of the police.   They even used the rooms of the State Archives building where Hormayr had offices, and they actually had a counter police system of their own. [2]   Once again, however, John and Hormayr were to find themselves pitted against the Fates.   Austria's famous police had news of the Klosterneuburg meetings as early as October, 1811, and Police Commissioner Pfleger, "the emperor's conscience," was at once put on the trail of the plotters.   Not until 1813, however, did Metternich have enough definite information to warrant governmental in-terference.   This information he received from one Anton von Roschmann, a friend of Hormayr, who had been taken into the *Bund* in January, 1813.   Roschmann, apparently

1 Horstenau, *op. cit.*, pp. 61-62.

2 *Ibid.*, p. 64.

frightened at the prospect of his fate in case the plot failed, and perhaps, also, aware of the opportunity for political preferment, informed Metternich of everything on February 12 and 13. There was no time to be lost now since the date set for the opening alarms was April 19, the anniversary of the Sicilian Vespers.[1] Metternich acted quickly. He foresaw all the difficulties which a revolt led by an Austrian archduke would cause for his government. He doubtless also realized the utter impossibility of success in the enterprise. The police were ordered to proceed with arrests. They did so in a most dramatic manner.

On the evening of March 8, Hormayr had a little party at his home in Vienna. During the course of the evening the host withdrew to a private room with his friends Schneider and Roschmann. Suddenly there was a knock at the door, and a voice announced the presence of an old friend. When the door was opened Hormayr immediately found himself surrounded by a group of policemen. A moment later Schneider and Roschmann found themselves in similar straits. All three were taken away[2] without a word of explanation either to themselves or to the company. Hormayr, after a nine-day trip in a wagon, was incarcerated, under the name of Hiller, at Munkacs. Schneider was taken to the Spiegelberg under the pseudonym Schuster (!). Gagern, as a less important leader, but as an undesirable visitor, was ordered to quit Austria. Archduke John was called before the emperor where he confessed to everything. Though he received no penalty, he was kept in ignorance of the whereabouts of his fellow-conspirators, and was virtually confined to Vienna, since his chief steward, Count Nimptsch, was

[1] Sicilian Vespers designates a revolt in the island of Sicily against the French ruler Charles I of Anjou. So-called because it broke out at the hour of Vespers on Easter Tuesday, 1282.

[2] *W. S. A., Staatskanzlei Vorträge, Fasz. 284, Vortrag Metternich's,* March 9, 1813.

ordered not to permit the prince to leave the city without the special permission of the emperor.[1]   Roschmann, whose arrest, of course, was only a sham, was kept in hiding for several weeks and then released.

The news of the arrest of these men traveled through the city quickly and spread consternation among Hormayr's friends. They were full of sorrow over the Baron's misadventure and were worried about his well-being, and yet they were unable to do anything for him since they were ignorant of his place of confinement.[2]

But it was fortunate that the campaign never materialized. John had been blinded by the glamorous accounts of his friends and was both too inexperienced and too little conversant with *Realpolitik* to fathom all the implications of the rash step.   Certainly his reputation remains brighter for the failure of the enterprise.   He was too eager to emancipate his fellow-Germans and to restore his beloved German fatherland.   He might have spoiled Metternich's plans completely, if he had had his way.

It was just ten days after the arrest of Hormayr that Prussia, as has been noted, joined Russia in that war against Napoleon which was a prelude to the Peace Congress at Prague.   Metternich was chiefly responsible for the calling of this Congress at which Austria would at last take a definite stand.[3] So carefully did the minister proceed, however, that few people in Austria knew in what direction the wind would blow.   The best that most sincere patriots could do was to hope that Francis would take what they considered to be the right step.   And while they hoped, some of the more daring Austrians indicated what they meant by the proper step. Thus, the *Eipeldauer* said:

[1] *W. S. A., Vortrag Metternich's*, March 6, 1813.

[2] Pichler, *op. cit.*, vol. ii, p. 233.

[3] Bibl, *op. cit.*, vol. i, pp. 157 *et seq.*

Some of these pessimists insist that Francis will take sides with the French. They envy the happiness which the Dutch, Swiss, Rhinelanders . . . and Saxons have enjoyed under French auspices, and they think we ought to strive to attain the same bliss. Fortunately, these people are nearly all beings who have been blown to Vienna from all the corners of the earth by the winds. The only reason they wear the blue livery is because they are being paid to do it. . . . Such people naturally have no fatherland. Indeed, if you please, they have no birthplace. Sorry to say, however, there are a few native fops who believe them and who walk around repeating this stupid French gospel. But the good patriots, in fact all the Austrians, refuse to believe that their honest emperor will be willing to help bring Germany completely under foreign control, or to obstruct the work of liberating the German fatherland.[1]

Even more directly did an anonymous poet express his sentiments, in these lines: [2]

> Awaken, Francis, hear your people calling!
> Awaken, see th'avenger's hand.
> Still under foreign horses' hoofs lies quaking
> Germania, the Fatherland!
>
> To arms, as long as the hated French Napoleon
> Makes Germania resound with woes.
> Rise, Francis, ties to bind you there are none,
> No son-in-law the Fatherland knows.

Francis did heed the call of the fatherland. On June 27, fifteen days before the Congress met, Austria had come to a secret agreement with Russia and Prussia at Reichenbach. By this convention the Habsburg monarchy promised to

---

[1] *Eipeldauer*, 1813, 10. Heft, p. 8.

[2] Quoted in Pfalz, A., *Aus der Franzosenzeit* (Deutsch-Wagram, 1906), pt. ii. Pfalz speaks of it as "*ein sehr verbreitetes Lied*," dated 1813. See Appendix p. 216 for German version.

assist the allies against Napoleon, if the latter did not accept Austria's peace proposals by August 10, the last day of the prolonged armistice.   The terms that Austria proposed were generous, involving as they did a general European peace based upon the reconstruction of Prussia, the restoration of the Illyrian Provinces to Austria, the repartition of the Grandduchy of Warsaw between Austria, Prussia and Russia, the break-up of the Confederation of the Rhine, and the return of their freedom to the North German Hansa towns.   But Napoleon did not want peace.   He merely wanted a rest period in which to collect reenforcements to renew the fight.   Metternich was aware of Napoleon's motives, and toward the end of July Gentz was ordered to prepare a war manifesto.[1]   In the first week of August the populace of Vienna sensed that war was in the air.[2]   On August 12, the armistice having expired, Austria declared war on France.   One week later the " Manifesto of the Emperor of Austria, King of Hungary and Bohemia," written by Gentz, was made public.   It explained the series of events that forced the hand of the peace-loving Francis.

Like a flash everyone now rallied to the cause.   The manifesto put an end to all uncertainty and the enthusiasm of the spirited patriots was carried over to those who hitherto had been hesitant and lukewarm.[3]   Said the *Eipeldauer:*

Now we have proof, black on white, of the real sentiments of our emperor. There is no more secrecy or lying about it. Our emperor is determined to free the poor Germans who for seven or eight years have been crushed by foreign intruders. . . . At seven o'clock yesterday morning the printed manifesto was put on sale at the government printing office on the Michaelerplatz, at a half-gulden per copy.   So eager were the

[1] *Gentz' Tagebücher*, p. 273.

[2] Rosenbaum's *Tagebuch*, entry for August 6, 1813.

[3] *A. f. o. G.*, vol. lxxix, p. 374.

crowds to get hold of it that the feathers began to fly in the tussle. The scene resembled receptions to which the Viennese had been invited gratis! . . . If the Austrians loved the emperor before the issue of the manifesto, they now idolize him.[1]

Metternich gleefully wrote his father: " Europe will be saved, and I flatter myself to think that I will be given a fair share of the credit for it. For years I have been heading toward this goal. It was not for nothing that I desired to become familiar both with my opponent, and with our own power, before I undertook the great task." [2] The emperor himself was delighted with the results of the proclamation, for it put everyone into the best of spirits.[3] Before long " all the streets were so plastered with patriotic handbills and proclamations that they presented the appearance of papered lanes. Every day brought with it a new batch of pamphlets." [4]

On August 27, however, Napoleon defeated the Austrians, Prussians and Russians under Schwarzenberg at Dresden.[5] It was Napoleon's last great victory, and it was more than counterbalanced by Blücher's victory over Macdonald on the Katzbach River, de Tolly's victory over Vandamme at Kulm, and Bernadotte's victories over Oudenot at Gross Beeren and Ney at Dennewitz.[6] Further disasters followed for Napoleon. On October 8, by the Treaty of Ried, Bavaria broke loose from the French emperor and joined the allies. Then, from October 16 to 19, was fought the Battle of Leipzig, the " Battle of the Nations ". Defeated, Napoleon turned his back upon Germany and never stopped

---

[1] *Eipeldauer*, 1813, 10. Heft, p. 23.

[2] Quoted in Bibl, *op. cit.*, vol. i, p. 162.

[3] *A. f. o. G.*, vol. lxxix, p. 374.

[4] *Eipeldauer*, 1813, 10. Heft, p. 54.

[5] Gottschalk, *op. cit.*, p. 406.

[6] *Ibid.*

marching until he had recrossed the Rhine into France. The Confederation went to pieces at his heels. The allies now took the offensive, and when Napoleon, late in 1813, refused what still were remarkably favorable peace terms, they inaugurated the new year by pouring three large armies across the northern and eastern French frontiers. Soon two additional armies threatened France from the south — a British and allied force in northern Spain, and an Austrian contingent in Lombardy. Napoleon's genius shone brighter than ever, but the odds were too great. Paris fell on March 31, 1814. Within a few days Napoleon abdicated and departed for Elba, while the Bourbons returned to the throne of France. In June Emperor Francis came back to Vienna in triumph.[1] A few weeks later the great men of Europe began to assemble in Vienna to participate in a Congress that would concern itself with the reshaping of the map of the continent.

It is necessary to go back a bit, now, and notice the effects of this series of military events upon the people of Austria. Although the government of Austria was not nearly so nationalistically inclined in its pamphlets and proclamations in 1813 as it had been in 1809, many of the people had neither forgotten nor lost the sentiments of the previous uprising. They were as " German " in their outlook now as on the former occasion. They did not write so many of their own German songs as in 1809, but at least they sang the songs written by such German, though non-Austrian, patriots as Körner, Max von Schenkendorf, Ernst Moritz Arndt and Friedrich Rückert.[2] Especially popular was the Prussian Schenkendorf, who called out to Francis:

[1] On this occasion even the inmates of the Viennese Deaf and Dumb Institution wanted to have a poem ready with which to welcome the returning emperor. Caroline Pichler wrote one for them, Pichler, *op. cit.*, vol. iii, p. 22.

[2] Pichler, *op. cit.*, vol. ii, p. 256.

> German emperor! German emperor!
> Come to rescue and to save;
> Loose the bonds that bind your people,
> Laurel wreaths await the brave.

" Almost more beautiful," said Caroline Pichler, was his " The Prussians at the Imperial Frontiers ", in which occur the lines:

> Germania is now united,
> North and south are not divided.
> One God, one life, one heart, one song,
> One fatherland sublime and strong.[1]

On the other hand, such veterans as Castelli, Posch, Schleifer and Rothkirch continued as active in 1813 as they had been in 1809, while new poets entered the lists, and anonymous works were plentiful.

In a *Wehrmann's Trinklied* (Militiaman's Drinking-Song) Castelli rendered a toast to the troops, saying:

> Hail to every German, hail!
> Who still his honor holds most dear,
> Who never will his country fail,
> In battle knows no fear.
> He shall of all be toasted first,
> With German wines shall slake his thirst,
> O'er the oppressor's bier.[2]

Schleifer composed a *Landwehrlied* in which he avowed:[3]

---

[1] Recalling this song (*Die Preussen an der kaiserlichen Grenze*) in her memoirs, Pichler wrote: "In those days we, too, counted as Germans, a designation which the people to the North and West frequently had refused to concede us before then, and again refuse to concede us now." Pichler, *op. cit.*, vol. ii, pp. 248-249.

[2] See Appendix p. 216 for German version.

[3] Schleifer, *Gedichte*, p. 233.

Most blessed land on all the earth,
Austria, home of loyalty,
E'er that thou becomest French
Thou a cemet'ry shalt be.

Later on he also celebrated the victory at Leipzig in a stirring
song entitled the " Battle of Leipzig." [1]

Even acrostics were used to sing and glorify the " beloved
fatherland " : [2]

An Mein theures Vaterland!

*E*rhebe Dich, mein theures Östreich! wieder,
*S*o gross wie sonst, zu Deinem Glanz empor!

*L*obsingend tönen Dir dafür der Musen Lieder:
*E*rhebe Dich! so schallt's im Dichterchor.
*B*is hieher half der Kriegsgott Dir im Streite,
*E*in Geist, ein Herz, ein Sinn steht Dir zur Seite.

*F*ür Alle stehest Du, und Alle stehn für Dich.
*R*udolph winkt Dir herab: Bleib' gross in Deinem Ich!
*A*uf! durch Beharrlichkeit erlangst Du nur zum Ziele;
*N*och keines war für Dich so gross, so schön;
*Z*um Kampf, zur Schlacht begleiten Dich Gefühle,

*D*ie nichts mehr schwächen kann: Du sollst, Du wirst bestehn!
*E*in edles Band knüpft Brüder fest an Brüder,
*R*ein ist der grosse Zweck, der es geknüpft, dies Band;

*E*rkämpfen wollen sie, als einer Kette Glieder,
*R*echtliebend, Freiheit nur fürs deutsche Vaterland.
*S*ey glücklich Östreich mit Deinen Streitgenossen!
*T*od, oder Sieg! so ward's im Bund beschlossen.
*E*s lebe hoch beglückt mein theures Vaterland!

[1] *Poetische Versuche von Matthias Leopold Schleifer* (Vienna, 1830),
pp. 152 *et seq.*

[2] *An Mein theures Vaterland! Ein Akrostichon für den gegenwärtigen
Zeitpunkt* (Vienna, 1813).

The reaching of an amicable agreement with Bavaria gave the editor of the *Eipeldauer* material for another " letter ", in which he wrote:

Now the Bavarians and Austrians form just one people. All dissension is forgotten. Once again we are good neighbors, German brothers. For a while we were angry at one another, but then that is not at all unusual among close relatives, in this world of ours. At present we are one heart and one mind, and we are going to drink and fight side by side to beat the band. . . . One of our army corps already has been united with the Bavarians under the command of the Bavarian cavalry general, Count von Wrede. The count is well-known as a brave and loyal German who has been impatiently awaiting the moment when his heart would again be allowed to beat for Germany.[1]

On occasion the government adopted a German tone, too. Just prior to the battle of Leipzig, for example, the following announcement was made from army headquarters in the name of the emperor:

At a time when the great struggle for the restoration of a European balance of power, and particularly for the liberation of Germany, offers reasonable hopes of success, His Imperial and Royal Majesty is convinced of the propriety of designating points of assembly at which the sons of the German fatherland may combine their own cause with that of the group as a whole. Accordingly, His Majesty has ordered the creation of a German legion in Austrian pay. . . . Every German who so desires may transfer to this German legion, where he will be enrolled in the same rank which he has held in other services.[2]

Then, when Francis entered the city of Frankfurt on November 6, 1813, he returned the keys of the city to the mayor, who had just presented them to him, with the words:

[1] *Eipeldauer*, 1813, 12. Heft, p. 17.
[2] Reprinted in *Wiener Zeitung*, no. 131, October 14, 1813.

"These keys cannot remain in the possession of a more appropriate owner than a city which ever has been so loyal a part of the German fatherland." He added that it was his own desire, as well as that of his allies, to bring about an era of peace and quiet in which "Germany would again enjoy its ancient happiness and freedom."[1]

Further, the *Wiener Zeitung,* on November 21, hailed the dissolution of the Confederation of the Rhine, saying:

> The Confederation has ceased to exist. All its members have deserted it. . . . All its members have renounced the foreign yoke and joined the cause of Germany. They are vieing with one another in contributing to the defense of German rights and liberty. . . . The people are arming everywhere, and in a few weeks Germany will have more united men in the field than at any time in its history. . . . All are filled with but one spirit: the conviction that only by such united exertions can freedom, independence and peace be secured. . . . Nations imbued with such a spirit have never been crushed. Germany, after long years of suffering, has finally reemerged as a nation![2]

The battle of Leipzig also provided another opportunity for Caroline Pichler to distinguish herself in the glorification of the German fatherland. All through the summer and fall of 1813 she worked on the production of a dramatic poem on Henry of Hohenstauffen. In her memoirs, written several decades later, she described her toil as follows:

> I no longer remember what it was that prompted me to select for my dramatic poem a phase of German history in which a

[1] *Wiener Zeitung,* no. 162, November 14, 1813.

[2] *Wiener Zeitung,* no. 169, November 21, 1813. On Christmas Day of this same year a delegation of Viennese citizens forwarded to Francis a message of "respect, loyalty and gratitude" on behalf of the city, in recognition of his work as "the savior of Germany". *W. S. A., Kaiser Franz Akten, Fasz. 82,* Count Saurau to Francis, Vienna, December 25, 1813.

German emperor of non-German birth, Frederick II,[1] came
into conflict with his son, Henry, because the latter objected to
his father's using the resources of Germany to serve his Italian
interests. . . . It was in the midst of prayers and tears and
hopes for success in the great struggle for the liberation of the
German fatherland that I worked on the play. And so more
than one reference to current conditions found its way into the
completed product, which thus, undesignedly, bore the mark
of having been written expressly in celebration of the victory
of October 18 [Leipzig].[2]

Upon its completion Pichler handed the play to the management of the Hoftheater, which decided to have it presented on the evening of October 27, as a benefit performance for the wounded veterans of Leipzig. Although not
particularly brilliant as a piece of dramatic composition,
Heinrich von Hohenstauffen was received with great enthusiasm because of its timeliness and sentiment.[3] Pichler,
now become popular,[4] continued to " compose diligently ",
and soon produced, among other things, a two-act play in
honor of Francis, entitled *Wiedersehn*. Toward the end of
this play one of the female characters is made to recite a
stanza to the effect that foreign slavery threatened the Austrians even through such media as foreign modes and
fashions, the tolerant reception of which gave clear proof of

[1] Frederick II, 1215-1250, of Italian birth, through the marriage of his
father with a princess of Sicily.

[2] Pichler, *op. cit.*, vol. ii, pp. 249 *et seq.*

[3] *Ibid.*, vol. iii, pp. 2 *et seq.*, and *Wiener Zeitung*, no. 149, November
1, 1813.

[4] Pichler was also asked to compose, first, the text of a cantata on
" The liberated Germany ", and then, the score for an opera on Rudolph
of Habsburg. The cantata was completed and set to music by the
musician Spohr. The opera, however, was rejected and did not become
known until published in a collection of her dramatic works in 1818.
Ibid., vol. iii, pp. 7-9.

an utter absence of that beautiful spirit of freedom and independence which had characterized the ancient Germans.
On one occasion when this stanza was recited from the stage,
a lady in the audience sighed: " *Ah! elle a bien raison* "(!).[1]

The victories of the year 1814, the return of Francis, the
anticipation of the meeting of the Congress of Vienna, and
the temporary renewal of warfare in 1815 after Napoleon's
escape from Elba were the stimuli for another flock of productions, some of which were indicative of a spirit of German nationalism.   By way of example, an *Epilogue of the
Year 1813,* recited from the stage of the Hoftheater early
in 1814, and then published in pamphlet form, read, in substance, as follows: The legions from the Loire and the Seine
were destroyed on the banks of the Elbe.   These men died
for oppression, not for the fatherland.   Hence no tombstone
marks the spot where they fell.   In this same manner did
Rome's proud legions fall in the valleys of Teutoburg.   They
were slain by the sword of Hermann, in Wodan's sacred
groves.   In vain did the pale and trembling imperator cry:
" Vàrus, Varus, give me back my legions."   They never
returned.   They remained on German soil as prey for the
beasts of the field.   Arise, then, brave and mighty sons of

---

[1] *Ibid.,* vol. iii, p. 38. Naturally, Pichler was not the only person who
continued to write such plays and poems in 1813 and 1814. Nor were
her plays the only " German " ones to be performed. Thus, November
27, 1813, saw the performance of Weissenthurn's *Hermann* in the
Burgtheater. (Wlassack, *op. cit.,* pp. 95, 127, 128). The *Wiener
Zeitung,* no. 206, December 28, 1813, carried an advertisement of a poem
*Der deutsche Geist. Ausgesprochen von Florian Pichlern, einem Sohne
Österreichs,* the publisher being J. B. Wallishausser. A new edition of
Tacitus' work on the Germans was advertised in the *Wiener Zeitung,*
no. 106, April 16, 1814. *Der Retter Germaniens, eine Ode in 18 Strophen
von Franz Fierlinger* was advertised in the *Wiener Zeitung,* no. 165,
June 14, 1814. In no. 117 of the same paper (April 27, 1814) Anton
Doll advertised two pamphlets: *Germanien, oder Miszellen und Denk-
würdigkeiten für das wiederbefreyte Deutschland,* 3 vols., and *Welches ist
die echte und natürliche Grenze zwischen Deutschland und Frankreich?*

Thuiskon! Arise, one and all, from the banks of the Danube
to the banks of the Oder! The moment for action has come.
Do not let it pass by, for it will never return. We have
already crossed the Rhine—that Rhine which has its source
on the St. Gotthardsberg in the fatherland of freedom
(Switzerland), and which loses itself in the sands upon the
completion of its course, thus refusing tribute to the very
ocean itself. It is a German river and represents the German spirit. And in its grandeur and glory, uniting all its
waters in one river bed, it also represents German might and
power.[1]

Schwarzenberg, moreover, was everywhere hailed as a
" German hero ",[2] while Francis, " the savior of Germany ",[3]
was praised in song and verse. The actor Friedrich Reil
recited a poem in the Hoftheater, in which occurred the lines :

Francis the German! Henceforth thou wilt be such to me ;
Such honorable name will history grant thee . . . [4]

Another faithful subject expressed his rejoicing over
Francis' glorious return by addressing him as God's chosen
savior of Germany, a hero who shunned neither danger nor

[1] *Epilog des Jahres 1813. Ein Gedicht von A. B. Deklamiert im k. k.
Hoftheater nächst der Burg, von Herrn Korn, k. k. Hofschauspieler*
(Vienna, 1814), esp. pp. 5-7.

[2] E. g. in the poem *Rückkehr des deutschen Helden Fürsten von Schwarzenberg an der Spitze der siegreichen Armee im Jahre 1814, nebst einem
patriotischen Volksgesang* (Vienna, 1814).

[3] *Die Sehnsucht der Wiener Bürger nach dem Einzug ihres Kaisers.
Ausgesprochen von Friedrich Reil, k. k. Hofschauspieler* (Vienna, 1814),
lines 1-2.

[4] *Ibid.*, lines 43-44. The ceremonies attending Francis' return included
the displaying of verses, poems and illustrated signs throughout the city.
The general trend in the poetry and displays seems to have been to call
Francis *Retter Deutschlands* and *Retter des deutschen Vaterlandes. Cf.
Denkbuch für Fürst und Vaterland*, edited by J. Rossi, 2 vols. (Vienna,
1814-1815), which is a collection of these materials.

hardships, so that his people might be freed from bondage. Further, this same writer urged all men of German blood to banish lying and trickery as the characteristics of treacherous foreigners, and, instead, to honor faith and loyalty, thus becoming more like Francis, more like the German forefathers, every day.[1]

Truly "German" in spirit was a booklet entitled *Retrospect of the Remarkable Year 1813,* which was published by Anton Strauss in 1814. Its contents, in summary, read: The German nation sank so low relative to its former lofty position that it seemed idle even to hope for a resurrection. The very name of " German " fell into disuse among the other European nations. They spoke of Bavarians, Saxons, Württembergers and so on, but not of Germans. German unity disappeared, and with it went German independence. The glorious heritage of our venerable ancestors was forgotten. Even the famous German word of honor lost its significance, because there were no Germans left to pledge with the ancient German courage. All the bonds which united the members of this manly, powerful nation were loosened. Despite all this the German princes long withstood the onslaughts of revolutionary France. Napoleon's triumphs, however, finally left Austria as the only German representative on the battlefield. Austria alone remained as the defender of German liberty and German independence, and in 1805 and 1809 Austria undertook to renew the struggle for honor and fatherland single-handed. (Actually, Austria was a member of a coalition with England and Russia in 1805.) Then, with the formation of the Confederation of the Rhine in 1806, German independence vanished. Germany ceased to be Germany. Still Austria

---

[1] Grüner, V. R., *Der treue österreichische Unterthan bey der glücklichen Ankunft unsers gnädigsten Monarchen zu Wien, nach dem siegreich erkämpften Frieden im Jahre 1814* (Vienna, 1814). See Appendix p. 217 for the poem.

refused to give up the fight. The events of 1813 made
neutrality on Austria's part impossible, but with its usual
unexampled moderation it attempted to tread the path of conciliation before resorting to arms. Austria's beloved emperor assumed the rôle of mediator in order to free the
German fatherland from its enemies without the further
shedding of noble German blood. Napoleon, however, refused all offers and determined to continue harassing Germany's flourishing fields. He probably hoped to add German
Austria, the only remaining independent German provinces,
to his empire. He expected to make himself monarch of the
universe by uniting the crown of the Holy Roman Empire
with his French crown. But before long a series of German victories cleared the French out of Germany. The
German princes, now, with a renewed sense of their dignity,
are coming together in order to decide ways and means for
lifting the German fatherland out of its sloth, and for
giving it unity and lasting independence. Everyone wants
to share in the distinction of helping to restore the noble
German name to its former position. When Napoleon is
completely crushed and no longer able to disturb the peace
of the world, we shall again become what we were for centuries, namely, Germans! Then, too, we will forever protect, with true German common spirit, the projected constitution which our rulers are preparing for the fatherland.[1]

Finally, Baron Rothkirch dedicated a poem of twenty-
seven stanzas to " Germania "[2] in which he boasted that the
Rhine no longer paid homage to the Seine, that German
might alone had driven out the ogre from the West, and that
there was nothing in the world that could withstand the
power of a league of the German people. He hoped, furthermore, that the " blessed bond of harmony " among the Ger-

[1] *Rückblick auf das denkwürdige Jahr 1813* (Vienna, 1814?).

[2] *Gedichte von Grafen von Rothkirch*, p. 162, " Germania " dated 1814.

mans would never again be loosed, for " Germania is the fatherland of all of us."

Despite this enthusiasm in 1814, the year 1815 again witnessed a period of calm and indifference. The danger was past. Napoleon was beaten. Europe was saved. Metternich was still in control — in fact, more so than ever. A natural reaction set in after the excitement of 1813 and 1814. The Tyrolese were probably elated at the return of Austrian rule.[1] The Styrian and Carinthian veterans went home to tell stories of heroic deeds and accomplishments. The Viennese resumed their normal life, though the round of festivals and parties was increased in honor of the plenipotentiaries who attended the Congress. A few nationalists continued to spread their ideas in word and deed, but their number was surprisingly small. Perhaps the indifference of the masses made the few apostles all the more fervent in their prosecution of the cause.

Matthias von Collin, for example, worked diligently to secure a popular reception in Austria for the numerous patriotic dramas and lyrical compositions that appeared throughout Germany. On one occasion, in a review of three German dramas (*The Battle in the Teutoburg Forest* by F. E. R.; *Hermann the Cheruscan* by Eckschlager; and *Caesar in Germany* by the same), he expressed a significant hope that the audiences might view them with a German heart and a lively feeling for the fatherland, rather than with the cold and exacting eye of literary criticism.[2]   On another

---

[1] Austrian control over the Tyrol was reestablished from the date of the signing of the Treaty of Ried with Bavaria. It was some time, however, before all the Tyrolese understood that the Bavarians now were their "brothers" rather than their oppressors, and for a while reprisals against the Bavarians continued.

[2] *Wiener allgemeine Literaturzeitung* (Vienna, 1815), pp. 108 *et seq.* The Austrian plays presented in 1814 and 1815 included Bäuerle's *Hugo der Siebente, genannt der Friedensgeber* and *Der Vater ist da*; Meisl's *Wiens frohestes Fest*; and Gleich's *Die Heimkehr ins Vaterland*. Cf. *Theaterzeitung*, 1814, nos. 56, 74, 76, 86 and 1815 *passim*.

occasion he praised the power and the " German air " which
characterized the patriotic works of men like Rückert, Schenkendorf and Stolberg.   To him these works represented the
most beautiful and dignified manifestation of the " rebirth of
a national life." [1]   A study of productions of this. type led
him to conclude that German song would only then reach the
heights of perfection " when it dared to be wholly and completely German." [2]   Collin's " Germanism " also cropped out
indisputably in the taunts and scornful words with which he
greeted Mme. de Staël's *De l'Allemagne,* containing dis-
paraging remarks about various phases of German life, in
particular of German art. [3]

Then, the return of " German freedom ", and the now
gradually increasing influence of romanticism once again
turned the thoughts of some of the people to the question of a
distinctive " German dress "—of a " German national cos-
tume ". [4]   Naturally, Caroline Pichler became prominent in
this movement.   An article of hers on " The Dress of German Women " was published in the popular *Fashion Journal*
edited by Friedrich Justin Bertuch. [5]   For a while it seemed
as though the idea might materialize.   Indeed, at a carnival
on Shrove Tuesday, 1815, held in the hall of the Imperial
Riding School, the cavaliers and ladies actually appeared " in
magnificent medieval costumes ". [6]   Pichler, moreover, determined at one time to come to another grand festival,
attired in medieval robes.   She planned to have her daughter
accompany her, and both of them, in masks, were to distribute to the other merrymakers copies of a poem in which

---

[1] Wihan, *op. cit.,* p. 161.

[2] *Wiener allgemeine Literaturzeitung,* 1815, pp. 1585 *et seq.*

[3] *Ibid.,* p. 776.

[4] Pichler, *op. cit.,* vol. iii, p. 50.

[5] *Ibid.,* p. 51.

[6] *Ibid.,* p. 50.

Germania's ancient daughters, temporarily resurrected, admonish their descendants to " wear German clothes ": [1]

For three hundred years [say the spirits] we had slept quietly in our graves. Suddenly the flare of torches, the clanging of arms, and the sound of cymbals awakened us from our slumber. Curiosity made us look about us and see what was going on. We were amazed to see splendid, princely figures celebrating a festival after our own ancient fashion . . . O, sacred dress! Mirror of good and pious times! We greet you with rejoicing. We expect much in the way of a better order in Germany because of your appearance. But you must assert yourself boldly, and not rest content to serve for mummery and play. German women must adorn themselves in German costumes, and break away from foreign dictates. Let our revered princesses of blessed memory point the way in this emancipation of German womanhood. We are not striving to impose a new fancy of fashion. Many a virtue is incidentally attendant upon our plan. Perhaps a better spirit and more pious life will return to us with the readoption of this German mode of dress.

The scheme to distribute copies of this poem under the indicated circumstances, however, was never carried out, since Pichler was kept at home by " migraine and a headache " on the day of the ball. Nevertheless, she later published the lines in a periodical.[2]

The acme of nationalistic adoration of " country " was reached at this time in a poem entitled " Yearning of a German for his Fatherland." [3] Its author was one Andreas

[1] Pichler, *op. cit.*, pp. 51-52. See Appendix, p. 219 for the German version.

[2] *Ibid.*, p. 52.

[3] " Sehnsucht eines Deutschen nach seinem Vaterlande ", in *Gedichte und Lebensgeschichte des Naturdichters Andreas Posch* (Vienna, 1821), pp. 116-117. Though this poem is not dated in the collection it appears to have been written either in 1815 or else shortly thereafter, since the entire group was published in 1821.

Posch, a poverty-stricken, self-taught poet, who was born in 1770 in Lower Austria, but whose date of death is unknown.[1] In this poem, Posch gave expression, in the first person, to the supposed sentiments of a German who was returning home after a prolonged sojourn abroad. The "German" began by enumerating the glories of his fatherland, glories which beckoned him to return no matter how great the span of rivers, seas and lands that separated him from his home. Germania, he vouchsafed, was the gem of the nations. Faith and loyalty, virtue and justice, hospitality and courage dwelt in every German hut and palace. Germania was the Eden of true-heartedness, the recognized fatherland of truth. Fortune, peace and contentment reigned supreme, he said, in those hallowed and thrice blessed regions. "Neither treasures, nor regal fortunes, neither space nor distance of a thousand seas," he concluded, "can make me waver from my desire to return to my fatherland."

Thus felt Posch and a few others. But Metternich felt differently. And it was Metternich who guided the Congress of Vienna when it decided upon the destiny of Europe in 1815. He steered it clear of nationalism of any kind, and of German nationalism in particular. Why did not Metternich take advantage of the opportunity to unite all Germany under the Habsburg aegis? Why did he attempt, as he did, to stamp out what little enthusiasm for an *Anschluss* remained? Why did the German nationalism which was so evident in 1809, and again in 1813, peter out toward the close of 1815? The answer is to be found in Metternich's political philosophy and his theory of the social order, to which we now turn.

[1] Goedecke, vol. vii, p. 575, and Wurbach, vol. xxiii, p. 644. Posch also wrote a fairly popular "Lied der Landwehr" in 1813, *cf.* p. 160 of his *Gedichte*.

CHAPTER VII

METTERNICH AND THE FATE OF GERMAN NATIONALISM AT THE CONGRESS OF VIENNA

METTERNICH [1] did not believe in the existence of isolated states as autonomous political organisms with interests entirely divorced from those of the community of nations. Each state, to him, was a part of a federative system of states bound together by the eternal law of social order and the idea of justice. No one state was to be allowed to become too powerful, and each was to respect the interests of all the others. Austria, Prussia, Russia, England and France as it was before the Revolution, were members, in particular, of a " moral pentarchy ", the duty of which it was to preserve society in a state of peace and order. It devolved upon this group, the membership of which had to continue intact, to maintain the proper balance of power and a fixed international organization. Unity among the five leading states was the only counterweight against " turbulence ", was the chief mainstay of the old social order, and was essential for the successful combating of the nationalist movement.

This nationalist movement, according to Metternich, was

[1] The following exposition of Metternich's theories of the state, the nation and nationalism is based largely upon the chapter entitled " Der Ideengehalt des Systems " which occupies pages 350 to 414 of the first volume of Bibl's biography, *op. cit.* Bibl's fully-documented chapter is the result of a thorough and painstaking study of Metternich's writings in every form. It presents a convenient synthesis and critical summary of the political ideas to which Metternich gave expression on various occasions—either in official memoranda, or in letters, or in private notes. *Cf.* also Metternich's *Nachgelassene Papiere*, edited by R. von Metternich, 8 vols. (Vienna, 1880-1884).

only one phase of the democratic movement which led straight to anarchy. The " worship of nationality " and the " rights of nationalities " were mere shibboleths, just as were " equality ", " constitution ", and such like. They were all worthless phantasms. Nationalism was but a blind for revolution. It envisaged the dissolution of existing social bodies, that is, of states composed of mixed nationalities. For, continued Metternich, there might be a vast difference between a state and a nation. " Cultural nations," as such, had no intrinsic right to exist. The interests of a group of political states, all of which might embrace members of a given single nationality, were far superior to the interests of that nationality. On the other hand, there was no reason why a state should not permit its diverse subjects to retain their national customs and traditions. True, national states were exceptionally strong internally and externally. But they had no greater right to exist than states whose population consisted of a multiplicity of nationalities.

Further, Metternich placed more emphasis upon race than upon nationality. He distinguished, in Europe, between the Teutonic, the Latin and the Slavic races. Each of these groups, he thought, had its special characteristics. Thus, the Teutonic race was stamped by the significance it attached to the word *Ehre* (honor), which degenerated into *point d'honneur* among the Latins, and was non-existent in the Slavic languages. " Peoples ", then, were simply branches of the three races, and only those " peoples " really deserved to be called nations who had historically demonstrated their desire and ability to live together in political unity regardless of language, traditions or origins. From this it followed that such leveling processes as the attempted Germanization of people, were both foolish and useless. The planned union of naturally and historically divided people was a misconception and misapplication of the idea of " natural rights." It could only lead to the creation of abortive monstrosities. Anyway, nobody but the troublesome middle class ever thought of such a forced unification. The masses everywhere were quite indifferent to national unity and were concerned with the task of securing a livelihood. They desired no change so long as they were satisfied economically. But they could be led astray with ease by fanatics, and they might readily be brought to demand things which they did not really want. Hence the state had to keep an eye on the middle-class intellectuals and preserve the people from the influences of agitation. The people did not care about high-sounding principles—they wanted peace. And peace could best be preserved by a " moral coalition of the governments."

So far as the governmental form of states was concerned, Metternich conceived federalism to be the ideal. He believed with the historian Niebuhr that " federalism favored the infinite diversification of institutions, and this diversity was the strongest guarantee against the introduction of revolutionary novelties." Every state that was made up of diverse parts, he felt, had to be federalized, in order that the schemes of the disturbers of the peace who agitated for unification might be obstructed. Thus, it was necessary for the European powers to unite on a righteous and moral basis in order to protect themselves against Napoleon's contemplated universal monarchy. Similarly, a German confederation had to serve to counteract the agitation for monarchic unity in Germany, and for a united German parliament expressive of a German national sovereignty. Moreover, within each state, the idea of federalism had to prevail to the extent of seeking to perpetuate the differences and peculiarities of language and customs of the subjects. Centralization in a state that was a composite of diverse parts was nothing short of tyranny, growing out of a mad desire for a general leveling of cultures. However, a strong central authority was not to be confused with centralization. The former was necessary for the maintenance of the social order. The latter was absurd.

Applying these theories to the concrete case of the Germanies, Metternich once remarked that the description " geographic expression " was as well suited to " Germany " as to " Italy." The term " German nation " was only an abstract conception since the history of centuries failed to uncover a single trace of a trend toward a unified external and internal life among the inhabitants of Central Europe. A nation was a historic political state, said Metternich now, regardless of the language or cultural traditions of the subjects.[1] He did recognize as " German race characteristics " a few traits such as separatism, loyalty and the rating of provincial patriotism above all other patriotisms; but he also differentiated between the dreamy, idealizing, mystical North German, and the active, practical South German. Moreover, he maintained that no Bavarian wanted to become Austrian, no Austrian Prussian, no Prussian Hanoverian, and so on for the whole German area. Every part of Germany wanted to remain what it was, distinct from all the rest, yet all German, and all together forming a large federation as a part of the European system. Anyone who thought he could unite these people was misjudging the German character which hated leveling and monotony. The fundamental justification of the separatist arrangement was its own long existence. A confederation was the proper system for the Germanies, and Austria would have to uphold it. On the other hand, Austria and Prussia would have to adopt a common policy in order that they might definitely control Central Europe and make it the European center of gravity. Austria needed a German

---

[1] Thus, in 1812, he referred to the "Austrian nation." Not until many years later did he realize his error in this respect, and refer to Austria-Hungary as an "agglomeration of peoples of different races."

confederation as a bulwark against external aggression, while the confederation needed Austria since the latter would be ready at any time to call on its non-German elements to help defend the system.

Here, then, was the crux of the whole matter of a disposition of the Germanies. Austria was uppermost in Metternich's mind, and if necessary he was willing to sacrifice the other German states for Austria. Whatever nationalistic aspirations for unification were voiced in the period of the Congress of Vienna, and later, fell on deaf ears so far as he was concerned, since nationalistic considerations did not exist for him. Under a federative system Austria would have all the advantages that might accrue to her under an imperial arrangement, and yet she would be relatively free from the inevitable obligations which the latter system would entail. In a confederation the friendship of the lesser states could be retained without difficulty through a series of treaties and alliances, while the bugbear of constant quarrels with a jealous Prussia would be obviated. Moreover, Metternich felt that the establishment of a strong German empire at this time would destroy the hallowed " moral pentarchy ", would upset the historic balance of power, and would be regarded in an unfriendly way by England for economic reasons, and by France and Russia for military and political reasons. Besides, Francis *was* an emperor, anyway, and since there no longer was any special prestige in the title of Holy Roman Emperor, the imperial standard with its double-headed black eagle on a field of gold might just as well be called Austrian as Roman. These views had probably become crystallized in Metternich's mind by the spring of 1813, when he confided to Wilhelm von Humboldt that Francis would never accept the imperial crown with his consent.[1]

[1] Gebhardt, B., *Wilhelm von Humboldt als Staatsmann*, 2 vols. (Stuttgart, 1896-1899), vol. i, p. 418.

With this background of Metternich's views in mind it is necessary now to return to the story of events in 1813. Before Austria joined the coalition in that year, some German patriots believed that the dreams of men like Stein, for a united Germany raised upon the ruins of Napoleon's power, might come true. Indeed, Stein was made president of a committee to administer the revenues of all territory that should be invested by allied troops. No one knew as yet whether or not the lesser princes would be permitted to keep their thrones, but Stein and Hardenberg and others hoped that in either event there would be only one sovereign power in a recreated German Empire. The princes, it was thought, might be retained as officials, but not as sovereigns. The entry of Austria into the war, however, gave the matter a different aspect. Metternich, with his hatred of change and agitation of any sort, regarded Stein as a troublesome politician, little better than the Jacobins of 1792. Upon Metternich's advice, accordingly, Francis refused the offer of a new German imperial crown.[1] Then, " with characteristic sense of present difficulties, and blindness to the great forces which really contained their solution, Metternich argued that the minor princes would only be driven into the arms of the foreigner by the establishment of any supreme German power." [2] In other words, he wanted to reassure the smaller states that riddance from French tyranny would not mean subjection to Austrian domination. At the same time, he strove to secure for Austria the leading position in the new " Germany "—whatever political form this might take—by

[1] Years later, in 1850, Metternich remembered Francis' words at this time: "*Ich bin nicht zu einem Kaiser geschaffen, der die Fürsten und die ihnen treuen Unterthanen zu Feinden und nur die Tugendbündler zu Bundesgenossen haben würde.*" Cf. *Aus dem Nachlasse des Grafen Prokesch-Osten*, 2 vols. (Vienna, 1881), vol. ii, p. 355.

[2] Fyffe, C. A., *A History of Modern Europe, 1792-1878* (New York, 1899), p. 344. Also Bibl, *op. cit.*, vol. i, p. 195.

a series of friendly agreements with the lesser areas.   As soon as Metternich had won Tsar Alexander over to these viewpoints, Austria, Russia and Prussia, on September 9, 1813, signed an agreement at Teplitz guaranteeing " full and unconditional independence " to all the states of the former Confederation of the Rhine.   And at Châtillon and Chaumont, in March, 1814, and Paris, on May 30, 1814, it was again affirmed that the states of Germany were to remain independent, though united by a federal bond into some sort of German federation.

When the time for discussing the " German question " at the Congress of Vienna arrived, therefore, it was not to be expected that Metternich would approve any scheme of a national unification of Germany.   On the contrary, with the great emphasis which he placed upon a European federative system, it was evident that Metternich would try to make the Germany of 1815 a microcosm within the European macrocosm.   *Einheit in der Vielheit* (unity in multiplicity) was the slogan to which he would adhere.[1]   If he had his way, the committees in charge would provide for a German confederation in which Austria would simply be the first among a group of equal, separate, sovereign German states.   It may be said at this point, too, that Metternich could count with surety upon the support of the delegates from such states as Bavaria and Württemberg, in his attempt to help them retain their sovereignty against the wishes of the advocates of a " Greater Germany ".   Moreover, even Gentz had come to the conclusion that a German empire could not stand.   The failure of Prussia to come to Austria's aid in 1809, the disorganized state of Austria's internal affairs after 1809, and the doubtful attitude of Russia all contributed to a change of heart and mind in the publicist.   He now felt that the only solution was " a closely-knit mass of independent and happy

[1] Bibl, *op. cit.*, vol. i, p. 391.

German states " in which Austria would be *primus inter pares*. If Austria were above any other state, he thought, there would be anarchy, internal feuds and foreign cabals.[1]

Naturally, the nationalist viewpoint was brought forward, too, both by representatives at the Congress and by pamphleteers. Most of the people in this category, however, were non-Austrian, since Metternich was Austria's chief delegate and since the Austrian police and censors were ordered to prevent the publication or propagation of popular ideas as to what the Congress ought or ought not to do.[2]

Many were the plans that were proposed and the suggestions that were made as to the proper settlement of the German question. Under one plan Stein was to be made president over the emperor and the kings. Under another, Austria was to be nominal head of a unified Germany, with Prussia in control of the armies. Stein at one time suggested a regular empire with Austria as the chief member state and the imperial title hereditary in the Habsburg family. Others preferred an elective empire or even a directorate. Some proposed an Austro-Prussian diarchy, while a few recommended a triarchy or even a pentarchy. A scheme for a septarchy consisting of seven Circles each under a Circle Chief had serious proponents. The Princess of Fürstenberg, on behalf of the mediatized princes,[3] asked Francis to restore

[1] Wittichen, F. C., " Gentz und Metternich ", in *Mitt. des Instituts für österreichische Geschichtsforschung*, vol. xxxi, pp. 95-99, 104.

[2] Thus Metternich was angered even by the publication, in August, 1814, of an article advocating his own schemes, namely, " The Idea of a German Federative State." This article appeared in no. 97 of the *Archiv für Geographie, etc. Cf. W. S. A., Pol. Corresp., Fasz. 4*, Metternich to Hager, August 25, 1814. *Cf.* also Fournier, A., *Die Geheimpolizei auf dem Wiener Kongress* (Vienna and Leipzig, 1913), and Weil, M. H., *Les dessous du Congrès de Vienne*, 2 vols. (Paris, 1917).

[3] The mediatized princes were those ex-rulers of German principalities who had irretrievably lost their possessions during the Napoleonic struggles.

the old German Empire, but he answered evasively on October 22, 1814.[1] There was talk of a religious unification of Germany " since states become stronger when no group of citizens feels that it is different from the rest." [2] Rumor had it that there would be a wedding of the King of Prussia and the emperor's daughter, Leopoldine,[3] and on January 10, 1815, was proposed a unification of the entire German nobility into a so-called " Chain ".[4] Finally, every type and grade of federalization found support with one group or another.

The people of Vienna were relatively little interested in the political discussions and decisions of the Congress. They were more concerned and delighted with the pomp and ceremony and the round of entertainments that were provided for the victors. Open-air opera performances, splendid parades, medieval tourneys, magnificent sleigh-rides, numerous balls and processions, the solemn funeral of the Prince de Ligne who happened to die just then, and the presence of such internationally famous or notorious women as the Duchess of Sagan, Grandduchess Catherine (the Tsar's sister), Princess Marie Esterhazy (the " diamond queen "), and Countess Laura Fuchs were all more interesting and entertaining than the political future of Germany.[5] Perhaps it was a natural

---

[1] Kralick, *op. cit.*, p. 381.

[2] Quoted from a pamphlet in *ibid.*, p. 385. Baron Johann von Wessenberg, later Vicar of Constance, was a leader in the movement for securing a grant of a constitution to the entire Catholic Church in Germany. The Federal Act of the Germanic Confederation, in one of its earlier drafts, actually contained a promise for a common constitution for the Catholic Church in Germany, but this was striken out eventually, upon the proposal of Bavaria with the approval of Austria. Kralick, *op. cit.*, pp. 377-385 and *Cambridge Modern History*, vol. ix, p. 649.

[3] Kralick, *op. cit.*, p. 378.

[4] Klüber, L., *Akten des Wiener Kongresses*, 8 vols. (Erlangen, 1817) vol. vi, pp. 452 *et seq.*

[5] Gervinus, G. G., *Geschichte des neunzehnten Jahrhunderts*, 8 vols.

reaction, now that the Napoleonic terror was dissipated. Furthermore, although the entertainments provided by Francis necessitated great outlays of money, and therefore heavier taxes, many of the citizens of Vienna were more than compensated for this increased burden by the profits made from sales to the wealthier " guests ". The rentals in Vienna and its thirty-one suburbs, for example, rose from three to eight million guldens in a few months.[1] These people were too busy making money to worry about what was going on at the conferences between the diplomats. As for the people in the remainder of German Austria, outside Vienna, they were so occupied with problems of reconstruction, with hard times and crop failures, with complaining about the heavy taxes, and with meeting the requisitions levied by the government in preparation for further military ventures,—this time in Italy and the Balkans—that they could pay but little attention to the game of diplomacy that was being played in the capital.[2] Only once, on November 24, 1814, did even the *Österreich- ische Beobachter* break its silence and carry a fairly long article on the political activities of the Congress. And then, " as if ashamed of its talkativeness," the paper explained that the article had been copied from a provincial newssheet. An ironic fate, however, made the article appear in this pro- vincial paper on the day following its printing in the *Beobachter*.[3]

(Leipzig, 1855), vol. i, p. 175. According to another historian " the government forbade its subjects any thought of public interest, but allowed them to amuse themselves freely. Vienna acquired the reputation of a capital given over to amusements." *Cf.* Seignobos, Chas., *A Politi- cal History of Europe since 1814* (New York, 1899), p. 406.

[1] Kralick, *op. cit.*, p. 377.

[2] Salzburg asked for free corn and a suspension of tax payments. The Tyrol clamored for its old constitution and strove to convince Francis that the province was much more valuable strategically than financially. Springer, *op. cit.*, vol. i, pp. 257 *et seq.*

[3] *Ibid.*, vol. i, p. 255.

Under these circumstances nothing better than the Federal Act of June 8, 1815,[1] could be expected from the Congress. The Act provided for a loosely-organized Germanic Confederation made up of the thirty-eight German states that still remained, and for a Federal Diet consisting of delegates chosen by the rulers of the respective member states. This Diet was to be presided over by Austria. Further, members were forbidden to enter into alliance with a foreign power if the alliance were aimed either at the Confederation as a whole or against another member. But aside from this each state was practically sovereign—free to have its own tariffs, its own coinage, its own army. There were no means of enforcing the decrees of the Diet. There was no Confederation flag, and no Confederation army. There was no German fatherland! Moreover, by the terms of the Final Act of the Congress, as signed on June 9, Francis was confirmed in his possession of new, large areas in the Italian peninsula as compensation for the release of the Belgian Netherlands to Holland. Thus Austria bequeathed to Prussia the task of defending the Germanies against France, while she herself turned her gaze in the direction of Italy and the Balkans.

And the Germans in Austria accepted the decisions of the Congress without ado. Their leaders had spoken. The people were weary of war. They were weary of agitation. They were busy reconstructing the damages of the Napoleonic wars. Their enthusiasm had reached a climax and was now rapidly approaching an apathetic nadir. Francis and Metternich were triumphant and Austria's secret police entered upon an era of unprecedented activity. Lord Russell, who traveled through Austria several years later, was amazed at the " political atrophy, indifference and ignorance " of the people.[2] The very people who a few years earlier were ready

[1] Klüber, *op. cit.*, vol. ii, p. 598.

[2] Quoted in Gervinus, *op. cit.*, vol. i, p. 442.

to lay down their lives that the cause of the German nation might triumph, now were utterly indifferent to the fate of their fellow-Germans across the Austrian border. Evident as German nationalism had been in Austria in the period from 1806 to 1814, it appeared to have been driven into hiding in 1815. One might have thought that Metternich was correct when he wrote that " German spirit " was a mythical expression so far as the Austrians were concerned.[1] But, as events proved, Metternich was wrong. The " German spirit " was not mythical. It was only dormant. And it reawakened before many years passed by.

[1] Quoted in Bibl, *op. cit.*, vol. i, p. 163. It may be noted here that an excellent description of the German Nationalist movement in Austria since 1848 is to be found in Molisch, P., *Geschichte der deutschnationalen Bewegung in Österreich* (Jena, 1926).

APPENDIX

Original German Versions of some of the Poems or Songs Referred to in the Text

(To page 68 of text)

Friedrich Schlegel
Gelübde
Zu Anfang des Jahres 1809

Es sey mein Herz und Blut geweiht,
Dich Vaterland zu retten.
Wohlan, es gilt, du seyst befreit,
Wir sprengen deine Ketten!
Nicht fürder soll die arge That,
Des Fremdlings Übermut, Verrat
In deinem Schooss sich betten.

Wer hält, wem frey das Herz noch schlägt,
Nicht fest an deinem Bilde?
Wie kraftvoll die Natur sich regt
Durch deine Waldgefilde,
So blüht der Fleiss, dem Neid zur Qual
In deinen Städten sonder Zahl
Und jeder Kunst Gebilde.

Der deutsche Stamm ist alt und stark,
Voll Hochgefühl und Glauben;
Die Treue ist der Ehre Mark,
Wankt nicht, wenn Stürme schnauben.
Es schafft ein ernster, tiefer Sinn
Dem Herzen solchen Hochgewinn,
Den uns kein Feind mag rauben.

So spotte jeder der Gefahr,
Die Freyheit ruft uns allen;
So will's das Recht, und es bleibt wahr,
Wie auch die Lose fallen.
Ja, sinken wir der Übermacht,
So woll'n wir doch zur Todes Nacht
Glorreich hinüber wallen.

[In Schlegel, F. von, *Gedichte* (Berlin, 1809), pp. 387 *et seq.*]

(To page 74 of text)

HEINRICH JOSEPH VON COLLIN
ÖSTREICH ÜBER ALLES
1809

Wenn es nur will,
Ist immer Östreich über Alles!
Wehrmänner ruft nun frohen Schalles:
Es will, es will!
Hoch Österreich!

Weil es nur will,
Seid stolz und sicher, Östreichs Bürger!
Ha was vermag der fremde Würger,
Wenn Östreich will?
Hoch Österreich!

Wenn es nur will,
Ist Östreich stark sich selbst zu retten,
Und lacht der angedrohten Ketten.
Es will, es will,
Hoch Österreich!

Weil Östreich will,
Ward unser Bund von Franz beschlossen.
Gesagt, getan! Er ist geschlossen.
Fragt noch, ob's will?
Hoch Österreich!

Und wie es will,
Soll unser Wehrbund siegend zeigen,
Wenn sich vor ihm die Feinde beugen.
Es will, es will,
Hoch Österreich!

Und weil es will,
Ruft Rudolph aus des Himmels Höhen
Zu Franz herab: es wird bestehen,
Weil Östreich will,
Hoch Österreich!

Und weil es will,
Belohnet Gott sein edles Streben
Und wird es höher, höher heben.
Es will, es will,
Hoch Österreich!

[In Collin, H. J. von, *Lieder österreichischer Wehrmänner*
(Vienna, 1809), pp. 28 *et seq.*]

(*To page 105 of text*)
ANONYMOUS
AUFSTEHEN ZUM FREYHEITSKAMPFE!
IM MÄRZ 1809

Lang' Unberührte! Staubhingegebene!
Zur Hand! O Leyer! Stimme zur Höhe dich,
  Die nur der Jubel übertreffe,
Welcher den fröhlichen Sieg verkündet!

Schon flieht der Kummer, der mir das Herz zerfrass,
Und Hochgefühle flammen im Busen nun!
  Aufs Neue streben der Begeistrung
Mächtige Fittig' empor zur Sonne.

Aufstehen sah ich mutvoll mein Vaterland,
Aufsteh'n zum Kampfe, welcher für Freyheit gilt!
  Ha! Kampf für Weib und Kind und Selbstthum!
Werth, dass des Edelsten Herzblut ströme!

Werth des Gesanges! Heiliger, schöner Kampf!
Für eig'ne Sitte! Eigenen Herrscherstamm!
 Für unsre Sprache! Ha! die hohe,
Die in den Feind stürzt in Donnerwetter!

Nie bog der Deutsche feig sich dem fremden Joch',
Er ist ein Löwe, zornig entflammter Kraft,
 Warf fremde List ihm an den Nacken,
Bis er sie sprengte, die Sklavenkette.

Du hast's gefühlet, Allesbeherrscherinn!
Du hast's gefühlet, Roma! dein Schutt bezahlt
 Dem Deutschen noch die Sklavenjahre,
Die du ihm aufzwangst nur durch Entzweyung.

Hör't! Deutsche! Höret! Nur durch Entzweyung ward
Das Schnöde Werk einst; nicht durch der Männer Kraft!
 Senkt tief in eure Brust die Lehre!
Nur durch Entzweyung besiegte Rom uns!

Gezittert hat die Allesbesiegerinn,
Als an der Weser Hermann, als Marawod
 Am Ister hier die deutschen Stämme
Gegen die freche Tyranninn einte.

Und soll ein Römling, welcher die Römer äfft—
In ihren Lastern, aber an Tugend nicht,
 Mit feinverschlung'nen wälschen Ränken
Wieder umnetzen die deutsche Manneskraft?

Ach! Schande! Schande! Flavier gibt es nun
Wie in den Tagen Hermanns! Es gibt, die um
 Ein Handbreit Land des deutschen Namens,
Deutscher Verbrüderung froh vergessen!

Ein Handbreit Landes! Deutschen entrissen nur!
Auf Zeit gelehnet! Und mit der Schande Pflicht,
 Wohin der stolze Imperator
Winket, zu senden zum Tod die Söhne!

Traut nur ihr Schwachen! Traut dem Verrätherwort!
Auch Rom gab willig Fremden den Freundeskuss,
  Um ihrer Freunde schöne Reiche
Leicht zu ererben, statt zu erobern.

Wo ist die Stadt des Bundes? der Bundesrath?
Wann spricht von Deutschlands Wohle der Rednerstuhl?
  Dekrete von Paris befehlen,
Wie er sich füge, der deutsche Lehnsmann.

Schon schlichten fremde Tafeln den deutschen Streit;
Schon tönt die fremde Sprach' in der deutschen Burg,—
  Auf deutscher Bühne, die geschliff'ne,
Gleisende, Gift zu versüssen, fertig.

Ha! Deutscher! Deutscher! Du nur bewahretest
Der Väter Sprache zwanzig Jahrhunderte!
  Es klingt um dich, bei deinem Nachbar
Noch in der Sprache des Römers Fessel.

Doch kochend rollet Deutschen das edle Blut.
Der Ärger naget wüthig am fremden Zaum;
  Bald bricht er los zum Freyheitskampfe,
Was auch die schwächlichen Fürsten rathen;

Voran wallt Östreichs Fahne; voran im Kampf!
Die Stärke hält sie; Klugheit ist Führerinn.
  Wo ist der Deutsche, der nicht muthig
Zu den bekannten Panieren träte?

Doch euch besing' ich, Taurische, Heldenvolk!
Fest, wie die Felsen, die ihr bewohnet! Euch!
  Ihr Noriker! Ihr! deren Eisen
Einstens der listige Cäsar zagte!

Und die ihr fertig euch in die Reiterschlacht
Mit Schwertern menget! Euch! Ihr Pannonier!
  Und Euch! Ihr Bojer! Deren Rache
Rom nur durch List sich kaum entwandte!

Und Euch: Ihr raschen Söhne der Heruler!
Der Väter würdig, denn nicht vergessen ist's!
  Die ersten waren sie der Deutschen,
  Die der Tyrannen Verbrechen rächten.

Euch nenn't mein Päan! Und die Unsterblichkeit
Empfängt die Namen! Völker voll deutschen Sinns!
  Denn aufstehn sah ich Euch voll Ingrimms
  Und die geheiligte Wehr ergreifen,

Zu rächen eure Brüder am neuen Rom,
Das Netz zu reissen, das es für euch gewebt,
  Für Weib und Kind, für deutsche Freyheit
  Und für die Herrscher sie stolz zu schwingen.

Er wag's, der kühne Cäsar von Gallien,
Wag's, Euch zu stehen! ha! die zerhauenen
  Cohorten seiner Heer' am Tagus
  Zeugen, wie Völker für Freyheit streiten.

[Broadside (Vienna, 1809)].

(*To page 106 of text*)
ANONYMOUS
AN MEINE DEUTSCHEN BRÜDER!
VON EINEM RITTERLICH-BÜRGERLICHEN SCHARFSCHÜTZEN
AUS DER 8TEN COMPAGNIE
1809

  Soll Hermanns hoher Stamm vermodern?
    Teutoniens Name untergehn?—
  Brecht auf! des Krieges Fackeln lodern,
    Lasst uns mit Muth den Kampf bestehn!

  Für Deutschlands Freyheit kühn gefochten,
    Ihr deutschen Brüder zückt das Schwert!
  Befreyt von Schmach die Unterjochten,
    Durch fremde Tyranney entehrt.

Wollt ihr noch länger knechtisch tragen
  Das eh'rne Joch der Sklaverey?
Durch Heldenthaten—nicht durch Klagen,
  Wird der verhöhnte Sklave frey.

Kein Freygeborner soll erliegen,
  Den Unterjochungs Wuth bezwang;
Drum sei, zu sterben oder siegen
  Der deutschen Völker Schlachtgesang!

Ihr Väter! sagt dem deutschen Sohne,
  Das mächtig war sein Vaterland.—
Ein Fremdling raubt' die Kaiserkrone,
  Und Deutschlands Ruhm und Grösse schwand!

Die ihr noch ehrt der Fürsten Ahnen,
  Weil ihr aus deutschem Blute stammt,
Auf! eilt zu Östreichs tapfern Fahnen,
  Wo deutsches Recht den Muth entflammt.

Die Adler fremder Legionen
  Verwüsten frech das deutsche Reich;
Um fremde Krieger zu belohnen,
  Erpresst der Rheinbeschützer euch!

Zerreisset kühn die Sklavenketten!
  Bald nahet die Entscheidungsschlacht:
Der Doppeladler wird euch retten,
  Euch bietet Östreich Schutz und Macht.

Ein zweiter Hermann geht zum Streite,
  Den Gott für Deutschlands Rettung schuf,
Ein Held, der nie Gefahren scheute:
  Ihr Völker! Folget seinem Ruf!

Auf! lasst uns schnell und muthig eilen,
  In fest geschloss'nen Bundes Reih'n,
Der deutschen Länder Wunden heilen,
  Den Unterdrückten Retter sein!

Der Knechtschaft nicht sich hingegeben!—
Uns treffe nicht der Enkel Fluch!
Als Deutsche lasst uns ewig leben,
   In der Geschichte Richter-Buch!

Drum fasset! Brüder, rasch die Waffen
   Mit Selbstgefühl und fester Hand,
Den süssen Frieden uns zu schaffen
   Für Franz und deutsches Vaterland!

Der Deutsche, müde sich zu schmiegen
   In fremder Fesseln hartem Zwang,
Will sterben oder rühmlich siegen;
   Das sey des Bundes Schlachtgesang!

[Broadside (n. p., 1809)].

(*To page 106 of text*)

MATTHIAS LEOPOLD SCHLEIFER
DIE STIMME AUS DER WÜSTE
MÄRZ 1809

Niebesiegter! Deine Stunde naht,
Die verhängnissvollen Würfel fliegen,
Unglück dräuend rollt des Schicksals Rad!
Soll auch jetzt dein böser Dämon siegen?
Muss die Welt sich in die Fesseln schmiegen,
Die ihr deine Wuth bereitet hat?
Menschheit zittre! Donner zieh'n heran;
Siegt sein Dämon, ist's um dich gethan.

Und Europa wird ein Sklavenland,
Wird verdammt zu schweigen und zu zittern,
Und die Freiheit wird hinaus verbannt;
Muth der Wahrheit wird von Hochgebietern
Fest geschmiedet hinter eh'rnen Gittern;
Erst das Weltmeer wird die Scheidewand,
Wo der Britten Schutzgeist donnernd spricht:
"Bis hieher, Tyrann! und weiter nicht!"

Und es harret Deutschlands Männerschaar,
Bis der neue Cäsar naht und fodert:
"Kommt und streckt dem Joch die Hälse dar!"
Und was unsrer Ahnherrn Brust durchlodert
Wäre ganz erloschen? ganz vermodert?
All ihr Muth und Mannstrotz in Gefahr?
Ganz gewichen wäre Hermanns Geist?
Rettungslos Germania verwaist?

Nein, du Liebe für das Vaterland!
Noch erlosch es nicht, dein göttlich Feuer;
In der Brust, wo es sein Schirmdach fand,
In der Brust der Vaterlandsbefreier
Flammt es und zerreisst den dumpfen Schleier,
Den der Kleingeist um die Menschheit wand;
Glorreich durch die Nebeln bricht sein Glanz,
Über'n Sternen strahlt des Siegers Kranz!

Auf dann! wer die Milch der Freiheit sog!
Auf! wen keiner Sklavin Schooss geboren;
Wen Natur nicht zum Bastard betrog;
Wer für deutsche Treue nicht verloren;
Wer nicht feig dem Fremdling sich verschworen,
Nie das Knie vor seinem Machtwort bog,—
Auf! und lehrt ihn, dass die Menschheit frei
Und kein Spielzeug für Tyrannen sei!

Auf! und kündigt ihm's in Donnern an—
Mild're Stimmen dürft' er überhören,—
Schreibt mit Blut—das liebt er—nimmer kann
Seine Sultanslaun' ein Volk zerstören,
Dessen Männer, treu umschlungen, schwören,
Frei zu sterben trotz dem Gengis-Chan!
Ist der Römer nicht von unserm Schwert,
Nicht der Hunne blutend heimgekehrt?

Schliesst euch dann zusammen Herz an Herz,
Männer Deutschlands! unsre Waffen tönen,
Unsre Banner flattern himmelwärts;
Lächelnd harrt der Sieg, um sie zu krönen;
Nimmer darf uns der Barbar verhöhnen,
Wenn wir kämpfend steh'n—ein Wall von Erz!
Deutschland, blick auf uns! nein, eher nicht
Sollst du fallen, bis der Erdball bricht!

[In Poetische Versuche von Matthias Leopold Schleifer
(Vienna, 1830), pp. 147 et seq.]

(*To page 107 of text*)

JOHANN GUSTAV FELLINGER

MARSCH FÜR DIE STEIERMÄRKISCHE LANDWEHR

1808

Auf, Brüder! auf, die Fahnen wehen!
Versammelt euch zum Waffenspiel!
Einst wollen wir wie Männer stehen,
Wie Deutsche steh'n im Schlachtgewühl!
Reiht euch in kampfgeübte Schaaren,
Nur Übung bildet uns zum Krieg,
Und einst in drohenden Gefahren
Ist unser, unser stets der Sieg.

Im Schutz der Waffen blüh'n die Saaten,
Den langen Frieden stört kein Feind,
Wo sich die volle Kraft der Staaten
Zu einem hohen Zweck vereint;
Der Bürger tritt dem Krieger näher,
Der ihn als Schlachtgenossen ehrt,
Und jeder Busen hebt sich höher,
Denn jedes Herz fühlt seinen Wert.

Des Herrschers gütiges Vertrauen
Macht uns des Tages Mühen leicht,
Wir scheuen nicht des Wetters Grauen,
Das an den fernen Grenzen schleicht,

Wir fürchten keines Feindes Rache,
Und trotzen kühn dem Wetterstrahl,
Gerecht, gerecht ist unsre Sache,
Und unser Gott ist überall.

Voran dem Brüderheere glänzet
Ein junger, allgeliebter Held,
Den treuer Völker Liebe kränzet
Und seiner Ahnen Geist beseelt;
Prinz Johann führt des Landes Söhne
Herbei zum Waffentanz, herbei!
Und Franz' und Johanns Name töne
In unser lautes Feldgeschrei!

Auf, ordnet euch zur Fahnenweihe!
Schwingt hoch die Wehr' in starker Hand,
Und schwöret echte Bürgertreue
Dem Kaiser und dem Vaterland!
Wenn einst des Krieges Schrecken dräuen,
Dann schliesse fest sich Mann an Mann,
Dann wollen wir den Schwur erneuen,
Und muthig geh'n die Ehrenbahn!

Wir schlagen ja für Franzens Rechte,
Für Weib und Kind und eig'nen Herd!
Dem Guten stählet im Gefechte
Sein Selbtbewusstsein schon das **Schwert.**
Und soll ein Bruder kämpfend sinken,
Wohl ihm! er stirbt in edlem Streit,
Und seine Heldenväter winken
Ihn segnend zur Unsterblichkeit.

[Quoted in *Achtzehnhundertneun*, pp. 30-31].

(To page 108 of text)

JOSEPH FRIDOLIN LEHNE
LIED EINES DEUTSCHEN MANNES
1809

(stanzas 1 and 2)

Gottlob, dass frey ich singen kann,
Wohl mir, ich bin ein deutscher Mann!
Was auch verfluchtes sie geseh'n,
Was ihr auch Böses ist gescheh'n,
Ich bleibe meiner Heimath Freund,
Worin das Herz es herzlich meint;
Willkommen wer da sagen kann,
Wohl mir, ich bin ein deutscher Mann.

Nicht störet mir der Herrschsucht Knecht
Mein Hochgefühl, mein Menschenrecht;
Kein fremder König hudelt mich,
Und tränkt von meinem Schweisse sich;
Das freye, deutsche Völkerreich
Erlieget keinem Sklavenstreich;
Willkommen, wer es sagen kann,
Wohl mir, ich bin ein deutscher Mann.

[Dated 1809 in Lehne, J. F., *Gedichte* (Vienna, 1817), vol. i, pp. 92-94.]

(To page 110 of text)

JOACHIM PERINET
WIR KENNEN DICH
EINE VOLKSSTIMME AUS TAUSENDEN AN SE.K.HOHEIT DEN
ERZHERZOG KARL ALS GENERALISSIMUS DER K.K.ARMEE
1809

" Ihr kennt mich! " Ja das sind die Worte,
Die jüngst Dein Aufruf zu uns sprach,
Und ging' es an die Höllenpforte,
Wir folgten Dir mit Muthe nach.
Wer wird den grossen Tag vergessen,
Den schönen Tag, den neunten März?

Tief wurzelt er und unermessen
  In jedes Österreichers Herz.

Dies war der Tag, an dem die Wehre
  Des Landes zu den Fahnen schwor
Und sich zum Wahlspruch deutsche Ehre!
  Im Fall des Angriffs auserkohr,
Dies war der Tag, wo sich in allen
  Ein Will', ein Sinn, ein Herz verband
Und jedem ohne Zwanges Qualen
  Nur Franz und Karl im Herzen stand.

Kein Feind, wer er auch sei, soll dräuen,
  Wir schützen unser Vaterland,
Und jeden soll der Angriff reuen,
  O glaub' uns Karl! wir halten Stand.
Wir wissen alle, was wir sollen
  Und sehen Deine Absicht ein,
Auch Du kennst uns und weisst, wir wollen
  Nicht Sklaven fremder Herrscher sein.

Wir sehen Dich in unsrer Mitte
  Und Deiner Augen Heldenglanz,
Voraus nach alter deutscher Sitte
  Bringt Dir das Volk den Lorbeerkranz.
Es winken Dir von allen Seiten
  Erworbner Ruhm und neuer Sieg,
Wenn man den Frieden will verbreiten,
  Bereite man vorher den Krieg.

Ja Treue schwören wir hier Alle
  Freiwillig ohne allen Zwang:
Wer immer uns beleidigt, falle!
  Dies ist der wahre Freiheitsdrang.
Droh'n einstens Österreich Gefahren,
  Dann schwören wir Dir deutsch und warm,
Wir wollen stets Dein Wort bewahren:
  "Ich zähle dann auf Euern Arm."

Ja, zähle keck! Du sollst nicht irren,
  Es prüf' uns jede Heldenbahn.
Wir werden sicher triumphieren,
  Führt uns Dein hohes Beispiel an.
Dein Aufruf liess es uns vermelden,
  Wir prägten tief die Lehre ein:
" Patriotismus zeuget Helden,"
  " Und er verbürgt den Sieg allein."

Ihr kennt mich! Ja, ja, Karl, wir kennen
  Dein Herz wie Deinen Ruhm nun ganz,
Und unsre Kindeskinder nennen
  Mít Ehrfurcht einst noch Karl und Franz.
Wo Ehre ruft, wirst Du uns finden,
  Auch Dich trifft man dort sicherlich—
Bei Gott! Wir müssen überwinden,
  Du kennst ja uns—Wir kennen Dich!

[Broadside (Vienna, 1809).]

(To page 110 of text)
IGNAZ FRANZ CASTELLI
KRIEGSLIED FÜR DIE ÖSTERREICHISCHE ARMEE
1809

Hinaus, hinaus mit frohem Muth!
  Hinaus in's Feld der Ehre,
Damit der Feinde Übermuth
Nicht unsrer Brüder Hab' und Gut
  Und unser Land verheere!

Soldaten! lasst uns zieh'n mit Gott!
  Wohin die Fahnen winken;
Sie nicht verlassen, wenn auch Tod
Aus tausend Feuerschlünden droht,
  Wir siegen oder sinken.

Zwar sind wir nicht aus einem Land,
    Doch einer Kette Glieder;
Denn Franzens milde Vaterhand
Herrscht segnend über jedes Land,
    Und so sind wir ja Brüder.

Einst hatte auch der Römer Heer
    Die halbe Welt verschlungen,
Da traten unsre Väter her
Und stellten muthig sich zur Wehr',
    Und Roma ward bezwungen.

Noch erbte Euer Sinn sich fort,
    Ihr Väter! auf die Söhne,
Wir dulden auch kein schimpflich Wort,
Ein Schuft nur leidet es hinfort,
    Dass man uns Deutsche höhne.

Was, Feinde! Euer Stolz entwarf,
    Das sollt mit Blut ihr büssen,
Beweisen wollen wir's Euch scharf,
Dass man nicht Jahre lernen darf,
    Um auf den Feind zu schiessen.

Vom Rechtsumkehrteuch!—wollen wir
    Im Schlachtgewühl nichts wissen,
Nur vorwärts wehe das Panier,
Für diesmal wollen wir dafür
    Euch auf den Rücken schiessen.

Dem Vaterland bleibt jeder treu,
    Im Tode wie im Leben,
Und schleichet Ihr mit Gold herbey,
So wollen wir mit unserm Bley
    Euch kräftig Antwort geben.

Was Franz befiehlt, das thun wir gern,
    Und keiner wird da weilen;
Doch lassen wir,—nein, das sey fern!—
Von keinem andern fremden Herrn
    Befehle uns ertheilen.

Was Ihr uns einst in Schlachten nahmt,
　Damit müsst Ihr nicht prahlen,
Wir handeln nun das Rächeramt,
Ihr müsst uns Alles insgesammt
　Und die Intressen zahlen!

Vertraut nicht jener Völker List,
　Die sich Euch überliessen,
Denn, wie Ihr Euren Freund begrüsst,
Wenn er Euch nicht mehr nöthig ist,
　Das habt Ihr ja bewiesen.

Baut nicht auf Eure Kriegerschaar,
　Auf jene leichten Kinder,
Oft dreht das Glück sich wunderbar,
Sie laufen schnelle vorwärts zwar,
　Doch rückwärts noch geschwinder.

Ihr droht der ganzen Welt den Krieg,
　Fröhnt sie nicht Euern Winken,
Bisher bekrönt' Euch zwar der Sieg,
Doch was so schnelle aufwärts stieg,
　Pflegt schneller noch zu sinken.

Hoch lebe unser Herrscherpaar;—
　Es enden, Franz! die Leiden,
Du fühltest viele Jahre zwar
Der Krone Last nur immer dar,
　Nun fühl' auch ihre Freuden.

Es lebe Carl! der deutsche Held,
　Dem neue Lorbeern grünen,
Er führt uns selber in das Feld,
Auf Kameraden! zeigt der Welt,
　Dass wir es auch verdienen.

Ihr Lieben! reicht uns noch die Hand,
　Und weinet keine Zähre!
Ihr wollt ja nicht der Kinder Schand',
Es gilt für Fürst und Vaterland,
　Für Eigenthum und Ehre.

Und nun Ihr Brüder! was auch droht,
    Hinaus, hinaus zur Rache!
Scheut keine Lasten, keine Noth,
Wir siegen, denn mit uns ist Gott
    Und die gerechte Sache.

[Broadside (Vienna, 1809).]

(*To page 164 of text*)

THEODOR KÖRNER
JÄGERLIED
1813

Frisch auf, ihr Jäger frei und flink!
    Die Büchse von der Wand!
Der Muthige bekämpft die Welt!
Frisch auf den Feind! frisch in das Feld
    Fürs deutsche Vaterland!

Aus Westen, Norden, Süd und Ost
    Treibt uns der Rache Strahl,
Vom Oderflusse, Weser, Main,
Vom Elbstrom und vom Vater Rhein
    Und aus dem Donauthal.

Doch Brüder sind wir allzusamm';
    Und das schwellt unsern Muth.
Uns knüpft der Sprache heilig Band,
Uns knüpft ein Gott, ein Vaterland,
    Ein treues deutsches Blut.

Nicht zum Erobern zogen wir
    Vom väterlichen Herd;
Die schändlichste Tyrannenmacht
Bekämpfen wir in freud'ger Schlacht.
    Das ist des Blutes werth.

Ihr aber, die uns treu geliebt,
    Der Herr sei euer Schild,
Bezahlen wir's mit unsrem Blut!
Denn Freiheit ist das höchste Gut,
    Ob's tausend Leben gilt.

Drum, muntre Jäger, frei und flink,
  Wie auch das Liebchen weint!
Gott hilft uns im gerechten Krieg!
Frisch in den Kampf!—Tod oder Sieg!
  Frisch, Brüder, auf den Feind!

[In Streckfuss, K. (ed.), *Theodor Körners sämmtliche Werke*
(Berlin, 1861), pp. 20-21.]

(To page 169 of text)

ANONYMOUS
1813

Wach' auf, Franciscus, Deine Völker rufen,
Wach' auf, erkenne des Vergelters Hand!
Noch dröhnet unter fremder Rosse Hufen
Der deutsche Boden, unser Vaterland.

Zum Kampf, so lang' auf uns'rem deutschen Boden
Noch einen Finger drückt Napoleon.
Franciscus auf! Dich binden keine Bande,
Das Vaterland hat keinen Schwiegersohn.

[Dated 1813 and quoted without title in Pfalz, A.,
Aus der Franzosenzeit II.]

(To page 173 of text)

IGNAZ FRANZ CASTELLI
WEHRMANN'S TRINKLIED
1813
(last stanza)

Es lebe jeder Deutsche hoch,
  Der für die Ehre glühet,
Der von sich schüttelt fremdes Joch,
  Das Schwert für Freiheit ziehet.
Ihm sei das erste Glas gebracht
Wenn nimmer unter fremder Macht
  Der deutsche Weinstock blühet.

Chor

Dem Deutschen sei ein Glas gebracht,
Ihm sei das erste Glas gebracht
Wenn nimmer unter fremder Macht
Der deutsche Weinstock blühet.

[Broadside (Vienna, 1813).]

(To page 180 of text)

V. R. Grüner

Der treue österreichische Unterthan bey der glücklichen Ankunft unsers gnädigsten Monarchen
zu Wien, nach dem siegreich erkämpften
Frieden im Jahre 1814
1814
(stanzas 1, 3, 4, 10 and 11)

Aus schweren Wolken, nach der Wetter Toben
Bricht himmlisch schön der Sonne Strahl hervor.
Er naht! Er naht! Der uns der Schmach enthoben,
Den Gott zum Retter Deutschlands uns erkohr;
Der nicht Gefahr und nicht Beschwerden scheute
Bis Er sein Volk vom Sklavenjoch befreyte.

Ihr Brüder Östreichs! Männer deutschen Blutes,
Ruft froh mit mir: Die neue Zeit erwacht!
Der Vater Franz, die Zier des Heldenmuthes
Hat hochbeherzt viel Opfer ihr gebracht.
O, lasst auch uns! dass wir ihm wieder gleichen,
Den alten Ruf des Biedervolks erreichen.

Verbannt des Fremdlings Lügensucht und Ränke;
Die alte Treu', der Glaube sey geehrt!
Wie sonst der deutsche Bürger dachte, denke,
Was sich auf Östreichs edlem Boden nährt:
Dann wird uns Franz als Vater froh umfangen,
Wenn wir, was Er verlanget, nur verlangen.

Nun komm' und rufe deine Waffenbrüder
Herbey, zu unserm freudenvollen Mahl;
Stimmt ein, in warme, frohe, deutsche Lieder,
Dem Vater Franz leert diesen Lustpokal;
Mit diesem Trunke werde Franzens Throne
Die sorgenfreyste Zukunft jetzt zum Lohne!

Auf Brüder! trinkt, jetzt ist die Zeit der Freude!
Nach langer Qual erschien der Tag der Lust;
Europa ist entbunden niederm Neide,
Frey schlägt das Herz in eines Deutschen Brust.
Trinkt, Brüder! trinkt! und lasst Gesang erschallen,
Auf deren Wohl, die Franzen wohl gefallen.

[Broadside (Vienna, 1814).]

(*To page 181 of text*)

LEONHARD VON ROTHKIRCH UND PANTHEN

GERMANIA

1814

(2 stanzas out of 27)

Jetzt können wir uns deine Söhne nennen,
Jetzt kann von dir kein Machtgebot uns trennen,
    Der *Seine* dient nicht mehr der alte Rhein;
Wir haben uns in uns'rer Kraft erhoben,
Der Schreckkoloss aus Westen ist verstoben,
    Nichts wiedersteht des deutschen Volks Verein.

Lasst denn der schönen Zukunft uns erfreuen,
Und in der Brust den Entschluss stets erneuen,
    Zu lösen nie der Eintracht segnend Band.
Wo kraftvoll frei erklingen deutsche Töne,
Sind Brüder, sind Thuiskon's edle Söhne,
    Germania ist aller Vaterland.

[Dated 1814 in Rothkirch und Panthen, L. von, *Gedichte*
(Vienna, 1848), p. 162.]

(To page 184 of text)

CAROLINE PICHLER
1815

Lautlos und ruhig haben wir geschlafen,
Dreihundert Jahr' in unsrer Ahnen Gruft,
Als plötzlich Fackelschein und Glanz der Waffen,
Und Cymbelnklang uns aus dem Schlummer ruft.
Die Neugier treibt uns an uns aufzuraffen,
Uns umzuschauen in der freien Luft.
Da sehn wir wundernd fürstliche Gestalten
Ein Ritterspiel nach unsrer Weise halten.

. . . .
. . . .

O holde Tracht! Bild guter, frommer Zeiten!
Wir grüssen dich mit freudigem Gefühl!
Ein schön'res Dasein kann sich jetzt bereiten,
Wir hoffen schon von deinem Anblick viel.
Doch siegreich musst du erst ins Leben schreiten
Nicht dienend bloss zu Mummerei und Spiel.
Die Deutsche muss im deutschen Kleide prangen,
Nicht mehr vom Ausland das Gesetz empfangen.
Das sollen unsre Fürstinnen uns geben,
Mit hohem Sinn für deutschen Frauenstand.
Sie, die als Vorbild längst schon vor uns schweben,
Geliebt, verehrt in dem beglückten Land.
Nicht Modethorheit nur ist unser Streben,
Mit mancher stillen Tugend ist's verwandt.
Es kehrt ein bess'rer Geist und fromm're Sitte
Vielleicht mit dieser Tracht in uns're Mitte.

[In Pichler, C., *Denkwürdigkeiten* (Vienna, 1844), vol. iii, pp. 51-52.]

(To page 184 of text)

ANDREAS POSCH

SEHNSUCHT EINES DEUTSCHEN NACH SEINEM VATERLAND

1815 (?)

Mich trennen Flüsse, See und Lande
Von dir, du heimatliche Flur;
Wie herrlich prangt an jedem Strande
Mir manche Schönheit der Natur.
Wie labend mildern dort die Weste
Des Erntemondes Sonnengluth.
Als Zeuge spricht so manche Veste
Von Völkerkraft und Heldenmuth.
Die Treue herrscht in diesen Zonen,
Der Biedersinn der Redlichkeit;
In Hütten und Palästen wohnen
Huld, Freundschaft und Gerechtigkeit.
Germania, du Völkerzierde,
Dich sieht Europa segnend an;
Du Aufenthalt der Menschenwürde,
Du Eden für den Biedersinn,
Dich nennen alle Erdenkreise
Der Wahrheit echtes Vaterland.
Statt Eiden gilt nach deiner Weise
Ein ernstes Wort, ein Druck der Hand.
Erhab'ner Wohnsitz meiner Brüder,
Du Pflanzstadt alter Redlichkeit,
In deinem Innern glänzt mir wieder
Glück, Ruhe und Zufriedenheit.
Gelobt sey an den Deutschen allen
Das ernste Wort, der Druck der Hand;
Mein Ruf soll hin durch Länder schallen,
Gesegnet sey mein Vaterland!
Dahin will ich nun wiederkehren;
Nicht Schätze, nicht ein Fürstenglück,
Kein Zwischenraum von tausend Meeren
Bringt mich von meinem Wunsch zurück.

[In Posch, A., *Gedichte und Lebensgeschichte* (Vienna, 1821), pp. 116-117.]

BIBLIOGRAPHY

This essay has been based upon manuscript archival materials, upon printed matter published in Austria, chiefly Vienna, during the decade from 1806 to 1815, and upon some general secondary works. The appended bibliographical lists include all of the archival sources used, but only a representative selection of contemporary newspapers, pamphlets, proclamations, poems and other materials of a similar nature. Practically all of the cited source materials are located in one or another of the following depositories: the Archives of the French Foreign Office in Paris, the *Wiener Staats-Archiv*, the Austrian *Nationalbibliothek* in Vienna, the *Wiener Stadtbibliothek*, and the library of the University of Vienna. The list of secondary works includes such books as were useful in furnishing the historical setting, discussing the philosophy of nationalism, or tracing the development of German nationalism in non-Austrian areas.

ARCHIVAL MATERIALS

Archives du Ministère des Affaires Etrangères, Autriche, Correspondance Politique, Vienne, 1806-1813, vols. 378-396, and *Supplément*, vols. 27-30 (1804-1818).

Publicationen aus den k. Preussischen Staatsarchiven, vol. vi: *Geschichte der Preussischen Politik 1807 bis 1815*, part i, 1807-1808 (Leipzig, 1881).

Wiener Staats-Archiv, Correspondenz des Grafen Ph. von Stadion 1807-1808.

> *Corresp. Gr. Ph. von Stadion 1801-1814.*
>
> *Dépôt Stadion, Acta des Herrn Grafen Friedrich von Stadion in Staats- Kriegs- und anderswärtigen Angelegenheiten aus den Jahren 1800-1810.*
>
> *Kabinets Akten, 1806-1815.*
>
> *Kaiser Franz Acten, 1806-1815.*
>
> *Polizei Corresp. Noten an die Polizei Hofstelle,* Faszikel 2: 1807-1810; Faszikel 3: 1811-1812; Faszikel 4: 1813-1815.
>
> *Staatskanzlei Korrespondenz, 1806-1815.*
>
> *Staatskanzlei Vorträge, 1806-1815,* especially 1809-1813, Faszikel 268-286.

CONTEMPORARY NEWSPAPERS AND PERIODICALS

Annalen der Literatur und Kunst des In- und Auslandes (Vienna, 1810).

Archiv für Geographie, Historie, Staats- und Kriegskunst (Vienna, 1810-1815).

Archiv für Geschichte, Statistik, Literatur und Kunst, edited by J. von Hormayr (Vienna, 1809-1815).

Briefe des jungen Eipeldauers an seinen Herrn Vettern in Kakran (Vienna, 1809-1813).

Briefe des neu angekommenen Eipeldauers an seinen Herrn Vettern in Kakran (Vienna, 1813-1815).

Der Österreichische Beobachter (Vienna, 1810-1815).

Der Sammler (Vienna, 1806-1815).

Lebens-Accorde, Zeitschrift von Freyherrn von Putlitz (Vienna, 1808).

Thalia (Vienna, 1814-1815).

Vaterländische Blätter für den österreichischen Kaiserstaat (Vienna, 1808-1815).

Wiener allgemeine Literaturzeitung (Vienna, 1814-1815).

Wiener Zeitung (Vienna, 1806-1815).

PAMPHLETS, POEMS, PROCLAMATIONS AND OTHER PRINTED MATTER SERVING AS ILLUSTRATIVE SOURCE MATERIAL

A. B., *Epilog des Jahres 1813. Deklamiert im k. k. Hoftheater nebst der Burg, von Herrn Korn, k. k. Hofschauspieler* (Vienna, 1814).

An Deutschland (Vienna, 1809).

An Erzherzog Carl zu seiner Ankunft bey der Armee. Von einem Grenadier (Vienna, 1809).

An meine deutschen Brüder! Von einem ritterlich-bürgerlichen Scharfschützen aus der 8ten Compagnie (n. p., 1809).

An mein theures Vaterland. Ein Acrostichon für den gegenwärtigen Zeitpunkt (Vienna, 1813).

An Vater Franz. Ein Gelegenheitsgedicht (Vienna, 1814).

Armbruster, J. M., *Wer ist ein österreichischer Patriot im Geist und in der Wahrheit? Im August 1813* (Vienna?, 1813).

Armee Befehl (Vienna, April 6, 1809).

Armee Befehl (Dotis, October 24, 1809).

Aufruf an die Baiern (Vienna?, 1809).

Aufruf zum Kampf für die tapferen Krieger der hohen verbündeten Mächte (Vienna, 1815).

Aufstehen zum Freyheitskampfe (Vienna, March 1809).

Bäuerle, A., *Spanien und Tirol tragen keine fremden Fesseln* (Vienna, 1809).

Bemerkungen eines österreichischen Patrioten über verschiedene in fremde Zeitungen eingerückte Artikel (Vienna?, 1809).

(Berchtold), *Beiträge zur Veredlung des österreichischen Landwehr-Mannes. Von einem Patrioten.* (Vienna, 1809).

Bergenstamm, A. G. von, *Denkmahl rühmlich erfüllter Bürgerpflichten in der Geschichte der Bürger und Einwohner Wiens,* 2 vols. (Vienna, 1806).

——, *Materialien zur Geschichte der österreichischen Landesvertheidigung, insbesondere der Landwehre, bis auf die neuesten Zeiten. Für den Patrioten und Geschichtsforscher* (Vienna, 1809).

Bleibtreu, L., *Das Acrostichon des allgemeinen Friedens im Jahre 1814* (Vienna?, 1814).

Castelli, I. F., *Ein Wort zu rechter Zeit eines Österreichers an seine verzagten Mitbürger* (Vienna, 1813).

——, *Kriegslied für die österreichische Armee* (Vienna, 1809).

——, *Volksstimme* (Vienna, 1809).

——, *Wehrmann's Trinklied* (Vienna, 1813).

(Chasteler, J. G. von), *Brave Tyroler, theure Waffenbrüder!* (April 18, 1809).

Collin, H. J. von, *Gedichte* (Vienna, 1812).

——, *Lieder österreichischer Wehrmänner* (Vienna, 1809).

——, *Sämmtliche Werke,* 6 vols. (Vienna, 1812-1814).

Das bedrängte und befreite Österreich im Jahre 1809 (Vienna, 1809).

Der deutsche Geist. Ausgesprochen von Florian Pichlern, einem Sohne Österreichs (Vienna, 1813).

Die Sehnsucht der Wiener Bürger nach dem Einzug ihres Kaisers. Ausgesprochen von Friedrich Reil, k. k. Hofschauspieler (Vienna, 1814).

Die treuen Männer der Landwehre Ihrem guten Kaiser zur Fahnenweihe. Von einem Gemeinen bey des sechsten Bataillons sechster Compagnie (Vienna, 1809).

Feichtinger, J., *Gelegenheitsgedichte* (1808).

Fellinger, J. G., *Heeresruf der Steyermärkischen Landwehr* (Grätz, 1809).

——, *Marsch für die Steyermärkische Landwehr* (Grätz, 1808).

Fierlinger, F., *Der Retter Germaniens, eine Ode in 18 Strophen* (Vienna, 1814).

Flugschriften: Österreich, Karton 2: 1700-1808; Karton 3: 1809-1847; in Österreichische Nationalbibliothek, Vienna.

Freimüthige Gedanken einiger Österreichischer Patrioten über den wahren und falschen Patriotismus (Vienna, 1813).

Gaheis, F. de P., *Denkwürdigkeiten Wiens während des Krieges zwischen Österreich und Frankreich im Jahre 1805* (Vienna, 1808).

——, *Hochgesang auf die Vermählung Seiner k. k. Apost. Majestät Franciscus des I. mit Ihrer königl. Hoheit Maria Ludovica Beatrix* (Vienna, 1808).

Genersich, J., *Geschichte der österreichischen Monarchie von ihren Ursprüngen bis zum Ende des Wiener Friedenscongresses*, 8 vols. (Vienna, 1810 and 1815).

Gentz, F. von, *An die deutschen Fürsten. Und an die Deutschen* (1812).

Germanien, oder Miszellen und Denkwürdigkeiten für das wiederbefreyte Deutschland, 3 booklets (Vienna, 1814).

Geusau, A. von, *Geschichte der Haupt- und Residenzstadt Wien in Österreich*, 6 parts (Vienna, 1810).

——, *Historisches Taschenbuch aller merkwürdigen Begebenheiten welche sich ... in Wien in dem Jahre 1809 zugetragen haben* (Vienna, 1810).

Gleich, J. A., *Untertanenliebe* (Vienna, 1809).

Grillparzer, F., *Briefe und Tagebücher*, edited by K. Glossy and A. Sauer, 2 vols. (Stuttgart and Berlin, 1903).

——, *Werke*, edited by J. Minor (Stuttgart and Leipzig, 1903). In this especially his *Alfred der Grosse*, a fragment written in 1810.

Grüner, V. R., *Der treue Österreichische Unterthan bey der glücklichen Ankunft unsers gnädigsten Monarchen zu Wien, nach dem siegreich erkämpften Frieden im Jahre 1814* (Vienna, 1814).

Gundelfinger, G. A., *Lagergespräch der österreichischen Krieger* (Vienna, 1809).

Hormayr, J. von, *Österreichischer Plutarch*, 20 vols. (Vienna, 1807-1814).

Jenull, J. von, *Wer soll im gegenwärtigen Kriege sich dem Soldatenstand widmen?* (Vienna, 1814).

Kumar, J. A., *Versuch einer vaterländischen Geschichte Ottokar VI., ersten Herzogs von Steyermark* (Graz, 1808).

Kurz, F., *Geschichte der Landwehre in Österreich ob der Enns*, 2 parts (Linz, 1811).

Landwehr Patent (Vienna, June 9, 1809).

Lehne, J. F., *An Bonaparte* (Vienna, 1809).

——, *An den grossen Herrn* (Vienna, 1809).

——, *Gedichte* (Vienna, 1817).

——, *Lied eines deutchen Mannes* (Vienna, 1809).

(Lêhmann), *Aufruf an Österreichs Völker* (Vienna, 1809).

Lied der Landwehrmänner, für den Marsch (Vienna, 1809).

-lsk-, *An Frankreichs Heer: Von einem Österreicher* (Vienna, 1809).

Müller, J. von, *Sämmtliche Werke*, 40 vols. in 14 (Stuttgart, 1831-1835).

Österreich im Jahre 1809 (Germanien, 1809?).

Patriotische Gesänge, den wackeren Streitern Österreichs geweiht von einem Mitgliede der k. k. Armee (Vienna, 1809).

Perinet, J., *Wir kennen Dich*, second edition (Vienna, 1809).

Pezzl, J., *Neue Skizze von Wien*, 3 vols. (Vienna, 1805 and 1812).

Pichler, C., *Germanicus* (Vienna, 1813).

——, *Kaiser Ferdinand der Zweyte* (Vienna, 1809).

——, *Sämmtliche Werke*, 45 vols. (Vienna, 1813).

——, "Über den Volksausdruck in unserer Sprache: Ein ganzer Mann", in *Vaterländische Blätter für den österreichischen Kaiserstaat* (Vienna, April 1809).

——, "Über die Bildung des weiblichen *Geschlechts*", in *Vaterländische Blätter* (Vienna, January 10, 1810).

Posch, A., *Gedichte und Lebensgeschichte des Naturdichters Andreas Posch* (Vienna, 1821).

Reissig, C. L., "Kriegslied", in *Blümchen der Einsamkeit von Christian Ludwig Reissig* (Vienna, 1809).

Rohrer, J., *Versuch über die deutschen Bewohner der österreichischen Monarchie*, 2 yols. (Vienna, 1804).

Rothkirch und Panthen, L. von, *Gedichte* (Vienna, 1848).

Rückblick auf das denkwürdige Jahr 1813 (Vienna, 1814?).

Sammlung der Aktenstücke über die spanische Thronveränderung, 4 parts, 2 vols. (Germanien [Vienna], 1809).

Sannens, F. K., *Aufruf an die Landwehre vor ihrem Auszuge* (Vienna, 1809).

(Schlegel?), *An die Deutschen. Aufruf eines Deutschen zum Zerbrechen drückender Fesseln* (Vienna?, 1809).

Schlegel, F. von, *Gedichte* (Berlin, 1809).

Schleifer, M. L., *Die Stimme aus der Wüste* (March 1809).

——, *Gedichte* (Vienna, 1841).

——, *Poetische Versuche* (Vienna, 1830).

Spanien noch nicht erobert (Vienna?, 1809).

Stubenrauch, E. von, *Der österreichische Bauer und sein Weib* (Vienna, 1814).

Suntinger, C. F., *Staatsgeschichte Innerösterreichs von den ältesten Zeiten bis zur Vereinigung der verschiedenen Länder unter dem Scepter des Hauses Habsburg* (Vienna, 1808).

Tagesberichte von der kaiserl. königl. Armee, Hauptquartier (1809).

Unser Volk. Ein Blick in Vergangenheit und Zukunft (Vienna, 1813?).

Versuch einiger historischen Reden über Österreich und seine Helden, von I. G. von C. (Vienna, 1809).

Völker Deutschlands (April 8, 1809).

Volkslied auf die dermahligen Verhältnisse gestimmt in Haydn's herzerhebende Melodie: Gott erhalte unsern Kaiser (Vienna, Oct. 1813).

Warum ist dem Österreicher seine Heimath theuer? Warum gibt er dafür Gut und Blut? (Vienna, 1813).

Warum wird der jetzige Krieg geführt? Von einem österreichischen Landmanne (Vienna, 1809).

Was verdankt Deutschland seit Jahrhunderten dem Hause Habsburg? (Vienna, 1813?).

Welches ist die echte und natürliche Grenze zwischen Deutschland und Frankreich? (Vienna, 1814).

Wieland, L., *Was ist gegenwärtig das Eine was Noth thut?* (Vienna, 1813).

(Ziegelhausen, G.), *Rückkehr des deutschen Helden Fürsten von Schwarzenberg an der Spitze der siegreichen Armee im Jahre 1814, nebst einem patriotischen Volksgesang von Bürgern, Österreichs Töchtern, Kriegern, Jünglingen und Mädchen* (Vienna, 1814).

Zoller, F. K., *Lied im Tiroler Dialekt nach dem Ausbruche der Insurrektion im Jahre 1809* (n. p., n. d.).

MEMOIRS, DIARIES AND CONTEMPORARY COLLECTIONS AND ACCOUNTS

Adair, R., *Historical Memoir of a Mission to the Court of Vienna 1806* (London, 1844).

Aus dem Tagebuche Erzherzog Johanns von Österreich 1810-1815, edited by F. Krones (Innsbruck, 1891).

Ausgewählte Schriften von K. A. Varnhagen von Ense, third edition, vol. ii (Leipzig, 1871).

Beobachtungen und historische Sammlung wichtiger Ereignisse aus dem Kriege zwischen Frankreich, dessen Verbündeten und Österreich im Jahre 1809, 5 vols. (Weimar, 1809).

Castelli, I. F., *Aus dem Leben eines Wiener Phäaken 1781-1862* (Stuttgart, 1912).

Correspondance de Marie Louise, 1799-1847 (Vienna, 1887).

"Erzherzog Johann's Feldzugserzählung 1809" contributed by Alois Veltzé to *Mitt. des k. k. Kriegsarchivs*, Supplement 4 (Vienna, 1909).

Friedrich Schlegel's Philosophische Vorlesungen aus den Jahren 1804 bis 1806, edited by I. C. H. Windischmann (Bonn, 1846).

Gassicourt, C. L. de, *Voyage en Autriche, en Moravie et en Bavière fait à la suite de l'armée française pendant la campagne de 1809* (Paris, 1818).

Hammer, P., *Actenstücke und Materialien zu der Geschichte des grossen Kampfes um die Freiheit Europas in den Jahren 1812 und 1813*, 4 vols. (Germanien, 1813-1814).

Hormayr, J. von, *Das Heer von Innerösterreich unter dem Befehl des Erzherzogs Johann im Kriege von 1809, von einem Stabsoffizier* (Leipzig, 1817).

Humboldt, W. von, *Gesammelte Schriften*, edited by A. Leitzmann and B. Gebhardt, 15 vols. (Berlin, 1903-1918), especially vols. x, xi and xii on *Politische Denkschriften 1802-1834*, edited by B. Gebhardt.

Lilienstern, R. von, *Reise mit der Armee im Jahre 1809*, 3 vols. (Rudolfstadt, 1810-1811).

Metternich, C. von, *Aus Metternich's nachgelassenen Papieren*, edited by R. von Metternich, 8 vols. (Vienna, 1880-1884).

Müller (?), *Interessante Beyträge zu einer Geschichte der Ereignisse in Tyrol vom 10. April bis zum 20. Februar 1810* (n. p., 1810).

Perthes, M. F. (*Praktikant im k. k. Oberst- Hof- und Landjägermeisteramte*) "Tagebuch eines Wieners", contributed by Karl Glossy to *Wiener Neujahrsalmanach* (Vienna, 1900).

Pichler, C., *Denkwürdigkeiten aus meinem Leben*, 4 vols. (Vienna, 1844).

Prokesch-Osten, A. von (ed.), *Aus dem Nachlass Friedrichs von Gentz*, vol. i (1867).

Reeve, H., *Journal of a Residence at Vienna and Berlin in the Eventful Winter of 1805-1806*, published by his son (London, 1877).

Reichardt, J. F., *Vertraute Briefe geschrieben auf einer Reise nach Wien und den Österreichischen Staaten zu Ende des Jahres 1808 und zu Anfang 1809*, vols. i and ii (Munich, 1915).

Rosenbaum, K. J. von, *Tagebuch 1797-1829*, manuscript in *Österreichische Nationalbibliothek* (Vienna).

"Steuermarkisch-Grätzerisches Tagebuch" in *Mitt. des hist. Vereins für Steiermark*, vols. 35-36 (Graz, 1887-1888).

Stutterheim, K. von, *Geschichte des Krieges 1809* (1811).

Tagebücher des Carl Friedrich Freiherrn Kübeck von Kübau, edited by his son, vol. i (Vienna, 1909).

"Tagebücher des Stiftes Klosterneuburg über die Invasionen der Franzosen in Österreich in den Jahren 1805 und 1809", contributed by Berthold Cernik to *Jahrbuch des Stiftes Klosterneuburg*, vol. ii (Klosterneuburg, 1909).

Tagebücher von Friedrich von Gentz—Aus dem Nachlass Varnhagens von Ense (Leipzig, 1861).

Thürheim, Lulu, *Mein Leben*, edited by René van Rhyn, vol. i (Munich, 1913).

Venturini, K., *Chronik des neunzehnten Jahrhunderts*, vol. vi: 1809 (Altona, 1811).

General Secondary Aids

Allgemeine Deutsche Biographie, 56 vols. (Leipzig, 1875-1912).

Archiv des Vereins für siebenbürgische Landeskunde, n. s. vol. xxii (Hermannstadt, 1890).

Arnold, R. F., "Achtzehnhundertneuner Nachlese", in *Zeitschrift für die österreichischen Gymnasien*, vol. lxiii (Vienna, 1912).

Arnold, R. F. und Wagner, K., *Achtzehnhundertneun: Die politische Lyrik des Kriegsjahres* (vol. xi of *Schriften des literarischen Vereins in Wien*), (Vienna, 1909).

Aus dem Nachlasse des Grafen Prokesch-Osten, 2 vols. (Vienna, 1881).

Bartholdy, J. L. S., *Der Krieg der Tiroler Landleute im Jahre 1809* (1814).

Batka, R., "Grillparzer und der Kampf gegen die deutsche Oper in Wien", in *Jahrbuch der Grillparzer Gesellschaft*, vol. iv (Vienna, 1894).

Beitzke, A., *Geschichte der Deutschen Freiheitskriege in den Jahren 1813 und 1814*, third edition, 3 vols. (Berlin, 1864).

Bernatzik, Ed., *Die Ausgestaltung des Nationalgefühls im 19. Jahrhundert* (Hannover, 1912).

Beurle, K., *Beiträge zur Geschichte der deutschen Studentenschaft Wiens* (Vienna, 1892).

Bidermann, H. J., *Geschichte der österreichischen Gesamtstaatsidee 1526-1804*, 2 vols. (Innsbruck, 1867, 1889).

Boguth, W., "Die Okkupation Wiens und Niederösterreichs durch die Franzosen im Jahre 1809 und ihre Folgen für das Land", in *Jahrbuch für Landeskunde von Niederösterreich*, n. s. vol. vii (Vienna, 1908).

Brockhaus' Konversations-Lexikon, fourteenth edition (Leipzig, 1902).

Bücher, W., *Grillparzers Verhältnis zur Politik seiner Zeit* (Marburg, 1913).

Busse, P. G. A., "Grillparzer und Napoleon", in *Jahrbuch der Grillparzer Gesellschaft*, vol. xix (Vienna, 1910).

Chapman, C. E., *A History of Spain* (New York, 1918).

Charmatz, R., "Napoleon und die Wiener", in *Neue Freie Presse* (Vienna, June 10, 1909).

Criste, O., *Das Buch von Erzherzog Carl* (Vienna and Leipzig, 1914).

Die Männer des Volks in der Zeit des deutschen Elends 1805-1813 (Berlin, 1864).

Droysen, J. G., *Vorlesungen über des Zeitalter der Freiheitskriege*, second edition, 2 vols. (Gotha, 1886).

Duller, Edm., *Erzherzog Carl von Österreich* (Vienna, 1847).

Egger, J., *Geschichte Tirols*, vol. iii (Innsbruck, 1880).

Erzherzog Karl, der Feldherr und seine Armee (Vienna, 1913).

Fournier, A., *Die Geheimpolizei auf dem Wiener Kongress* (Vienna, 1913).

——, *Historische Studien und Skizzen* (Prague, 1885).

——, "Österreichs Kriegsziele im Jahre 1809", in *Beiträge zur neueren Geschichte Österreichs*, booklet iv (Vienna, Dec. 1908).

Fuchs, K., "Neue Forschungen zur Geschichte des Kriegsjahres 1809", in *Zeitschrift für die österreichischen Gymnasien*, vol. lx (Vienna, 1909).

Fyffe, C. A., *A History of Modern Europe 1792-1878* (New York, 1899).

Gebhardt, B., "Wilhelm von Humboldt als Gesandter in Wien 1810-1813", in *Deutsche Zeitschrift für Geschichtswissenschaft*, vol. xii (Freiburg, 1894-95).

——, *Wilhelm von Humboldt als Staatsmann*, 2 vols. (Stuttgart, 1896-1899).

Gentz, F., *Österreichs Teilnahme an den Befreiungskriegen*. *Hrsg. von Richard Fürst Metternich-Winneburg. Geordnet und zusammengestellt von Alfons Freiherrn von Klinkowström* (Vienna, 1887).

Gervinus, G. G., *Geschichte des neunzehnten Jahrhunderts*, 8 vols. (Leipzig, 1855).

Glossy, K., "Hormayr und Caroline Pichler", in *Jahrbuch der Grillparzer Gesellschaft*, vol. xii (Vienna, 1902).

Goedecke, K., *Grundriss zur Geschichte der deutschen Dichtung*, second edition, vols. vi, vii (Leipzig, Dresden, Berlin, 1898).

Gottschalk, L. R., *Era of the French Revolution* (New York, 1929).

Gross-Hoffinger, A. J., *Leben, Wirken und Tod des Kaisers [Franz]* (Stuttgart, 1835).

Gugitz, G., "Ein Pamphlet gegen das Burgtheater", in *Jahrbuch der Grillparzer Gesellschaft*, vol. xx (Vienna, 1911).

Guglia, E., *Friedrich von Gentz* (Vienna, 1901).

——, "Geschichte der Wiener Zeitung im Zeitalter der Revolution und Napoleons", in *Jubiläums-Festnummer der kaiserlichen Wiener Zeitung, 8. August 1703-1903*.

——, *Kaiserin Maria Ludovica von Österreich* (Vienna, 1894).

Hagen, K., *Über die öffentliche Meinung in Deutschland von den Freiheitskriegen bis zu den Karlsbader Beschlüssen* (Leipzig, 1846).

Hamberger, J., "Die französische Invasion in Kärnten im Jahre 1809", in *XXXII. Jahresbericht der Staats-Oberrealschule zu Klagenfurt* (Klagenfurt, 1889).

Hayes, C. J. H., *Essays on Nationalism* (New York, 1926).

Helfert, C. von, *Das Kriegsjahr 1809. Nach den Erinnerungen des Grafen Czernin von Helfert* (Heimat, 1877).

Hirn, J., "Literarische Vorläufer des Tiroler Aufstandes 1809", in *Beiträge zur neueren Geschichte Österreichs*, booklet iv (Vienna, Dec. 1908).

——, *Tirols Erhebung im Jahre 1809*, second edition (Innsbruck, 1909).

Hormayr, J. von, *Das Land Tyrol und der Tyrolerkrieg von 1809*, 2 vols. (Leipzig, 1845).

——, *Geschichte Andreas Hofers* (Leipzig, 1817).

——, *Lebensbilder aus den Befreiungskriegen*, 3 vols. (Jena, 1841-1845).

Horstenau, E. G. von, *Die Heimkehr Tirols* (Vienna, 1914).

Hottenroth, F., *Handbuch der deutschen Tracht* (Stuttgart, 1892).

Ilwof, F., "Johann Georg Fellinger 'der steirische Theodor Körner'", in *Jahrbuch der Grillparzer Gesellschaft*, vol. xix (Vienna, 1910).

Just, G., *Als die Völker Erwachten* (Vienna and Leipzig, 1907).

Kaltenborn, K. von, *Geschichte der deutschen Bundesverhältnisse und Einheitsbestrebungen von 1806 bis 1856*, 2 vols. (Berlin, 1857).

Kink, R., *Geschichte der kaiserlichen Universität zu Wien*, 2 vols. (Vienna, 1854).

Klüber, J. L., *Akten des Wiener Kongresses*, 8 vols. (Erlangen, 1817).

——, *Übersicht der diplomatischen Verhandlungen des Wiener Kongresses überhaupt, und insonderheit über wichtige Angelegenheiten des Teutschen Bundes*, 3 vols. in one (Frankfurt am Main, 1816).

Klüpfel, K., *Die deutschen Einheitsbestrebungen in ihrem geschichtlichen Zusammenhang* (Leipzig, 1853).

Krones, F., *Aus Österreichs stillen und bewegten Jahren, 1810-1813 und 1813-1815* (Innsbruck, 1892).

——, *Zur Geschichte Österreichs im Zeitalter der französischen Kriege und der Restauration 1792-1816* (Gotha, 1886).

Laban, F., *Heinrich Joseph Collin* (Vienna, 1879).

Lamprecht, K., *1809, 1813, 1815 Anfang, Höhepunkt und Ausgang der Freiheitskriege* (Berlin, 1913).

Löwenthal, E., *Die deutschen Einheitsbestrebungen im neunzehnten Jahrhundert* (Berlin, 1899).

Luckwaldt, F., "Österreich und die Anfänge des Befreiungskrieges von 1813", in *Historische Studien*, booklet x (Berlin, 1898).

Mager, A., *Österreichische Dichter des XIX. Jahrhunderts* (Vienna, 1898).

Mailath, J. von, *Geschichte des österreichischen Kaiserstaats*, vol. v (Hamburg, 1850).

Malcher, F. X., "Wien während der Anwesenheit der Franzosen", in *Vogl's Volkskalender, 1888* (Vienna, 1888).

Mayer, F. M., *Geschichte Österreichs*, 2 vols. (Vienna, 1909).

——, *Steiermark im Franzosenalter* (1888).

Metternich, Prince R. (ed.), *Memoirs of Prince Metternich 1773-1815*, translated by Mrs. Alexander Napier, vol. ii (New York, 1890).

Meyer, Chr., *Die Erhebung Österreichs, insbesondere Tyrols, im Jahre 1809, mit einem Anhang: Aus Deutschlands trübsten Tagen* (Dresden-Blasewitz, 1909).

Meynert, H., *Franz I., Kaiser von Österreich und sein Zeitalter* (Leipzig, 1834).

——, *Kaiser Franz I. Zur Geschichte seiner Regierung und seiner Zeit* (Vienna, 1872).

Minor, J., "August Wilhelm von Schlegel in den Jahren 1804-1815", in *Zeitschrift für die österreichischen Gymnasien*, vol. xxxviii (Vienna, 1887).

Mitscherlich, W., *Der Nationalismus Westeuropas* (Leipzig, 1920).

Molisch, P., *Geschichte der deutschnationalen Bewegung in Österreich von ihren Anfängen bis zum Zerfall der Monarchie* (Jena, 1926).

"Österreich nach dem Frieden von Wien 1809—Politisch-Militärische Studien eines Zeitgenossen", in *Mitt. des k. k. Kriegsarchivs für das Jahr 1882* (Vienna, 1882).

Österreichs Kriege seit 1495. Chronologische Zusammenstellung... Zusammengestellt aus den Mitt. des k. k. Kriegsarchivs, Jahrg. 1876, 1877, 1878 (Vienna, 1878).

Oncken, H., *Österreich und Preussen im Befreiungskriege, 1813-1815*, 2 vols. (Berlin, 1876-1879).

Paller, H. von, *Der grossdeutsche Gedanke* (Leipzig, 1928).

Perthes, C. T., *Politische Zustände und Personen in Deutschland zur Zeit der französischen Herrschaft*, 2 vols. (Gotha, 1869).

Pertz, G., *Das Leben des Ministers Freiherrn vom Stein*, 6 vols. (Berlin, 1849-1855).

Pfalz, A., *Österreichische Krieger- und Wehrmannslieder aus dem Jahre 1809* (Deutsch-Wagram, 1905).

Ploy, H., "Die Rückwirkung der spanischen Ereignisse auf die österreichische Politik", in *Neuntes Programm der k. k. Lehrerbildungs-Anstalt in Salzburg 1910* (Salzburg, 1910).

Poppe, Max, *Chronologische Übersicht der wichtigsten Begebenheiten aus den Kriegsjahren 1806-1815*, 2 vols. (Leipzig, 1848)

Raich, J. (ed.), *Dorothea Schlegel und deren Söhne...Briefwechsel*, 2 vols. (Mainz, 1881).

Redlich, J., *Das österreichische Staats- und Reichsproblem*, 2 vols. (Leipzig, 1920-1926).

Rehtwisch, Th., *Geschichte der Freiheitskriege in den Jahren 1812-1815* (Leipzig, 1880).

Richter, H. M., *Geistesströmungen [in Österreich]*, (Berlin, 1875).

Rose, J. H., *The Revolutionary and Napoleonic Era*, sixth edition (New York, 1913).

Rossi, J. (ed.), *Denkbuch für Fürst und Vaterland*, 2 vols. (Vienna, 1814-1815).

Sauer, A., "Erzherzog Carl in Grillparzers Dichtung", in *Jahrbuch der Grillparzer Gesellschaft*, vol. xx (Vienna, 1911).

Schallhammer, A. von, *Kriegerische Ereignisse im Herzogthume Salzburg in den Jahren 1800, 1805 und 1809* (Salzburg, 1853).

Scheuer, O., *Die geschichtliche Entwicklung des deutschen Studententums in Österreich, mit besonderer Berücksichtigung der Universität Wien* (Vienna and Leipzig, 1910).

Schimmer, K. A., *Die französischen Invasionen in Österreich* (Vienna, 1846).

Schindel, C. W. O. A. von, *Die deutschen Schriftstellerinnen des 19. Jahrhunderts*, vol. ii (Leipzig, 1825).

Schlossar, A., "Die 'Wiener Zeitschrift' von J. Schickh und F. Witthauer. Ein Beitrag zur Geschichte des österreichischen Journalwesens in vormärzlicher Zeit", in *Zeitschrift für Bücherfreunde*, vol. v[2] (Bielefeld and Leipzig, 1901-1902).

——, *Erzherzog Johann von Österreich* (Graz and Vienna, 1908).

——, "Ungedruckte Briefe des Erzherzogs Johann aus 1808-1809", in *Wiener Zeitung* (Vienna, April 19, 1908).

Schneidawind, F. J. A., *Der Krieg Österreichs gegen Frankreich, dessen Alliirte und den Rheinbund im Jahre 1809*, 2 vols. (Schaffhausen, 1842).

Springer, A. H., *Geschichte Österreichs seit dem Wiener Frieden 1809*, 2 vols. (Leipzig, 1863).

Srbik, H. von, *Metternich, der Staatsmann und der Mensch*, 2 vols. (Munich, 1925).

Starzer, A., "Aus den Polizei-Rapporten des Jahres 1809", in *Mitt. des Archivs für Niederösterreich*, vol. ii (Vienna, 1909).

Stern, A., *Geschichte Europas seit den Verträgen von 1815 bis zum Frankfurter Frieden von 1871*, vols. i and ii (Berlin, 1894-1924).

Veltzé, A. (ed.), *Österreich in den Befreiungskriegen, 1813-1815*, 10 vols. (Vienna, 1911-1914).

Voltelini, H. von, "Die Klausel *Non Autrement* des Pressburger Friedens", in *Mitt. des Instituts für österreichische Geschichtsforschung*, vol. xxxii (Innsbruck, 1911).

——, *Forschungen und Beiträge zur Geschichte des Tiroler Aufstandes im Jahre 1809* (Gotha, 1909).

Wackernell, J. C., *Beda Weber 1798-1858 und die tirolische Literatur seiner Zeit 1800-1846* (Innsbruck, 1903).

Wagner, K., "Der Einzug der Romantiker in Wien und die Wiener Presse", in *Die Kultur*, vol. ix (Vienna, 1908).

——, "Die Flugschriftenliteratur des Krieges von 1809", in *Anno Neun, Bücherei des Österreichischen Volksschriftenvereins*, vol. v (Brixen, 1912).

——, "Die Wiener Zeitungen und Zeitschriften der Jahre 1808 und 1809", in *Archiv für österreichische Geschichte*, vol. civ (Vienna, 1915).

Ward, A. W., *The Period of Congresses* (New York, 1919).

Weil, M. H., *Les dessous du Congrès de Vienne*, 2 vols. (Paris, 1917).

Weiss, K., *Geschichte der Stadt Wien*, second edition, 2 vols. (Vienna, 1883).

Werner, R. M., "Aus dem Wiener Lager der Romantik", in *Österreichisch-Ungarische Revue*, n. s. vol. viii (Vienna, Oct. 1889-March 1890).

Wertheimer, Ed., *Die drei ersten Frauen des Kaisers Franz* (Leipzig, 1893).

——, *Geschichte Österreichs und Ungarns im ersten Jahrzehnt des 19. Jahrhunderts*, 2 vols. (Leipzig, 1884-1890).

——, "Metternich und die Presse", in *Neue Freie Presse* (Vienna, July 13, 1899).

——, "Wien und das Kriegsjahr 1813", in *Archiv für österreichische Geschichte*, vol. lxxix (Vienna, 1893).

——, "Zur Geschichte Wiens im Jahre 1809", in *Archiv für österreichische Geschichte*, vol. lxxiv (Vienna, 1889).

Wiesner, A., *Denkwürdigkeiten der österreichischen Zensur* (Stuttgart, 1847).

Wihan, J., "Matthäus von Collin und die patriotisch-nationalen Kunstbestrebungen in Österreich zu Beginn des 19. Jahrhunderts", in *Euphorion*, supplementary vol. v (Leipzig and Vienna, 1901).

Winckler, J., *Die periodische Presse Österreichs*, vol. i (Vienna, 1875).

Wittichen, F. C., "Gentz und Metternich", in *Mitt. des Instituts für österreichische Geschichtsforschung*, vol. xxxi (Innsbruck, 1910).

Wlassack, Ed., *Chronik des k.-k. Hofburgtheaters* (Vienna, 1876).

Wurzbach, C. von, *Biographisches Lexikon des Kaiserthums Österreich*, 60 vols. (Vienna, 1856-1890).

Zenker, E., *Geschichte der Wiener Journalistik von den Anfängen bis zum Jahre 1848* (Vienna, 1892).

Zimmerman, W., *Die Befreiungskriege der Deutschen gegen Napoleon*, third edition (Stuttgart, 1859).

Zwiedeneck-Südenhorst, H. von, *Erzherzog Johann von Österreich im Feldzuge von 1809* (Graz, 1892).

INDEX